# SOMME SUCCESS

# Somme Success

### THE ROYAL FLYING CORPS AND THE BATTLE OF THE SOMME, 1916

## Peter Hart

LEO COOPER

First published in Great Britain in 2001 by Leo Cooper and reprinted in this format in 2012 by Pen & Sword Military
an imprint of Pen & Sword Books Limited
47 Church Street, Barnsley, South Yorkshire S70 2AS

*For up-to date information on other titles produced under the Pen & Sword imprint, please telephone or write to:*
Pen & Sword Books Limited
FREEPOST
47 Church Street
Barnsley
South Yorkshire
S70 2BR

Telephone (24 hours): 01226 734555

**ISBN 978 1 84884 882 5**

British Library Cataloguing in Publication Data

**Printed by CPI  UK**

# Contents

# Prelude

*Each of us crouches in a little hole that he has dug out for himself as a protection against possible splinters and stares at nothing but the sky and the black wall of the trench. And the airmen circle over us and try to do us some damage, but only enemy ones, for a German airman will not dare to come here - far too much afraid - only behind the front a great crowd and here not one makes an appearance.*[1] Anon German Soldier, The Somme, 1916

# Preface

This account, based as it is on diaries, letters, memoirs and oral history recordings, leaves me incredibly indebted to the people who have actually created and preserved those sources. I would like to thank all those people who have given me permission to include extracts from sources in which they hold the copyright. I hope that this book will encourage more people to delve into the original archives and literary sources. My grateful thanks are therefore as ever due to Margaret Brooks and her staff at the IWM Sound Archive: Jo Lancaster, Richard McDonough, Lyn Smith, the ridiculously ramshackle Rosemary Tudge and Conrad Wood. I freely acknowledge my debt to David Lance who initiated the IWM oral history programme on the RFC way back in those far off 1970s. I would also thank Rod Suddaby and his staff in the IWM Department of Documents, with particular reference to the indefatigably patient Tony Richards. My thanks to the executors of Wing Commander E J D Routh for permission to use his evocative drawings in the text. Thanks are due to the staff of the IWM Photographic Archive for their kindness and their permission to use the photographs included in this book. I would particularly mention Rose Gerrard who has brought an unaccustomed order to that graveyard of generations of sad cataloguers. Although the acknowledged IWM expert in the RFC and RNAS has been temporarily transported to the far off Dorsetshire Archives, Brad King remains an inspirational mentor! Come back soon! My grateful thanks go to the redoubtable, if slightly crumpled, Simon Moody of the Department of Research and Information Services at the RAF Museum, Hendon who provided many valuable sources and much innocent amusement besides. Most of the photographs of the individual pilots come from the collection of the Royal Aero Club held by the RAF Museum whom I would like to thank for their permission to reproduce them. Thanks also to Peter Boyden and his staff at the National Army Museum.

The hard work of specialist aerial researchers seems to be never ending and an object lesson to a dilettante such as myself. The finest work of aerial reference I have ever seen is that compiled by Trevor Henshaw, *The Sky their Battlefield: Air fighting and the Complete List of Allied Air Casualties from Enemy Action in the First World War* published by Grub Street in 1995. This masterpiece is invaluable for checking names, dates, squadrons and - oh just about everything! I really urge you to buy it if you have a serious interest in First World War aviation. I would also particularly like to express my admiration for the often unsung writers and members of 'Cross and Cockade'. Their brilliant research work has uncovered many little known contemporary sources that I have been able, with due acknowledgement, to weave into this general account. Amongst those whose work I would particularly wish to personally salute are: Barrington J Gray for his article, *'Number One of Jasta 2: An account of Oswald Boelcke's Twentieth Victory'*; Barrington J Gray and the Cross & Cockade DH2 Research Group, *'The Anatomy of an Aeroplane: The de Havilland DH2 Pusher Scout'*

This book marks an important step in my relationship with Pen & Sword. The baton of designer has been passed from the aged, yet still talented, hands of Roni Wilkinson to the next generation – in this case literally as it is his son Paul Wilkinson who has turned a collection of jumbled text and images into a book. Thanks Paul.

The very wonderful Nigel Steel has done a brilliant job of editing this book for which I shall ever be in his debt! Polly Napper and Bryn 'Tanky' Hammond were also kind enough to check early versions of the script. As ever any remaining errors are entirely my own fault. My thanks are due to Sukbhir Singh of our IWM Information Systems Department who rescued this book from a damaged hard disk.

The original quotations that are such an important part of this book have where necessary been lightly edited for readability. Punctuation and spellings have been largely standardized, material has occasionally been re-ordered and irrelevant material has been omitted usually without any indication in the text. However, changes in the actual words used in our original sources have been avoided wherever possible.

1. The Times, 24/8/1916

Chapter One

# In the Beginning...

In the beginning there was the ground war. The entrenched armies faced each other across No Man's Land all along the Western Front; an inviolable line that marked the end of the brief period of open warfare in 1914. As the armies crashed into each other the soldiers scratched themselves impromptu cover when it seemed certain death to stay above ground. They sought sanctuary from the streams of machine gun bullets and crashing detonations of artillery shells that typified modern warfare. Gradually these tentative scrapings were deepened and extended until an unbroken front was created from which they could pour fire into any attack made upon them. So the line froze into immobility. Gradually a second or third line was dug and the whole system interconnected with communication trenches that allowed the troops to come into the line without ever raising their heads above the trench parapets. At first both sides were relatively confident that these trenches were temporary resting places, while they girded their metaphorical loins for the next great attack that would

*German troops relaxing in a shallow trench.*

surely rupture the enemy's line, allowing a resumption of old style open warfare, culminating in an enjoyably satisfying advance to victory in Berlin or Paris depending on perspective. However, for all their initial optimism, it was an intractable problem that faced the generals in 1915 and their pre-war experience was to prove of little or no value.

There was another new factor. Though before the war the military value of the aeroplane had been clearly recognized, the first powered flight by the Wright brothers had only taken place eleven years earlier in 1903. Aircraft were developing rapidly, but their limitations in 1914 were considerable. Speeds were dangerously low and the margin between safe flying and stalling speed was often extremely narrow. Although some aircraft had flown at over 100mph the bulk of aircraft flew at between 60 and 80mph. Methods of controlling movement in the air were not fully understood and consequently aerial manoeuvres were often carried out on the basis of guesswork; simply repeating actions that had not actually resulted in disaster last time they were tried. The science of aeronautics was literally in its infancy. Underpowered as they were, the amount of weight that each aircraft could lift was severely limited and this hindered any attempt to develop any real military 'strike' role by deploying bombs or machine guns. The immediate practical military interest in the aircraft centred on the obvious possibilities of aerial reconnaissance. Aircraft offered the embattled general the opportunity for observers to rise above the confusion of battle and gain access to the minutiae of his opponent's

*By 1912 the military was showing a keen interest in aviation; here British Army Aeroplane model No.1, designed by Samuel Cody, is being wheeled out for a test flight. The classic aircraft shape had yet to emerge.*

dispositions and movements. Reams of vital intelligence could be harvested at the risk of just a few daring aviators flying deep into enemy territory, rather than the much more limited results offered by the conventional reconnaissance in force by cavalry. Although the Great Powers invested to some degree in aircraft before the war, rigid airships were seen by many as a far more promising method of pursuing aerial warfare. Not only did airships have a far greater range of operations, but they could also lift significant bomb loads, with which to hopefully destroy their enemies when they found them.

The Royal Flying Corps (RFC) had gone to war under the command of Sir David Henderson with just four squadrons, that in all totalled some 63 serviceable aircraft. The primitive state of aircraft technology can be judged by the fact that it was still considered a remarkable feat that they had managed to cross the English Channel under their own power. After all, the first successful cross-Channel flight by the redoubtable Louis Blériot had only been completed five years previously. Once there, the RFC soon proved its value by helping to expose the workings of the German Schlieffen plan to the initially sceptical British Commander in Chief Sir John French. It was their reconnaissance reports that provided a basis for the Allied reorganization and counter-attack at the Battle of the Marne.

The most crucial advances in aerial warfare were made incredibly early in the war. Aerial photo-reconnaissance began on 15 September with a mission undertaken by Lieutenant G F Pretyman above the emerging German trenches in the Aisne hills which had blocked the Allied advance. Aerial photography greatly expanded the reconnaissance capabilities of aircraft. The plates exposed could be examined when developed safely back on the ground and so the science of photographic interpretation was born as the slightest traces of German activity could be exposed to the camera in the sky. At the same time the first wirelesses were carried into the sky where they provided aerial observation that allowed the British artillery to range onto targets invisible to their ground level forward observation posts. Thus, just a month after the RFC had landed in France their two most important roles in the First World War had been defined and refined. In addition small bombs, had been carried into the air to attack targets of opportunity such as columns of troops. Meanwhile the Royal Naval Air Service (RNAS), which was the Royal Navy equivalent of the RFC, had begun to experiment in 'strategic' bombing raids on Zeppelin sheds, naval bases and even German towns. Small-scale and ineffectual they may have been in the context of later events, but the first steps had been taken that would lead in time to the wholesale devastation of cities from the air.

However, it was equally apparent that their German opposite numbers were performing the same function - the curtain had been lifted for both sides. It was obvious that a great advantage would be gained by blinding the aerial eyes of the opposing forces. Thus, although they were hamstrung by the weakness of their aircraft, right from the start aviators harboured murderous designs against each other. Observers carried rifles or shotguns and they exchanged fire with their counterparts wherever possible. The sheer difficulty of aiming at a relatively fast-moving target with a single shot weapon meant that casualties from enemy action were rare in the opening months of the war. Efforts to carry the light Lewis machine gun into the air floundered because even the extra weight crippled the performance of the aircraft. Seemingly, you could have speed and altitude, or a machine gun, but not both. Nevertheless the first German aircraft were forced down just two days after the Battle of Mons; the first British pilot to be wounded in combat with a German aircraft was Lieutenant G W Mapplebeck on 22 September; while the French scored the first real aerial victory when a Voison shot down a German Aviatik on 5 October.

Although few aviators were killed directly by enemy action, the multifarious dangers of flying caused a constant haemorrhaging of men and machines in accidents. At the front the RFC was withering away, but their importance had been officially recognized. A rapid expansion was ordered by the Minister of War, Field Marshal Lord Kitchener, to achieve a target of some 100 squadrons. Unfortunately, this was far easier envisaged than carried out. Britain did not have an aeronautics manufacturing industry that could suddenly turn on the tap to build the hundreds of aircraft that would be required. Pilots, observers and ground mechanics were also in scarce supply and their training would take time. To simplify matters all round, it was decided early on to concentrate on producing just one aircraft as the workhorse for most of these putative squadrons. Because of the time it took to build the aircraft and train the pilots it was to be this decision, taken in 1914, that would decide what machines the pilots in 1915 and 1916 fought in. The choice settled on the BE2 C.

The BE2 C was a variant of the 'Blériot Experimental' series of all-purpose tractor aeroplanes (the engine was at the front of the aircraft) designed in sequence from the BE1 at the Royal Aircraft Factory, (RAF) Farnborough. It had many advantages as a photographic reconnaissance and artillery observation aircraft in that it was designed to be inherently stable. In this it was remarkably successful as once aloft it could almost fly itself. The aircraft were powered by the new RAF 1 90hp engine that generated a flying speed of 72mph at 6,500 feet and 69mph at its service ceiling of 10,000 feet, although it took a lamentable 45 minutes to reach that height. Production was bedevilled by frequent design modifications and the difficulties inherent in placing contracts with firms that in some cases had never before built aircraft of

*The BE2 C was the workhorse of the RFC in the first three years of the war.* IWM Q 56847

any type. Nevertheless, the BE2 C was reaching the front in ever increasing quantities by mid-1915. Here it proved a safe flying machine that would provide yeoman service in its designed role. Unfortunately it had one serious flaw that would become apparent as the air war developed that year - it was not, and never would be an effective aircraft for the rigours of aerial combat.

It was recognised that pilots had got to be trained quickly and would not have a great deal of experience and so an aircraft was needed which would be simple to fly and between them they produced the BE2 C. The BE2 C was the first aircraft that was to be really inherently stable. The dihedral on the wings gave it lateral stability; the dihedral at which the tail plane was set in relation to the main planes gave it fore and aft stability. The lateral stability was very strong indeed – it would correct anything by itself. A very stable aircraft. From the flying point of view this had the very great disadvantage that as the machine wanted to stay on a level keel, right way up, it was very difficult to make it do anything else.[1] *Lieutenant Charles Chabot, 4 Squadron, RFC*

\*   \*   \*   \*

The problems of trench warfare that both sides faced were a direct consequence of the application of the industrial might of nation states to the process of war. The mass production of rifles, machine guns and artillery for the use of citizen armies numbering millions took the whole business of war to a new pitch. To launch a successful attack the infantry had to first cross an area covered by long-range enemy artillery. Units could be devastated before they even reached the front

*13*

line. Once in their 'jumping off trenches' they remained vulnerable to shell fire until the whistles blew for Zero Hour. At this point they had to leave all cover and venture across a No Man's Land swept by bursting shells, the deadly stutter of machine guns and concentrated rifle fire. When they got near their enemies they were baulked by an impenetrable wall of barbed wire. The obvious answer to the conundrum lay in their own artillery. It could destroy, or at least suppress the enemy artillery batteries; smash the machine gun posts; flatten the trenches; kill the front line garrison and blast apart the barbed wire defences. Unfortunately there were problems in this theoretical approach. It pre-supposed the enemy would do nothing, but of course they too concentrated their guns in the disputed area and inevitably every battle became a huge artillery duel. Pinpoint accuracy was essential to destroy reinforced earthwork defences, but the science of gunnery was not well advanced enough to secure precision gunnery. The only alternative lay in deluges of shells to annihilate everything in the target area, but such wasteful practices were effectively debarred by the crippling shortages of modern guns, shells and trained gunners.

The first British attempt to break out of the strait jacket of trench warfare was made by the First Army commanded by General Sir Douglas Haig in the Battle of Neuve Chapelle launched on 10 March 1915. Haig built the pioneering work of the RFC into his overall plan and relied on the artillery using aerial observation to overcome the identified German batteries and German strongpoints. The RFC produced a photographic map of the whole of the German defensive

*This BE2 A was observing when it was struck in flight by a large British shell in the Neuve Chapelle area. The crew of two were killed.* IWM Q 49212

trench system. Some of the technical problems of aerial artillery observation were gradually being overcome following the introduction of accurate mapping and the 'clock code' which allowed the observer to relay the fall of each round to the Royal Artillery gunners. The RFC were also responsible for bombing raids on German troops in their bases behind the lines and for interdiction attacks to disturb the movement of troops and munitions by destroying key transport installations. The actual assault was to be carried out by Lieutenant General Sir Henry Rawlinson's IV Corps and Rawlinson had carefully calculated the amount of shells required to smash down the German trenches. In the event the German line was indeed breached. However initial hopes of a decisive breakthrough were soon quashed as the Germans simply brought up their reserves. A new defensive line sprang up that within days was as strong, if not stronger, than their original front line.

The next attempt was launched by the Germans in the Second Battle of Ypres, when they tried to cut the Gordian knot of trench warfare by their use of poison gas on 22 April. They too found initial success to be an illusion as British reserves proceeded to plug the gap. During the battle, one young pilot distinguished himself by conducting a series of reconnaissance 'contact patrols' designed to accurately establish the location of the fluctuating British and German front lines in an effort to bring sense to the extreme confusion that pervaded the Ypres battlefield.

> I had a very careful look at that bit of ground, circling and going over it again and again till I could make sure of the exact positions we held. It was while flying low over a big farm to the north of this bit that I received a bullet just above my left ankle that solved the problem as to who held the farm! It was remarkably painful at first and I headed for home but as I could use my foot I turned back to deny the Germans the satisfaction of having driven me off, placed the farm carefully on the map and then turned and went home.[2] *Captain Lanoe Hawker, 6 Squadron, RFC*

*Lanoe Hawker.* RAFM/RAeC435

Subsequent offensives conducted by the British at Aubers Ridge and Festubert were doomed to failure by an insufficient concentration of artillery and an increasing shell shortage, which meant that not even the German front line could be effectively breached.

As the trench systems grew ever more complex there was a pressing need to know what was happening on the other side of the barbed wire. The location of German machine gun posts, saps, mortar pits, command posts, signals stations and artillery gun positions had a crucial significance should the British intend to make an attack. But the varying intensity of road and railway traffic coupled with the establishment of camps and dumps could also signal an impending German offensive. Conversely it was increasingly important to deny the same intelligence to the Germans. Anti-aircraft guns were making their appearance on both sides and although they rarely scored a direct hit, as they increased in number they became gradually more inconvenient and threatening, especially to low flying aircraft committed to flying in straight lines for their reconnaissance and observation duties. However it was inevitable that the first real 'fighter' aircraft armed with machine guns should appear as the rapid improvements in aircraft performance allowed more weight to be carried aloft. The Bristol Scout was the best known of the first generation of single-seater aircraft designed to rapidly fly ahead of the army to 'scout' and report what they had found. Blessed with a speed of over 80mph they were the obvious choice to hunt down and attack the German reconnaissance aircraft that implicitly threatened the operations on the ground. As single-seater tractor aircraft they were difficult to arm as the propeller naturally got in the way of a machine gun firing straight ahead. A variety of ingenious methods were devised and deployed to overcome this problem and Captain Lanoe Hawker, who had been assigned to the Bristol Scout attached to 6 Squadron RFC, mounted a Lewis gun on the left of his cockpit trained to fire obliquely past his propeller. Aiming was difficult in the extreme, for the extra problem of an inbuilt deflection was added to the normal difficulties of aerial gunnery. Yet Hawker persevered, and on 25 July he earned a Victoria Cross by shooting down two German aircraft over Ypres. These 'scouts' in time bequeathed their name as a generic type to the early fighter aeroplanes.

The first purpose built British aircraft designed to destroy German aircraft was the Vickers FB 5 biplane pusher. With the engine tucked behind the pilot and observer, it was armed with a pillar mounted Lewis gun in the observer's front nacelle. Powered by a 100hp Gnome Monosoupape engine it could reach 70mph at 5,000 feet with an effective ceiling of 7,000 feet. The Vickers Fighter enjoyed considerable success, but the summer of 1915 was marked by the gestation of the next generation of scout aircraft that would change the whole complexion of war in the air.

On 1 April 1915, the French pilot Roland Garros claimed his first victory. Garros had fitted deflection plates to the propeller of his Morane-Saulnier Type L Parasol Monoplane. This allowed him to fire straight ahead, through the arc of the propellor and hence to aim his guns by aiming the whole aircraft at the target. After shooting down three German aircraft he was brought down himself while attacking a train behind the German lines on 18 April. The remains of his Morane were quickly handed over to Anthony Fokker, a Dutch aircraft designer and manufacturer working in Germany. The Garros device acted as a spur to Fokker's brilliant design team who developed a successful cam-operated synchronized machine gun which eliminated the need for deflector plates. Fokker fitted this to his copy of the Morane-Saulnier Monoplane. The end result was the Fokker Eindecker E1. The Fokkers reached the front and scored their first victories over their flabbergasted opponents in July and August, 1915. This marked the beginning of the Fokker scourge and the end of a period of relative security for the RFC over the Western Front. At first the number of casualties was small as the Fokkers were largely used in a defensive capacity to escort German reconnaissance aircraft. The language of aerial fighting had not yet been written and the young German pilots had to evolve their tactics from scratch. Unfortunately for the British, in *Leutnants* Max Immelmann and Oswald Boelcke, the Germans had two young men with both the courage and brains to exploit the superiority that the Fokker gave them over any British aircraft then available on the Western Front. Gradually they learnt to use the relatively high altitude ceiling of the Fokker to lurk far above the lines until they sighted

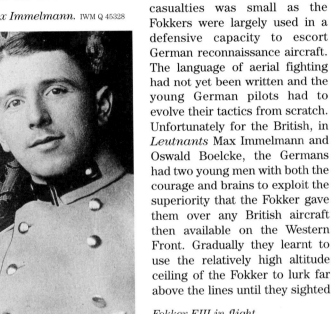

*Oswald Boelcke.* IWM Q 63147    *Max Immelmann.* IWM Q 45328

*Fokker EIII in flight.*

*The Fokker EIII flown by Boelcke showing his machine gun and interrupter gear which allowed the gun to fire through his propeller.* IWM Q 58037

their prey, upon which they would dive down out of the dazzling sun to attack their prospective victim from behind to capitalize on their advantage in being able to fire straight ahead. They also began to hunt together as a pair and soon informal gatherings of three or four Fokkers would work together to maximize their deadly effect, whilst reducing the collective risk as far as possible.

With the advent of the Fokker, the terrible and unforeseen weakness in combat of the BE2 C was fully exposed. Its inherent stability now became a severe handicap, as it could not be swiftly and effectively manoeuvred to take rapid evasive action. Furthermore as a tractor aircraft, the engine was in front of the aircraft and like all its brethren that meant that it was exceedingly difficult to arm in the absence of an effective British synchronization gear. The observer sat in the front cockpit where both his view and field of fire were obstructed by the wings and a linking forest of struts and wires that he would be well advised not to shoot away. Many and varied were the solutions that were tried to mount Lewis guns, but the most common involved the use of four socket mountings around the observer's cockpit from which he could make his choice depending on the position of the enemy. This was obviously totally inadequate in the face of ever more deadly Fokker attacks. Without parachutes the crews were often left imprisoned in a flaming coffin. Although the casualties were infinitesimal in comparison with those suffered in the trenches below them, it became apparent that something would have to be done if the RFC was to continue to carry out its duties effectively. Back in Britain the obsolescent BE2 Cs continued to roll off the production lines. The contracts had been signed and there was insufficient flexibility in the system to change course.

The RFC were heavily engaged at this time in the myriad preparations for the Battle of Loos launched on 25 September. Loos had been launched as the British flanking contribution to the co-ordinated French offensives in Champagne and Artois. The British artillery concentration in terms of guns and shells per yard of German trench attacked was a great deal less than had been achieved at Neuve Chapelle. To compensate for the insufficient artillery support it had been decided to use poison gas in an attempt to decisively rupture the German front line. After a patchy first day, the offensive ground to a halt and failed in a welter of blood and guts. The fighting dragged on into October, by which time the Fokkers were increasingly making their presence felt.

*uglas Haig*

The Battle of Loos marked a further development in the careers and relationship of two officers who were to dominate the story of the RFC in the great Somme offensive of 1916 - General Sir Douglas Haig and Brigadier-General Hugh Trenchard. Sir Douglas Haig was a career army officer par excellence who had prospered in the pre-war army and developed many qualities that served him well in the encounter battles of 1914. In command of the First Army, he had overseen the bulk of the British offensives on the Western Front in 1915. The clumsy handling by Commander in Chief Field Marshal Sir John French of the reserve divisions on the first day of the Battle of Loos had provoked widespread condemnation. This was coupled with simmering general dissatisfaction with the overall failure to break through that year and stirred vigorously by a thoroughly disloyal campaign of whispering from Haig. As a result, French was dismissed in December and Haig appointed in his place. Haig had a clear understanding of the primary importance of the Western Front and was never tempted by the chimera of 'easier' options in Gallipoli, Mesopotamia, Palestine, Salonika or Italy. He saw that the main enemy of the Allies was Germany and correctly reasoned that the only way to beat Germany was to defeat her main army in the field. As such he was the arch 'Westerner' determined to concentrate all possible resources in the only place where they counted – on the Western Front. His task was made easier by the sheer confusion and woolly thinking proffered as global strategy by the 'Easterners' such as Winston Churchill and David Lloyd George. Haig could easily be characterized as a dour Scot and his unfortunate verbal inarticulacy made it easy to underestimate his intelligence. Although undoubtedly stubborn, not necessarily a disadvantage at times in a military command, he had a willingness to accept new technologies. Early on in the war he had recognized the prime importance of artillery and therefore the crucial importance of the RFC in directing it to best effect; but he was also fully aware of the importance of the machine gun and was quick to see the possibilities

*jh Trenchard*

*19*

lurking in the slowly lumbering early tanks. His support for the cavalry has been frequently cited as a sign of a hidebound nature, but it remained the only fast moving arm of exploitation available to him at that time.

Lieutenant Colonel Hugh Trenchard had commanded the First Wing, RFC and had worked closely with Haig during the Battle of Neuve Chapelle earlier that year. In one sense their association went back even further for it was Trenchard's role as an aerial observer in the Annual Army Manoeuvres of 1912 that had allowed Haig's opponent to thwart his planned attack! After the withdrawal of Major General Sir David Henderson to take up the key post of Director General of Military Aeronautics, Trenchard was promoted to Brigadier and given the command of the RFC on the Western Front in August 1915. A brash, booming man who was intolerant of failure, he nevertheless had a certain panache that let him get away with statements that might seem inflammatory from a lesser man.

> I'm not asking you to do anything I wouldn't do myself. Just because I'm condemned to ride about in a big Rolls-Royce and sit out the fighting in a chair, you mustn't think I don't understand.[3]
> *Brigadier General Hugh Trenchard, Headquarters, RFC*

Such phrases became almost catch phrases in the RFC. Trenchard was greatly assisted in his task by the tact and outstanding competence of his ADC, Captain Maurice Baring.

> Trenchard's personality and abilities took him to the top early on. He was that peculiar thing. A totally inarticulate genius. He had no power of expression whatsoever either verbally or on paper. He always had to have by him somebody to collect and correct his English, his thoughts and so on. During the whole war this was performed by Maurice Baring, one of the most charming men that ever lived, brilliant writer, charming person - and he knew all the squadrons which 'Boom' visited very frequently. It became a catchword, "Take that down, Baring!" He always followed up everything, trivial or of major importance, that came under his notice.[4] *Captain Archibald James, 2 Squadron, RFC*

Trenchard had a remarkable gift for prophecy coupled with a peculiar ability to develop policy almost by instinct. His regrettable inarticulacy was counter-balanced by the verbal dexterity of Baring who could translate his wishes into clear statements of intent in orders and official papers. Trenchard had developed an unswerving belief that the RFC was part of and entirely subordinate to the requirements of the army; hence they must do whatever was required and bear the inevitable losses to service those needs. As a result over 50 RFC pilots and observers were shot down between November 1915 and January 1916 as the Fokker scourge raged; but, following Trenchard's line, the RFC

*Fokker EIII in flight.*

had to continue to do its duty at all costs. Methods could be modified but not the overall aggressive aerial approach.

Until the Royal Flying Corps are in possession of a machine as good as or better than the German Fokker it seems that a change in the tactics employed becomes necessary. It is hoped very shortly to obtain a machine which will be able to successfully engage the Fokkers at present in use by the Germans. In the meantime, it must be laid down as a hard and fast rule that a machine proceeding on reconnaissance must be escorted by at least three other fighting machines. These machines must fly in close formation and a reconnaissance should not be continued if any of the machines become detached. This should apply to both short and distant reconnaissances. Aeroplanes proceeding on photographic duty any considerable distance east of the line should be similarly escorted. From recent experience it seems that the Germans are now employing their aeroplanes in groups of three or four, and these numbers are frequently encountered by our aeroplanes. Flying in close formation must be practised by all pilots.[5] *Brigadier General Hugh Trenchard, Headquarters, RFC*

Trenchard did not intend to give up the dangerous reconnaissances, he was merely modifying his tactics to reflect the changing circumstances. This approach was naturally more than acceptable to Sir Douglas Haig.

Trenchard had also developed a policy of replacing all casualties on the day of their demise. A pool of pilots and observers were held at the base at St Omer to ensure that his insistence on "a full breakfast table, with no empty chairs" were not just empty words. This seemingly callous approach was in fact designed to help maintain squadron morale.

I always looked on the RFC as a family. I tried to put myself in the others' places and to consider the feelings of those who flew as if they had been my own. If as an ordinary pilot you see no vacant places around you, the tendency is to brood less on the fate of friends who have gone forever. Instead your mind is taken up with buying drinks for the newcomers and making them feel at home. It was a matter of pride and human understanding.[6] *Brigadier General Hugh Trenchard, Headquarters, RFC*

Meanwhile his pilots learnt to make the best of a bad job. They did not meekly surrender their lives but strove to overcome the manifest design faults of their aircraft. One observer flying in BE2 Cs codified the results of his hard won experience and the advice other survivors had given to him.

## NOTES ON COMBATS IN AIR

Attack on same level if possible. In BE2 C use side mounting. Don't open fire over 500 yards. You don't carry enough cartridges to waste. Fire in bursts of not over ten. Switch your gun quickly to back mounting as he passes and fire remainder of drum. i) If Hun dives replace gun on side bracket. ii) Attack as before. iii) Put gun on front mounting and dive for position under tail. Never follow a machine directly behind he will rake you through and through. Never let a machine get under your tail. Never let a machine swoop down on you unawares from behind. At first sound of a shot from behind turn to right and left with nose down before looking round even. It is with his first burst of fire that the Fokker Scout gets his machine down. If an EA Scout presses his attack home and persists in following go into a slow spiral losing as little height as possible.[7] *Lieutenant Bernard Rice, 2 Squadron, RFC*

*Bernard Rice.*

\* \* \* \*

By the end of 1915, the industrial bases of the warring nations were beginning to hit their stride and crippling shell shortages were addressed as ever more resources were redirected into the manufacture of munitions. Artillery of all types and sizes was being produced in ever increasing numbers and there was the tempting vista of almost unlimited shells raining down on enemy trenches. The recruiting fervour of 1914 had generated a harvest of fresh new divisions of partially trained and frighteningly keen soldiers. The early British attempts to break the line had concentrated on using artillery to rupture the line and then to pour troops through the gap to victory. The shortages of guns and shells, coupled with the ability of the German High Command to move in their copious reserves to seal the gap, had resulted in lengthy casualty lists and only minor advances measured in yards rather than miles. It was decided to raise the stakes by amassing ever more artillery and men at the selected point and to wear down the available German reserves by a process of attrition and coordinated attacks by all the Allies in the coming year. Unfortunately, the thought processes of the German High Command under General Ernst von Fallkenhayn were not dissimilar and it was he who launched the first blow at Verdun on 21 February 1916. The concept behind the Verdun offensive was blood curdling in its murderous simplicity. National pride would not allow the French to retreat from their frontier fortress town and Fallkenhayn had secured an unparalleled concentration of artillery to lash the eight mile Verdun sector

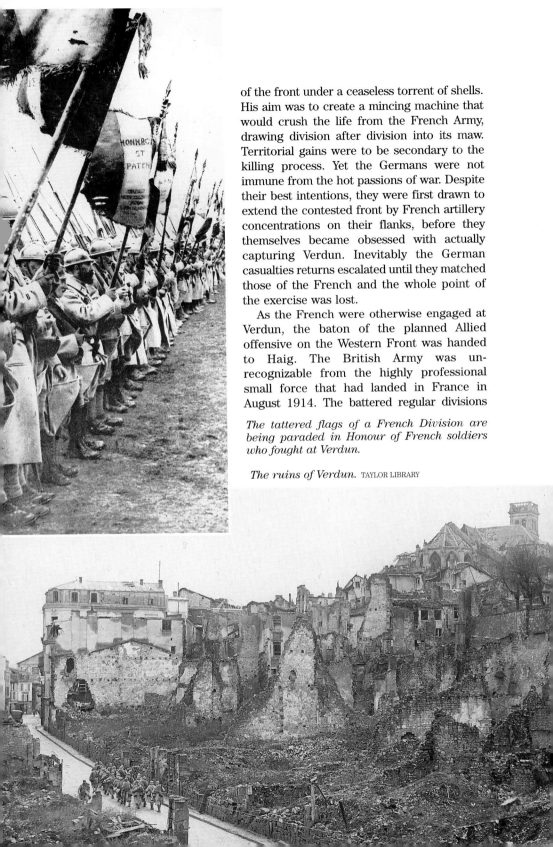

of the front under a ceaseless torrent of shells. His aim was to create a mincing machine that would crush the life from the French Army, drawing division after division into its maw. Territorial gains were to be secondary to the killing process. Yet the Germans were not immune from the hot passions of war. Despite their best intentions, they were first drawn to extend the contested front by French artillery concentrations on their flanks, before they themselves became obsessed with actually capturing Verdun. Inevitably the German casualties returns escalated until they matched those of the French and the whole point of the exercise was lost.

As the French were otherwise engaged at Verdun, the baton of the planned Allied offensive on the Western Front was handed to Haig. The British Army was unrecognizable from the highly professional small force that had landed in France in August 1914. The battered regular divisions

*The tattered flags of a French Division are being paraded in Honour of French soldiers who fought at Verdun.*

*The ruins of Verdun.* TAYLOR LIBRARY

had been rebuilt, the territorial divisions had arrived and the Kitchener New Army divisions were coming on stream in ever increasing numbers. This massive expansion generated its own problems. There were just not enough regulars with recent experience of war to train all these millions of men and in general the bulk of the officers and NCOs were as untrained as their men. These soldiers were enthusiastic amateurs in the rough business of war, all but blinded by their own delusions of glorious combat; hamstrung by their lack of personal skill in weapons handling; ignorant of all but the simplest battle tactics; above all, totally unfamiliar with the dreadful cocktail of confusion, fatigue and terror that made up the 'shock of war' which could strip a man naked in the face of his enemies.

Haig planned to launch 25 of his divisions supported by some 1,500 guns and howitzers into the attack along a wide frontage of 25,000 yards to the north of the River Somme. It was considered that the artillery would suppress resistance and that the infantry would have little problem in opening up a wide gap in the German line. This the Germans would find impossible to plug with their reserves and the cavalry could then go through the centre to penetrate deep behind the lines. The final stage would see an advance to roll up the German line towards Arras. Lieutenant General Sir Henry Rawlinson, now in command of Fourth Army, was given the responsibility for carrying out the initial attack, whilst the Reserve Army, commanded by Lieutenant General Sir Hubert Gough, would lead the exploitation to the north.

Whilst Haig and Rawlinson laid their plans, the war in the air was slowly beginning to develop a coherent pattern. Trenchard always sought to dominate the air space over the German lines, whatever the disadvantages his pilots may have been under. In April, he received a

*General Sir He[n]*
*Rawlinson*

*New battalion for the 'Tigers', the Leicestershire Regiment. Part of Kitchener's New Amy.* TAYLOR LIBRARY

letter from the commander of the French Air Service in the Verdun area that confirmed many of his instinctive beliefs.

Aircraft can be divided into two, army machines and combat machines. And these aircraft can be employed in two separate ways: either by using the combat machines to protect the army machines, or by letting the latter fend for themselves so that the combat machines can do their real job of fighting. We've employed both methods and here are the results. Like the Germans, we began by adopting the second method and thanks to our offensive efforts we attained a material and moral superiority so marked that the enemy were forced to protect their army machines. We were proud of this. It made us a little complacent; we yielded to the demands of our own army corps which wanted close protection for their hard-pressed co-operation machines. We in turn were driven to adopt the first method and were barely able to hold our own with the enemy. The strongest formations of aircraft proved themselves masters of the situation. We then resumed the second method – and immediately recaptured local air superiority by going after it. There were two main drawbacks. The first was this: the corps commanders, misunderstanding what was at stake, protested shrilly at being left in the lurch, despite the fact that their corps machines, by flying in formations of three, as ordered, managed to do their work, protect themselves and suffer relatively few casualties in the process. The second drawback has been the acute nervous strain imposed on our combat pilots, who are carrying the fight non-stop to the enemy's back areas, fighting and dropping their bombs far from their own bases and within constant range of the German anti-aircraft defences. Our losses in the air may be heavy, but they are much less than those we are inflicting on the enemy. And our air mastery is proving of enormous advantage to the troops on the ground.[8] *Commandant du Peuty, French Air Service*

The scene was set for the Battle of the Somme both on the ground and in the air.

1 . IWM SR: C. J. Chabot, AC 8
2. T. Hawker, *'Hawker VC'*, (London: Mitre Press, 1965), p85
3. A Boyle, 'Trenchard', (London: Collins, 1962), p199
4. IWM SR: A. James, AC 24 (Copyright Churchill College, Cambridge)
5. H. A. Jones, *'Official History of the War: The War in the Air, Being the Story of the part played in the Great War by the Royal Air Force'*, (Oxford: Clarendon Press, 1922-1937), Volume II, pp156-157
6. A Boyle, 'Trenchard', (London: Collins, 1962), p190
7. RAF MUSEUM: B. Rice, Manuscript notes
8. A Boyle, 'Trenchard', (London: Collins, 1962), pp169-170

Map of the Somme area.

Chapter Two

# An Aerial Offensive

The aerial offensive had to commence well before the first British guns had begun their preliminary bombardment. Artillery observation was required to identify and register the thousands of possible targets. Of course meanwhile the Germans had to be prevented from observing the British preparations and if possible driven from the sky. The BEF had taken over the Somme front from the French in July 1915. Immediately routine photographic reconnaissance had commenced, but it was only given a real impetus once the Fourth Army took over the sector in March 1916. The process of photographing every square inch of ground of the German front line trench systems and their immediate hinterland had to be carried out by the army or 'corps' aircraft on an almost daily basis in order to meticulously chart and interpret any changes. Thousands upon thousands of photographs were taken.

As far as possible the whole of the German front line would be photographed for a depth of about a thousand yards every month. The cameras that we used for this work were box cameras with an infinity focus, containing an auxiliary magazine or changing box of twelve plates. As each of these plates was exposed, they were

*A BE2 C fitted with a camera for aerial photography.*

transferred into a second changing box by means of a sliding handle that worked on top of the camera. This handle reset the shutter for another exposure at the same time. The shutter release had a piece of cord attached to it so that the pilot might pull it easily with his thick-gloved hands.[1] *Lieutenant Robin Rowell, 12 Squadron, RFC*

The pilot rather than the observer was given the task of actually taking the photographs.

The pilot had to look after the camera because at least from his seat you could look straight down. The camera was one of those real antiques made by the ancient Greeks! Good square mahogany box with a leather concertina pullout with a good big lens and a little

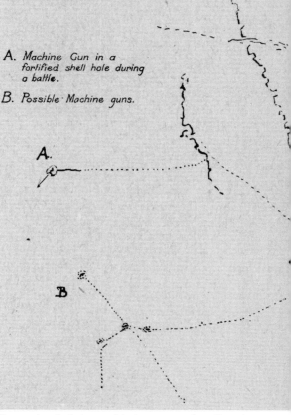

A. Machine Gun in a fortified shell hole during a battle.

B. Possible Machine guns.

*Example of photographic interpretation. See photo on next page.*

handle that you pushed and pulled to change the plates. Real good old glass plates. In addition to that a bit of wire or string with a ring on it, which was skittering around in the wind, to pull every time you wanted to take a picture. The whole thing was strapped on the outside of the aeroplane and you had a sort of ball and ring sight at the back. To take the photo you had to lean over the side of the cockpit and look down through this ball sight, fly the aeroplane with the left hand, move the camera handle changing the plates with the right. Every time you change the plate you pull the string, wait until you'd flown along a bit more, judge the overlap and did it again.[2] *Second Lieutenant Cecil Lewis, 9 Squadron, RFC*

However, things could easily go wrong.

Today I went up to take photos and went over the lines four times, carefully sighting the required trenches and taking 18 photos. I spent nearly two and a half hours in the air, and when I got back I found the string that worked the shutter had broken after my third photo, and the rest had not come out. It was disappointing, because my last three journeys over the lines need

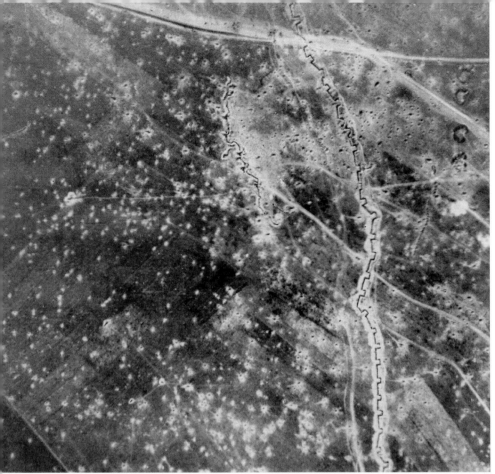

*Aerial photograph of Somme battlefields*

not have been made, and incidentally it would have saved getting a hole through one of my planes.[3] *Second Lieutenant Lessel Hutcheon, 5 Squadron, RFC*

In more fortunate cases, the overlapping results were developed and used to form a photographic map of that particular sector of the front.

Now the advantage of fixing the camera to the machine is that the pilot can only take photographs of objects directly below him, and in consequence his pictures are all small maps of the ground, with a correct perspective, and can be pieced together to form a large photo of the enemy's trenches and emplacements. One cannot underestimate the value of good results. In a good photo, taken from a reasonable height, 6 to 8,000 ft, and enlarged from a quarter-plate to a half-plate, it is wonderful what you can see. You can count railway trucks and engines in sidings; from their positions you can frequently tell whether they are empty or full. You can distinguish between main lines, temporary light railways,

*Examples of photographic interpretation locating entrance to German dugouts.*

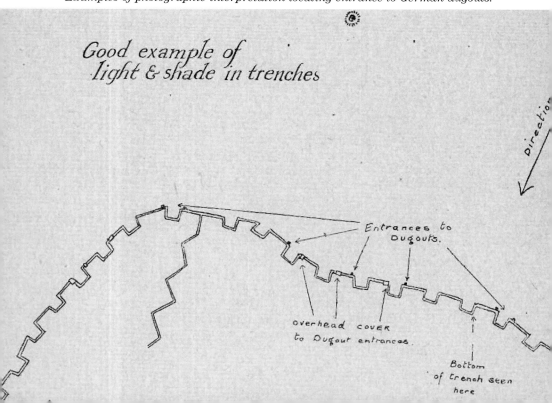

roads, cart tracks and footpaths; and if you march half-a-dozen men across a field in single file, their tracks can be picked up with a magnifying glass. The gunners spend half their lives trying to hide their guns or camouflage their battery positions and it frequently deceives the casual glance of an observer; but if you once get a photo of the field that they are in, you will even in all probability see the muzzle of their guns, to say nothing of the limber tracks along the hedges. If you made a trench and enforced it with barbed wire, you will not only be able to see if it is a deep trench by the shadows, or if it has water in it, but you will be able to see how many rows of barbed wire entanglement it has in front of it and which way the field was last ploughed.[4] *Lieutenant Robin Rowell, 12 Squadron, RFC*

Rowell was not exaggerating the potential of aerial photography and even by that stage the methods of interpreting aerial photographs had advanced considerably. To the untrained eye an aerial photograph reveals remarkably little; but an expert can, in conjunction with the associated features, determine the probable nature and purpose of an object by analysing aspects of the shape, size, shadow structure and tone.

1. The following points should be remembered when examining aeroplane photographs:-
a) Ascertain the direction of light.
b) Do not 'look' at a photograph; take a pencil and go carefully over each part; many details will thus be brought out which would otherwise escape notice.
c) Work in closest co-ordination with reports of visual observation and locations given in Intelligence Summaries. Eliminate all those which are obviously wrong; find out the likely places for the remainder and have these spots closely watched.
d) Study the configuration and nature of the ground in question very closely, in order to gain a correct impression of the siting of the points which are being observed on the photograph. This will assist in placing deductions on a correct basis.
2. Shadows play a most important part in the interpretation of photographs. It is therefore essential to ascertain the direction of light in order to decide whether the point under observation is convex or concave and to determine its relative height, depth and shape by the length of shadow cast.[5] *Notes on the Interpretation of Aeroplane Photographs, 1916*

Gradually characteristic features that exposed the inner workings of the German defences could be identified – machine-gun posts, trench mortar batteries, gun batteries, dugouts and mine shafts. The configuration of tracks and buried cables allowed the location of the various headquarters to be determined. However this expertise took time to codify and photographic interpretation was by no means an exact science in 1916.

As thousands of guns moved into the Somme area, the artillery observation aircraft had a ceaseless task seeking out the location of German gun positions in preparation for the inevitable duel as both sides flexed their artillery muscles.

> You went up for about an hour, an hour and a half, with the object of spotting enemy guns firing. You looked out across the lines into enemy territory and if a gun was operating you'd see a flash and then white smoke would be visible. You'd realise then that there was an enemy battery and on the large scale map you were carrying, you'd make a note of the exact position. During the period of that reconnaissance you might discover two or three batteries and you did the same thing for each case. There were occasions on which you reported them straight away back to one of your own batteries which were on the alert with the object of taking on any new battery but generally speaking on an artillery reconnaissance you made a note and then brought the intelligence back to your office – telephone up the batteries concerned and let them know what the situation was, or go down and see the battery commanders and let them know exactly where these batteries were so that they could take them on when they wanted to.[6] *Lieutenant Alan Jackson, 5 Squadron, RFC*

The methodology of aerial observation was well established and by then a matter of routine.

> Now ranging a gun from an aeroplane is the most perfect way that it is possible to devise and it naturally achieved

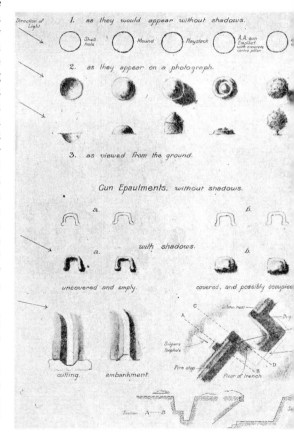

*Diagrams and an aerial photograph illustrating the importance of light and shadows in photographic interpretation.*

Direction
of
Light

Wood

Pit with
Water

Dugout

Dugout

Dugout

Dugouts

Dugout

A

A

Trench

Road

Trench

Overhead
Struts

Wood

A.A. *Breastworks*
shown ⍑⍑⍑⍑⍑.

6b 1079

*Example of aerial photograph interpretation.*

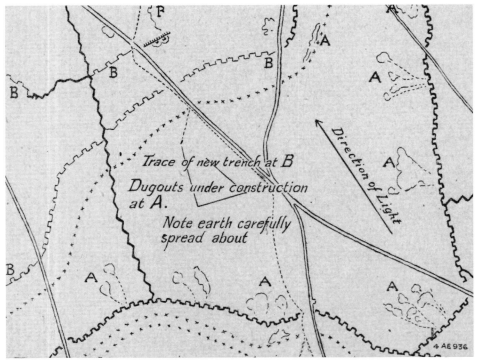

Trace of new trench at B

Dugouts under construction at A.

Note earth carefully spread about

Direction of Light

4 AE 936

extraordinary success. The rough principle of the game is this. Each aeroplane has a transmitting set of different note or frequency. Each battery of any consequence will have a receiving instrument, operators, and code letters by which it is known and can always be called upon to fire. In ordinary quiet times the targets that have to be ranged are pre-arranged before the machine leaves the ground, and when the machine gets up over the lines it will first go over and have a good look at the target. The observer will make a mental note of the distances of various objects round about the target, so that he will have something by which to judge his distances; he will also take note which is due north and set his imaginary clock dial with 12 o'clock pointing north. The machine then returns to the battery and warns them to prepare for the first round.[7] *Lieutenant Robin Rowell, 12 Squadron, RFC*

The clock code had been developed in 1915 and allowed the aerial observer to communicate within the same frames of reference with the battery on the ground.

You then, from a height of probably about 5,000 feet, proceeded to give the signal to fire, which was the letter 'G'. Having given the signal 'G' you watched the battery and you saw the flash of the guns. You then knew pretty well exactly how many seconds it would take for those shells to arrive at the target. You then shifted the wing of your aeroplane to have an unrestricted view of the target and you saw the fall of the shell or shells. The system of correcting faults was this. You had imaginary circles drawn round the target, 25 yards, 50 yards, 150, 200, 250, 300, 350, 400 – and you had a simple letter and figure code to indicate two things: the clock-face point at which the shells were falling, in other words whether they were falling at one o'clock or three o'clock from the target; and the distance as expressed in the imaginary circles which you visualised without much difficulty. With a good battery – batteries varied enormously – you should get them right on target at about the third salvo. They then fired as many shells as they had been instructed by the artillery authorities to fire.[8] *Captain Archibald James, 2 Squadron, RFC*

The practice of artillery observation may have been perfect in theory but it was not yet perfect in practice in 1916. A great deal of experience was needed to spot and identify the correct shell burst on the battlefield.

Obviously some guns were much easier to see than others. A gun was far more difficult to see the shell land and explode, far more difficult, than in the case of a howitzer. Obviously again, the bigger the calibre of the gun – say a 9.2″ which was an enormous gun – that gave a tremendous burst which was frightfully easy to see. Shrapnel bursting as it was timed to do in the air was awfully hard to judge from the very light smoke puff the bursting shell gave, how far above the ground it was and therefore exactly where the forward impetus would place the little round pieces of shrapnel.[9] *Captain Archibald James, 2 Squadron, RFC*

Furthermore, the Royal Artillery was a proud and august regiment and it harboured within it many traditionally minded officers who did not take kindly to being given fire orders by rank outsiders.

The real crux of the matter is that the artillery have a profound distrust and contempt for the Flying Corps, and have a terror of "allowing their guns to be run by the Flying Corps". This is the phrase which is always produced in such controversies. As a matter if fact there are many cases when the Flying Corps are the only people who can run the artillery, and if they are not even allowed to have priority in the use of one gun they are practically wasted. The artillery are apt to exaggerate their accuracy when firing without aerial observation I think. Both sides lost their tempers.[10] *Lieutenant Thomas Hughes, 1 Squadron, RFC*

\* \* \* \*

The German anti-aircraft fire, generally nicknamed 'Archie' after a popular musical hall song, plagued both the artillery observation and photographic reconnaissance missions. They were required by the nature of their duties to fly at a comparatively low altitude of around 6,000 feet in the case of aerial photography reconnaissances.

The anti-aircraft gun 'Archie' became extremely accurate with practice, and as it was almost essential to fly a straight course when photographing, the gunners had plenty of time to make the sky thick with bursting shell. In some parts of the line it was perfectly amazing to see the amount of stuff they could chuck up at you in a minute. The shells would burst far faster then you could count them, and you were compelled to change your direction every fifteen or twenty seconds or you would not last long. But it's well worth taking heavy risks to get good photos.[11] *Lieutenant Robin Rowell, 12 Squadron, RFC*

The practical menace of 'Archie' was little considered in the jovial atmosphere of the squadron mess, but in reality it was a constant source of danger that could suddenly leap into focus as shells suddenly burst all around the aircraft.

Yesterday I was some miles across the line with my observer, as an escort to another machine and was 'Archied' like the - er - dickens, shells bursting all round and some directly under me. Why the machine wasn't riddled I don't know. I was nearly 10,000

*el Hutcheon.* RAFM/RAeC 2086

feet up too. The 'Archies' burst, leaving black puffs of smoke in the air, so that the gunners could see the result. Those puffs were all over the sky. Talk about dodge! Banking both ways at once! 'Orrible. What's more, I had to stay over them, dodging about until the other machine chose to come back or finished directing the shooting.[12] *Second Lieutenant Lessel Hutcheon, 5 Squadron, RFC*

A few days later Hutcheon had an even worse experience.

I went out with an observer on a howitzer shoot, an officer in this case. We went over to the lines, arriving there about 11.15 am and 'rang up' the battery. All being well, we ploughed over the lines to have a look at the target in Hunland. The battery then fired and the observer watched for the burst and wirelessed back the correction. Each shot fired meant a journey over the lines and each time we went over the Huns got madder and madder and loosed off 'Archie' at us in bucketsful.

'Archie to right of us
Archie to left of us etc'.

We were fairly plastered in 'Archie'. Each time I crossed the lines I did so at a different altitude. The first five times I climbed higher each time to throw the range out, and the next five times I came down a bit each time. The last five times I was so fed up with their dud shooting that I went across at whatever altitude I happened to be at and that probably upset 'em more than ever! At any rate they fired about 600 shells at us in the course of that 'shoot', allowing roughly 40 shells per crossing (at least) and 15 crossings - and the only damage they did was to put a small hole through my top plane. My, they must have been disgusted! The strafe took place between 5,000 and 6,000 feet altitude. The 'Archies' got so near sometimes that we went through the smoke from the shell. Of course it would never do to go on flying a straight course; it is a case of dodge, twist, turn and dive at odd and unexpected moments - and when it gets really too hot, run away and come back at a different altitude.[13] *Second Lieutenant Lessel Hutcheon, 5 Squadron, RFC*

After a while the pilots developed their own methods of evading the shell bursts.

If you are getting badly hustled by German AA gunfire, you may find it of great use to sideslip your machine so that you are no longer travelling in the direction that your machine is heading, but at an angle, which is quite enough to throw all the AA calculations out. The fact that the machine has a list one way or another can rarely be seen from the ground. If you are being worried by an AA gun while you are ranging your own guns and you happen to know where the culprit is in hiding, you have only to fly straight until you see him fire and then, ten or fifteen seconds later, change your course one way or another and you will find the shells will explode where you would have been had you gone on straight. There are few things that annoy 'Archie' more than this trick because he doesn't get a ghost of a chance of even frightening you. If you are at a height of about 6 or 7,000 ft, it will take the shell about twenty seconds to explode from the time you see the flash of the gun.[14] *Lieutenant Robin Rowell, 12 Squadron, RFC*

For the pilots and observers of the corps aircraft it was a strange mixture of routine tedium and flashes of extreme nervous tension.

We were rather tired of flying up and down, being shot at continually by fairly accurate and remarkably well hidden anti-aircraft batteries, while we registered endless guns on uninteresting points. On the German side of the trenches, before the battle, the country seemed almost peaceful and deserted. Anti-aircraft shells arrived and burst in large numbers, coming apparently from nowhere, for it was almost rare to see a flash on the German side; if one did, it was probably a dummy flash; and of movement, except for a few trains in the distance, there was none. Only an expert observer would know that the thin straight line was a light railway; that the white lines were paths made by the ration parties and reliefs following the dead ground when they came up at night; that the almost invisible line was a sunken pipe line for bringing water to the trenches, and that the shading which crept and thickened along the German reserve trenches showed that the German working parties were active at night if invisible in the day time. For the shading spelt barbed wire. Only about half a dozen times during those three months did I have the luck to catch a German battery firing. When that happened one ceased the ranging work and called up something really heavy, for preference a nine-inch howitzer battery, which pulverized the Hun.[15] *Lieutenant A J Evans, 3 Squadron, RFC*

When they sighted their opposite numbers in German reconnaissance aircraft then they would inevitably try to bring them down.

One day I was ranging a battery and I was on our side of the lines over our battery, the visibility being very good. I looked over the side before sending a signal to our battery to fire and to my surprise saw a German two-seater almost directly below me well on our side of the lines and about 1,000 feet below me. I had in the front seat of the BE2 C as my observer and air gunner a corporal in my squadron who hadn't much experience in the air. So I throttled back, shouted to him what was happening, showed him the aeroplane and said, "Get your Lewis gun!" I omitted to say, "Don't start shooting till I tell you to!" With that I proceeded to go down circling on top of the all-unsuspecting German. Unfortunately, my Corporal got excited and when we were at least 150 yards away he opened fire and discharged the whole drum of his Lewis gun without any effect at all. Indeed the range was excessive. I then flattened out, very, very, close echeloned above the German. And I shall never forget the look of horrified surprise on the Germans' faces when they looked up alerted by the rattle of my machine gun and looked at me in sort of open mouthed astonishment. The German observer recovered his composure in probably two or three seconds and swung round the rotating mounting round his cockpit and pointed the gun at me and opened fire. Meanwhile my idiot Corporal was fumbling to try and get another drum on. We were so close that I actually saw the oil burning off the recoiling portions of the German machine gun. Well naturally, after two or three shots had been fired I banked steeply away at the same moment the German banked in the same direction. And we almighty nearly collided. That was the end of a thoroughly unsatisfactory episode.[16] *Captain Archibald James, 2 Squadron, RFC*

*German LVG CII.* IWM Q 66401

The BE2 C was generally inferior to the German two-seater LVG and Albatross reconnaissance machines, but the natural disparities of competence meant that a good British crew at least had a fair chance if they happened to meet a bad German crew. Second Lieutenant F C A Wright and Lieutenant Alan Dore of 13 Squadron proved themselves a determined team in combat.

> Doing artillery again but could get no batteries to put out ground signals. When at 9,000 feet we saw a Hun, probably LVG aeroplane below us. Wright, my pilot, who was going towards the enemy, swung the machine round and dived steeply. When 200 feet or more above, I let off a drum and saw the tracer bullets flicking all round the machine. He appeared to be hit, for he dived very steeply and we both thought he would crash to the ground on his own side; but when apparently about 1,000 to 2,000 feet above earth, he flattened out and continued his journey inland.[17]
> *Lieutenant Alan Dore, 13 Squadron, RFC*

A few days later, in very similar circumstances, Wright and Dore were to achieve the ultimate triumph of perseverance and luck.

> Left at 6.45 to do artillery. Gloriously fine. Wright, my pilot, at 9.30am saw a cloud of anti-aircraft shells bursting behind our lines. I signalled to my pilot to go in the direction of it. Suddenly two LVGs emerged. We turned and dived from 9,500 feet. The machine seemed almost vertical and the rush of wind terrific. When we were about 200 feet above I opened fire on the leading machine. Saw the tracer bullets go all round it. We were now all still diving like mad, we to get over the line, they to get away. I put another drum into the second machine as both disappeared beneath our wings. One only emerged which we chased over the trenches. On coming down we heard that one had fallen near Mount St Eloy, both pilot and observer being killed. It was all over in a few seconds, so infinitely fast do things happen in these fights. The debris of the fallen machine brought in today. Nothing but a tangled mass of wreckage remains; but the camera and lens, flying helmet, compass and other necessities for the aviator were practically uninjured. The anti-aircraft gunners are, apparently, claiming it as their bird, but all eye-witnesses at the batteries agree that the machine plunged directly after we had dealt with it. The batteries send us congratulations.[18] *Lieutenant Alan Dore, 13 Squadron, RFC*

As was often the custom when a German crashed on the British side of the lines, Dore went to see the results of his efforts.

> I go to Maroeuil to see the bodies of the two fallen Huns. Not out of morbid curiosity but to find out where they are hit with

GERMAN MACHINE,
L.V.G. TYPE.
Brought down by British
Airman in France.
PROPELL

*Captured LVG.* IWM Q 55547a

bullets and fix their burial place. Two bullet holes are discovered in the officer. A pitiful sight. It is war, though, and I must have no regrets. Everyone very kind and congratulations are frequent and

fervent. It is now officially recognised that we brought down the Hun. I am allowed to keep the pilot's helmet as a trophy.[19]
*Lieutenant Alan Dore, 13 Squadron, RFC*

Yet the LVGs were a very different kettle of fish from the threat of the Fokker that still loomed over the BE2 C squadrons. Although the casualties were not numerically high in comparison with the infantry, they still hit hard in the small world of the Squadron mess where every loss was a personal blow. So it was that Dore found that his usual pilot Second Lieutenant F C A Wright had more than met his match when flying with another observer.

News arrives that old Wright and Lucas are down behind the lines, but within reach of shells. Both wounded in fight with a Fokker. Powell and I go off to see the machine. It has a battered appearance. The front seat is covered with blood. Bullets have ploughed their way through everything. Many flying wires shot away. The throttle control out of action, the petrol tank punctured. We learn that a Fokker suddenly dived at them from a great height unawares. It passed right under them and then swung round, climbed and again attacked them in the rear. Lucas was shot after firing half a drum, and Wright soon after in the right shoulder and lung. He had to glide down without his engine and land with his left hand - a great performance. Lucas died immediately after landing. Saw Wright in hospital today; seems fairly cheerful. It is sad to have our partnership thus severed. The Doctor says he will get well.[20] *Lieutenant Alan Dore, 13 Squadron, RFC*

The situation improved gradually as the pendulum of aerial superiority began to swing back to the British as a new generation of aircraft that could compete on equal terms with the Fokker made their appearance. The first to arrive was the FE2 B, a two-seater pusher aircraft which could be regarded as a step forward from the near obsolescent Vickers Fighter. Again the gunner was perched in the front nacelle seat with a completely unobstructed forward view and armed with a Lewis gun. Although lacking in manoeuvrability and only capable of around 72mph at its service ceiling of 9,000 feet, it was a sturdy and reliable aircraft. The origins of the FE2 B lay in an aircraft designed by Geoffrey de Havilland as far back as 1910. The FE stood for 'Farman Experimental' marking the family resemblance to their early pusher aircraft. After a redesign, an order was placed for 12 of the FE2 A as it was then called on the outbreak of war. It would have been a formidable beast indeed, capable of effortlessly dominating the skies of 1914. Unfortunately, severe problems with the original engine provoked endless delays and by the time the first 12 were delivered in November 1915, it had been replaced with the more reliable 120 HP Beardmore and thus mutated into the FE2 B. The first squadron equipped

*British FE2 B.* IWM Q 63183

throughout with FE2 Bs was 20 Squadron, which arrived in late January 1916 to be followed shortly after by 25, 23 and 22 Squadrons.

The FE2 B was an advance on the Vickers Fighter and the BE2 C, but it could not be regarded as an intrinsically superior aircraft to the Fokker of 1916. As a pusher it was naturally vulnerable to the attacks from behind which had become the hallmark of the better Fokker pilots. The FE2 Bs and later variants with more powerful engines fulfilled a variety of roles, especially for the troublesome long-range reconnaissances and as a general escort aircraft to such as the BE2 Cs. Thus it was that on 31 May, five FE2 Bs of 23 Squadron accompanied by two Martinsyde Scouts were sent on a reconnaissance over the rear of the putative Somme battlefield.

Went up again at 7am, got into formation at 8,000 feet and crossed the lines at 8,500 at 9.30 keeping good station. Unfortunately, the wind got up at this time and when we turned at Cambrai were able to make but slow progress over the ground. When over Marquion, the Scouts suddenly swooped down and I knew we were attacked. I had ordered them to do this as I was well aware that they could not turn much to fight their fixed gun and hoped they would draw the enemy down on to the stern guns of the escort. I turned round after Solly and fired our drum back and he got in another one from the bow gun. I did not turn completely again after this as I realised that if we kept on turning with the wind, we should never get out. The Fokkers evidently worked on some pre-arranged plan as they were firing small white lights before swooping down. After the first attack which was made

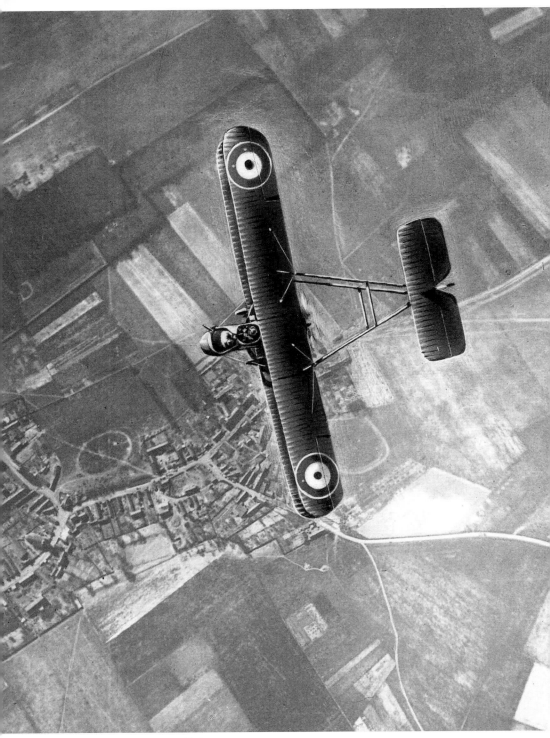

*FE2 B from above in flight.* IWM Q 69317

between us and the sun, the enemy showed much more caution in approaching near. It was in this first attack I think that Cairn Duff was shot down. Allen had his observer (Powell) shot dead as he was firing back and I rather think he got his man too as three of us saw one Fokker going down anyhow, side slipping and nose diving. Anyway Powell had his gun right 'on' as the bullet grazed his trigger finger and struck him in the eye. He fell back into the nacelle breaking one of his legs in the fall. Allen was now defenceless and in spite of the fact that the machine was shot to 'bits' just managed to scrape back over the lines, when his engine stopped. He got back into the aerodrome. While all this was going on Solly was making his notes in a most cool manner. I got him to man the after gun three times when I saw a Fokker coming up behind, but the escort kept him off.[21] *Captain Harold Wyllie, 23 Squadron, RFC*

The Fokkers soon found that the ungainly looking FE2 Bs were more than capable of looking after themselves.

Went on reconnaissance. Unfortunately the camera jammed. Five Fokkers hung on our tails but did not close in to fighting range. The wind was strong against us coming back. We were lucky not to have another running fight. Perhaps they realised we carry a sting in our tail. These running fights are the devil. It is annoying to have to be passive resisters, caring only about the Reconnaissance and getting back with the report and the photos.[22] *Captain Harold Wyllie, 23 Squadron, RFC*

*Fokker on the ground.* IWM Q 69182

*FE2 B on ground.* IWM Q 69650

The FE2 B Squadrons found that the best method of defence was to circle round to protect each other's vulnerable tail from the lurking Fokkers. It had already been found necessary to fit a second Lewis gun that was located on a telescopic mounting between the two cockpits. To use it the observer was required to stand on his seat and fire the Lewis backwards over pilot and the upper wing to partially cover the blind spot to the rear. Perched as he was with only his feet and ankles actually within the cockpit, the observer was almost completely exposed and could easily fall out to his inevitable death in the days before parachutes. In such circumstances the crews had to have total faith in each other.

Two-seater scrapping can be half won on the ground in this way. We will assume that the pilot is a thoroughly good pilot and can make his machine do anything he wants it to. Then we will take it that you have picked the best Observer in the Squadron and that he knows all there is to know about the Lewis Gun. Well, the essence of two-seater fighting is, without a doubt, thorough co-operation between Pilot and Observer. You want to get to know each other. To have absolute confidence, so that when it comes to a scrap you know what each other are going to do. You can talk things over; imagine all sorts of positions. You don't get time to think hard when it comes to a scrap, and if you get it mapped out before, the battle is half won. Say you are diving on your Hun. You are almost going to collide with him. Your Observer knows you will bank off to the left and he is ready with his gun. I believe in living with your Observer. When I was out there we lived in huts; each Pilot and Observer shared a hut. It is useful just before turning in to talk over what you have been doing. Several points may crop up; use them in the next scrap. Then with regard to actual tactics. With the F.E.'s the Hun will try and get on your tail. If you want to, the F.E. will turn very quickly. The Fokker is not able to turn as quickly as an F.E. and you will have a good chance of catching him as he is on the turn. The Fokker can only fire straight ahead. With the F.E. you have a very large arc of fire. The Pilot's maxim with a two-seater is to always give your Observer the best possible shot and the Hun the worst. Personally, I always went up with my gun pointing over the top of the plane ready for the Observer to use, and I remember one occasion when it came in useful. In all F.E.'s the Observer must face the rear. Unless the Observer is kneeling looking to the rear, you will get caught, because the Pilot can see nothing. Make the Observer responsible for all behind and the Pilot responsible for all machines in front. I remember on one occasion a Fokker was just about to fire and the Observer signalled to the Pilot to stall the machine. They got in a burst at the Fokker over the top plane with the rear gun mounting and brought him down.

This shows what can be done if you think it out. Don't go plump at all machines. Go for them as if you were attacking a hostile machine until you are absolutely certain it is friendly. Then of course with formation flying it is absolutely imperative that you keep your station and distance and watch your reconnaissance leader. All Hun machines are scared to death at an F.E. nose-diving down on them. The only machine to fight was the LVG because the Observer could stand up from the back. You must zigzag until you get right on top of him. It is the essence of two-seater fighting to be in close co-operation with the Observer, and when you once get onto a Hun never leave him until you have brought him down.[23] *Captain Sydney Harris, 23 Squadron, RFC*

With a well-trained confident crew such as this a lone FE2 B could even make a decent shift of single combat with a Fokker.

One fight in particular stands out in my mind. Just a tiny line in the sky, rushing at one with frightening speed, belching bullets which 'flick' on one's wings as they strike on either side. It is hard to fly straight and level to give Mann, my Scottish Rifles Observer, a good shot - and after a bit I don't - side-slipping like hell. By the grace of goodness the Hun misses our vital parts and either hit, or scared of Mann's fire, dives off groundwards in a trail of smoke. Thus we survive, victors over the plummeting enemy going down, down into the cloud towards the dark earth. Was he hit or just buzzing off? But it has been a very near thing . . .[24] *Lieutenant Ranald Macfarlane, 25 Squadron, RFC*

*Sydney Harris.* RAFM/RAeC )

The Germans soon recognized that the FE2 B was a dangerous opponent that was not to be underestimated.

The techniques and tactics of the English were amazing, their main principle being that each machine should not look after itself but its partner. Each one therefore protected the other against any attack by their German opponents, and each pair tried to attack the same foeman . . . The Englishmen refused to be rushed, and their steadiness gave them an absolute superiority. Meanwhile our machines tried to break their formation by a series of advances and retreats, like dogs attacking a hedgehog. They pirouetted and spiralled, but their movements exposed them to more risks than their opponents, who appeared to be invulnerable and unassailable.[25] *Hans Schroder, German Air Force*

One surrealistic tactic tried on the spur of the moment by a pair of FE2 Bs was certainly not to be repeated!

You had to fly over a German aerodrome for four hours waiting for a scrap and doing a reconnaissance at the same time. Two planes had to go on that job and my pal, a Sergeant Mottershead, who always took the job with me, started pointing down, but I could see nothing to worry us. Well, we had made it up to always stick together, no matter what happened, so, of course, I went down as well. We were down to 500 feet and still he went down and landed on the aerodrome. By the time I got down he and his observer had opened up with their guns at the hangars etc, so we did the same. I know we used about 200 rounds of tracer and the hangar was on fire; so I pointed up and off we went. We got back OK and made it up together to say nothing of what had happened. I'm afraid we were found out, as we were sent for to the CO's office and asked what we had done with our ammo. We never thought of that or perhaps could have made a tale up. Well, we had to admit the truth and we were put on the peg.[26] *Sergeant Sydney Attwater, 20 Squadron, RFC*

After threats of a court martial for such reckless behaviour they were eventually let off with extra parades. Mottershead was awarded the VC for his courageous actions later in the war.

The German tactics were also beginning to evolve as they made increasing use of decoys to lure the unwary into their fatal grip.

It was all a strange, other-worldly feeling. There, high above the battlefront, perhaps on a lovely, cold spring morning, peaceful seeming, and away on the distant ground, marvellously clear trails of smoke from enemy trains. Then far below, one spots a light grey shape moving between the clouds; an Albatross or Taube glides across the green-brown earth. One dives down to strafe it. The Boche pilot is alerted and dives away earthwards. But suddenly there is an unpleasant crackling behind. The Albatross has been a decoy, or it is being escorted and two or three nasty spitting little monoplanes come whizzing in to attack. A fierce turn or two but the odds are too great and despite the known danger of diving away one plunges earthwards like a stone, to luckily live and fight again.[27] *Lieutenant Ranald Macfarlane, 25 Squadron, RFC*

The beauty of the decoy system was that it provided an extra layer of protection for all unescorted German reconnaissance aircraft that may or may not be decoys. If a British pilot survived the trap once it had been sprung, then he would naturally be cautious about putting his head in the noose again. Caution became the watchword, and in a war of split second opportunities, many German two-seaters escaped while their opponents were carefully searching the heavens fearful of a trap.

When you see an old Albatross two-seater flying about on the other side of the lines a few thousand feet below you, watch his movements with great care before you go and attack him. If he is

*Albatross C1.* IWM HU 1815

busy ranging his guns, go straight ahead; but as likely as not he will be a 'decoy' and out to catch you. Directly you turn your head towards him you will find that he will make away back to his side of the lines, and he will encourage you to follow him, when all the time there are half-a-dozen fighting machines up above you waiting their chance when they can get you well across onto their side. So whenever you see any 'easy prey', mind it is not a trap to catch you . . . It is never sufficient just to look round the sky in a casual manner. You must turn your machine round and change your direction once or twice, so that any portions of the sky that were covered by the planes of your machine will be exposed. And never forget to look into the sun. The sun is often an enemy as it is a friend. An attacking machine will often fly miles round the sky, often completely out of sight, in order to get into the sun and make his attacking dive, so that the gunner defending the attacked machine has a very poor chance of any good shooting.[28] *Lieutenant Robin Rowell, 12 Squadron, RFC*

Despite this instinctive caution, the whole aggressive ethos inculcated by Trenchard meant that they could not just ignore any opportunity to shoot down an aircraft actively tormenting their comrades in the infantry below them. It was a difficult dilemma that every pilot had to resolve, balancing his sense of duty with the question of personal survival.

Another new British aircraft that made its debut early in 1916 was the DH2. A single-seater pusher fighter of slightly comical appearance it, perhaps more than any other aircraft was instrumental in winning domination of the Somme skies for the RFC. It was produced by the Aircraft Manufacturing Company and designed by Geoffrey de Havilland, the former designer at the Royal Aircraft Factory, who had joined the firm just before the outbreak of war. It is a reflection of his design skills that his aircraft were known by his name rather than that of the manufacturer. Thus his second design for the AMC was the 'de Havilland 2' soon shortened to the more familiar DH2. It was a small aircraft but strongly built and able to absorb a fair amount of punishment. Powered by the rotary 100 HP Gnome or Le Rhône engine it could generate 85mph at 7,000 feet, 77mph at 10,000 feet and had a service ceiling of 14,000 feet. Unfortunately the DH2 did have several disadvantages that had to be circumnavigated by its pilots. It was still not as fast as the Fokker and had a slower rate of climb. The engine had a hand controlled petrol induction system that in practice meant that it was always running flat out or not at all. Due to the risk of flooding the engine, the ignition invariably had to be switched off using a switch on the joystick during a dive. Furthermore, it was armed with just one Lewis gun on a flexible mounting in front of the pilot. The gun was almost always fixed to fire forward by aiming the aircraft, rather than make the futile attempt to manoeuvre and aim at the same time in

*DH2 on ground.* IWM Q 67534

frenetic combat. Finally, the combined effect of the torque of the propeller and the gyroscopic effect of the spinning rotary engine meant that the aircraft was essentially unstable which made the flying controls very sensitive. At first it was difficult to fly, being prone to spin if the pilot was inattentive or overly clumsy in his handling. This was compounded by the usual rash of engine failures that seemed to mar the launch of every new type of aircraft. After a particularly bad accident the aircraft was blessed with the gloomy sobriquet 'The Spinning Incinerator'.

The first unit to be wholly equipped with the new scouts was 24 Squadron that reached France under the command of Major Lanoe Hawker VC in February 1916. After two fatalities, morale declined as the pilots came to believe that the DH2 could not be got out of a spin. For a man like Hawker there was only one way to resolve this problem. Not for him patient lectures and diagrams. He took a DH2 up to 8,000 feet and there, in front of his men, put it into a series of spins. Left spin, right spin, engine on, engine off he tried them all and every time got out safely. Only after landing did he explain to his pilots exactly what they must do. When the necessary light touch had been developed, pilots came to love their DH2s for the ease with which they could out-turn almost any aircraft in combat situations. That is not to say that flying the DH2 was without risk. The pusher layout had an obvious danger in that engine problems or outright failure could damage or sever the tail boom structure and put the machine out of control. In a crash landing the engine could lurch forward to crush the pilot.

My engine was going splendidly, when all of a sudden at 4,000 feet (I had left the ground a few minutes only) there was a most awful bang and crash followed by frightful vibration and at the same time the whole machine shook convulsively in all directions. A cylinder with 100 horse power behind it had blown clean out of the engine going straight through the rear main spar of the top plane and shattering it, first ripping out one blade of a four bladed propeller. I at once switched off and shut off the power, but the engine was unfortunately able to revolve, as the remaining three blades of the propeller continued to revolve on account of resistance to the air as the machine descended. Because the engine minus a cylinder, and propeller minus a blade was shockingly unbalanced, therefore vibration and shaking took place and could not be stopped. Now imagine that descent to the ground (I descended as slow as possible, as the faster you went the worse the vibration), my gun in front jerked out of its mounting and was jumping from side to side, three drums containing 47 rounds of ammunition were caused by the vibration to leap from their positions and flew past me to make holes in the plane. Then the machine commenced to break up in the air, two

struts broke in two. Piloting the machine while being thrown about and with the controls jumping in my hand was not exactly ideal, but to my astonishment I made a good landing, in luckily a good field and was unhurt. Wonderful escape as everyone says.[29]
*Captain Robert Hughes-Chamberlain, 24 Squadron, RFC*

Captain Hughes-Chamberlain may well have been a somewhat insensitive young man as he included this vivid description of his death-defying escape in a letter to his mother. This cannot have alleviated her natural fears as to her son's welfare.

Hawker was the ideal commander for the first DH2 squadron. As a former officer in the Royal Engineers, he had a practical and inventive mind that he employed to devise solutions for the every-day problems of flying. He produced endless little gadgets – gun racks, engine modifications, a ring sight and even special thigh boots to keep the pilots feet from freezing.

The idea of devoting some method to practise allowances in shooting was solved by Major Hawker, who designed the first aiming off model, with the marked rod up the centre, which later became universal and was adopted by every training station in the RFC. We had been discussing aiming off and how much to allow at various ranges. Major Hawker, taking a pencil and paper and reckoning the pace of a bullet, showed us in a few minutes:- 1) That most of us were wide of the mark. 2) That range was a very essential factor, which we were largely overlooking . . . He was one of the first to realise that many a pilot can get close to his man, but few can shoot straight enough to shoot him down.[30] *Captain A M Williams, 24 Squadron, RFC*

The DH2s of Hawker's Squadron were initially assigned to escort reconnaissance missions undertaken by the BE2 Cs of 4, 9 and 15 Squadrons and the FE2 Bs of 22 Squadron. The DH2 may not have been able to match the Fokker in diving or climbing, but it could easily out turn-it in action without losing much height. On 24 April three DH2s flown by Lieutenant N P Manfield, Lieutenant J O Andrews and Lieutenant D Wilson were in action whilst escorting five BE2 Cs of 15 Squadron They ran into the ultimate test for the DH2, for one of their opponents was Immelmann himself.

I had a nasty fight in the air today. I took off at about 11am and met two English biplanes southward of Bapaume. I was about 700 metres higher and therefore came up with them very quickly and attacked one. He seemed to heel over after a few shots, but unfortunately I was mistaken. The two worked splendidly together in the course of the fight and put 11 shots into my machine. The petrol tank, the struts on the fuselage, the undercarriage and the propeller were hit. I could only save myself by a nose-dive of

1,000 metres. Then at last the two of them left me alone. It was not a nice business.[31] *Lieutenant Max Immelmann, Flying Section 62, German Air Force*

On 25 April, Second Lieutenant S E Cowan was escorting a BE2 C of 9 Squadron on a reconnaissance mission over Bapaume. In single combat the DH2 was evidently more than capable of holding its own with the hitherto dread Fokker.

When at 9,000 feet over Flers, I was attacked from behind and above by a Fokker. The bullets appeared to go off with a bang on striking the machine. Turning sharply, I saw a Fokker about 500 feet above me. I did an upward spiral following the Fokker and when about 100 feet below him, I pulled the nose of the de Havilland right up, training my gun on him and fired half a drum. I then held my fire and although my engine was missing badly I was able to reach his height. After some manoeuvring I got behind his tail, about two lengths away; finishing the first drum, I changed drums, and was able to do this very quickly meanwhile, I had got still nearer and was able to fire this drum right into him, although my aim was erratic, as the back draught of the Fokker bumped the de H. about. The Fokker dodged wildly but could not get away. He then suddenly put on vertical bank and side-slipped down about 500 feet. The side-slip developed into a nose dive, which he did not come out of until very low down. While he was diving I was able to get another drum in. I then picked up the BE2 C again and finished the escort.[32] *Second Lieutenant Sidney Cowan, 24 Squadron, RFC*

Just as the Fokker had preyed on the BE2 Cs, now the DH2 pilots culled the hapless German reconnaissance aircraft.

On reaching the lines I saw the Hostile Aircraft (HA) arrow at Bray pointing towards Mericourt, but, was unable to see any HA. After hunting around for about 30 minutes, I saw the arrow had changed and made to point towards Curlu. I then saw a hostile machine (Type 'A' LVG) flying south at about 1,500 feet between Hen and Clery. I dived; after chasing him round and gradually getting closer, I got within 50 yards of him; the observer was firing wildly over his tail. I fired about quarter of a drum and he immediately dived and endeavoured to land cross-wind, hitting a wire fence, his bottom plane was ripped off by a post, which bent back the left hand wings. The whole machine swung round again taking the undercarriage off. I then switched on, climbed to 200 feet and turned round, dived, firing the remains of my drum at the pilot and observer who were running across the field. I hit one of them who staggered and fell, the other took refuge in a shed nearby. Meanwhile, my thumb switch had stuck and I was forced

*Sopwith 1½ strutter.*

to land, but in doing so the bump loosened the spring and I was able to get off again. Climbing to about 500 feet, I came home along the Somme amidst a lively fusillade of shells and small arms.[33] *Second Lieutenant Sidney Cowan, 24 Squadron, RFC*

One more British aircraft was to add weight to the British air offensive on the Somme. The Sopwith 1½ Strutter, which first appeared over the Somme with 70 Squadron, was the first British aircraft to mount a synchronized Vickers machine gun firing through the propeller. Originally built for the RNAS, it was powered by a 110hp Clerget rotary engine, which allowed it to reach speeds of 99mph at 8,000 feet and it took only 17 minutes to reach 10,000 feet. The observer was armed with a Lewis gun mounted on a ring mounting. The Sopwith 1½ Strutter thus generated considerable firepower, which made it a formidable opponent even though it had severely limited manoeuvrability.

Once the three new British aircraft types were fully operational the swing of the aerial pendulum was at last reversed, but it was a slow process and many more British pilots would die in outclassed aircraft before there were sufficient numbers of the new types to wrest control. Thus Immelmann, undaunted, scored his fifteenth victory on 16 May 1916.

I flew up and down at 4,200 metres; after a while I saw three biplanes far below me. One was about 2,800 metres up, and the other two perhaps 2,400. I could not make out the nationality markings on account of the thick haze. But as they were over German territory and no one was shooting at them, I thought they might be Germans. There was something funny about one of them, however. He seemed to be flying peaceably behind the other two, and yet he looked a different type. I decided to have a look at the fellow. Down I go in a very steep dive, which brings me also horizontally nearer to him at a very great speed. When I have dropped down to 3,000 metres and am about 300 - 400 metres away from the three, I discover that the upper one is a Bristol biplane and the lower two LVGs. The Englishman is pursuing one of the two Germans. As he is concentrating all his attention on him, he has not noticed me yet. I dive still lower, and when I am within 30-40 metres of him and 10-20 metres above him, I got him in my sights and take careful aim. I fire both machine guns simultaneously, 15-20 rounds from each. I must have hit him, for never have I been able to aim so calmly and deliberately. The Englishman goes into a feeble right hand turn, which develops at once into a heel over by the right. Then, pushing his machine hard down, he flies a short distance westward, after which he promptly begins to spin - a sign that his fate is sealed. But he vanishes in the haze before he has finished his first spiral.[34] *Lieutenant Max Immelmann, Flying Section 62, German Air Force*

His victim was the Bristol Scout flown by Second Lieutenant M M Mowatt of 11 Squadron who died of his wounds. Mowatt had been enraged by a crash landing he had endured earlier that day and had taken off determined to redeem himself by shooting down a German aircraft. It is apparent that he had almost managed it before Immelmann had intervened to such deadly effect. One of Mowatt's squadron was upset by his death, "He was such a topping chap."[35] Second Lieutenant Albert Ball, who made the remark, would however begin his own remarkable career as a scout pilot that day, with an unconfirmed first victory whilst flying a Bristol Scout above Givenchy.

I was on patrol yesterday morning on my British Scout. I was at 12,000 feet and saw a Hun at 5,000. It started off and I went after it, catching it up when 20 miles over its own lines. It took 120 shots to do it in, but in the end it went down, upside down.[36] *Second Lieutenant Albert Ball, 11 Squadron, RFC*

Albert Ball was born in Nottingham on 10 January 1898, the son of a wealthy businessman who was prominent in local politics. Academically undistinguished, Ball had a mechanical bent, which he fully indulged in a variety of boyish hobbies before leaving school in 1913, and taking up a position in an engineering firm. On the outbreak of war he answered the call of adventure and enlisted in the ranks of the 2/7th Battalion, Sherwood Foresters on 21 September 1914. He was almost immediately commissioned as a second lieutenant and seconded to a Cyclist unit, but was anxious to get to the front and he paid privately for flying instruction to increase his chances of getting into the ever expanding RFC. He passed the Royal Aero Club pilot's examination and was transferred to the RFC for further training with 9 (Reserve) Squadron and a final polish at the Central Flying School. After a brief interlude with 22 Squadron at Gosport, Ball was posted out to France and joined 13 Squadron flying BE2 Cs on 18 February 1916. Here he engaged in the normal duties of a corps squadron pilot although he took every chance he could find to fly the attached Bristol Scout. His potential may well have been recognized, as on 7 May he was transferred to 11 Squadron, who were in the process of forming a flight of Bristol and Nieuport Scouts. Ball was destined to become the dominant British pilot throughout the Battle of the Somme. His name soon became linked with the French single-seater purpose built Nieuport 16 Scout a tractor biplane which ultimately replaced the Bristol Scout. The streamlined Nieuport 16 was powered by a 110 HP Le Rhône engine, which managed to generate speeds of up to 110 mph with a service ceiling of 15,000 feet. The Nieuport 16 was superior in every respect to the Fokker with the sole exception of armament - the only firepower was a fixed forward firing Lewis gun mounted above the wing centre section and fired by a Bowden wire grip on the joystick.

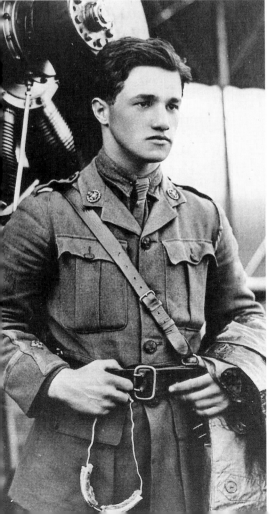

*Albert Ball.* IWM Q 69593

Again this dodged the central requirement for a synchronized gun by directing its fire above the span of the propeller. The French made a few of these magnificent fighting machines available to the British who at first doled them out to the scout pilots attached to their reconnaissance squadrons. As the scout pilot of 11 Squadron it was Ball's role to protect the slower and vulnerable recon-naissance machines whilst they trundled up and down above the battlefields and to engage in offensive patrols to seek out and destroy German aircraft wherever they might be found. On 29 May he was in four separate combats in rapid succession.

I had four fights in one patrol on my Nieuport, and came off top in every fight. Four Fokkers and an LVG attacked me about 12 miles over the lines. I forced the LVG down with a drum and a half, after which I zoomed up after the Fokkers. They ran away at once. Out of all the fights I only got about eight shots into my machine, one just missed my back and hit the strut. However, on my way back, the Hun 'Archie' guns hit the tail of my machine and took a piece away, but I got back and have now got a new tail. The other fights were with Albatross machines. General Higgins sent for me on landing, and was very pleased.[37] *Second Lieutenant Albert Ball, 11 Squadron, RFC*

In May and June the pace of the conflict grew ever more frenetic, as both sides fought desperately for control of the skies prior to the launch of the Allied offensive. For the BE2 Cs the requirements of the General Staff became ever more specific as they sought to complete their plans and preparations. They were desperate for information that only the RFC could realistically supply.

Evening patrol from 6pm to 8.15pm. XVII Corps want information of roads used by Germans when relieving. We patrol up and down our front, seeing and marking down several gun flashes. At last we find a gap and circling round in it get to 4,500 feet, cross lines over cloud and find a gap the other side of Bailleul. On Gavrelle-Bailleul road I pick out a dozen or more wagons proceeding North-West and immediately let off a drum from the Lewis gun into them. I think I must have stirred them up for some stopped. Others went on and formation was lost. Turning West again we crossed the lines, dived through the clouds and so home – only to run into the flares and set alight to the machine. Luckily it went out just as I was preparing to jump out.[38] *Lieutenant Alan Dore, 13 Squadron, RFC*

The aircraft would almost always attack targets of opportunity, but when flying low they had to bear in mind the intense volume of fire that infantry could generate against them.

On patrol I noticed at 7.15pm a column of infantry coming round bend at Bois du Bouval. Flew over to investigate. Through glasses could see men clearly standing in road and looking up at us. They were now stopped and bunched together at entrance to a trench. Called up guns furiously, but could get no-one to fire. Very angry. Decided with Wright my pilot to strafe them ourselves, so crossed at 3,000 feet and dived. I put two drums of Lewis gun into them from 1,800 feet to 2,000 feet. Return journey seemed endless. The whole line for miles seemed to be firing at us, the crackle of the machine guns continuous. In the waning light I could see volleys of flashes. The bullets were whistling all around and through the planes. Shall we never reach our side of the lines? A bullet struck the front gun mounting with a vivid splash not six inches from my head. At last we were back again. Wright having a bullet in his coat that did not penetrate him. We had 14 bullet holes in the machine.[39] *Lieutenant Alan Dore, 13 Squadron, RFC*

To maximise the damage and disruption caused to the Germans, all corps machines were ordered to carry bombs but, there was another reason.

> All machines that flew up to the lines and across had to always carry two 20 lb bombs and drop them on any target they thought was worthwhile. The object of this was to make quite sure that the pilots did cross the lines and go over enemy territory. Very often they rather shirked that through nerve tiredness - they preferred not to do it. Across the lines is always more dangerous than doing it on your own side. They had to get across the lines to do it and they would choose some railway station or whatever it might be that they thought it might be useful to bomb. As often as not they never hit them so it didn't much matter, but still they dropped the bombs and they got across the line which was the object of the exercise.[40] *Lieutenant Alan Jackson, 5 Squadron, RFC*

The inevitable casualties caused by the ever increasing pace of the fighting, coupled with the time required to train a competent pilot, meant that many pilots reached the front with a less than adequate number of training hours flown in the air. One young pilot's first flight in an FE2 D, soon after his arrival at his squadron in France, could well have been his last.

> It was a dizzy affair, right in front of my flight commander and the squadron commanding officer. I had studied all the plane's instruments and gadgets and could have located them blindfolded. I had checked and double checked fuel, oil, temperature, and other items and bumped off down that awful field for a take-off. Rising nicely and not too abruptly I was beginning to pat myself on the back when, "Whang! Bang! Bang! Wang!" The engine was stalling – one bank of six cylinders cut out. Down went the nose like a bullet and in the steepest bank I had ever made in my twenty-odd hours of flying I turned abruptly and glided back to the field with a dead engine and landed on the runway downwind with scarcely a bump.[41] *Second Lieutenant Harold Hartney, 20 Squadron, RFC*

This seemingly minor incident was actually the luckiest possible escape for the young pilot and his doubtless unimpressed gunner. His instructors had clearly failed to impress upon Hartney that in the event of the engine stalling on take-off a pilot should never, ever, attempt to turn back. Such a turn would sacrifice yet more flying speed and would in most cases result in a catastrophic smash up. Far better to attempt a controlled forced landing straight ahead.

Another inexperienced young pilot, Lieutenant Leslie Horridge joined his squadron in late May and like most new arrivals was almost immediately thrown into the fray. During the afternoon of 28 May he was sent up on line patrol duty. His training in England had omitted at least one vital component that might have been supposed essential before he could face the Germans in aerial combat.

> I carried an observer and two machine guns. One is fired backwards over my head by the observer and the other is mounted on the right hand side and is fired forward by the pilot. I have never fired a Lewis gun or been shown how to, but that is a mere detail. The cartridges are carried in drums which we put on when we had climbed to 5,000 feet. After we had put on the drums we went off to the lines. Patrol duty consists in moving about over the lines for a length of about 15 miles and chasing away any Huns. The Huns are always about 2,000 feet higher than a BE2 C will climb but that does not matter. The lines are very distinct. They run roughly parallel and zig-zag about all over. The No Man's Land between them was quite green. The whole ground on either side is covered all over with shell holes and looks exactly like a photo of the moon. Occasionally you see a gun flash but it seemed to me to be very hard to distinguish. When I got about half way along the patrol line and was about 7,500 feet up, I heard a sudden bang and looked round and saw an Archie 'puff'. They kept coming up but none of them were very near. It was not long before I was out of range, but it was not very comfortable. There are two Archies on the line and each time I passed over them they sent the things up. All the time we were keeping a look out for Hun machines but we did not see any. There seem to be absolutely no life on the German side of the lines. It was too misty to see clearly except right underneath and all you could see was the network of grey brown trenches stretching away on either side. We started to come down after we had been up 2½ hours. It was very boring work sitting there, especially as the machine had been slightly strained and would not fly hands off.[42] *Lieutenant Leslie Horridge, 7 Squadron, RFC*

*Leslie Horridge.* IWM HU 866

Horridge was lucky the skies were empty that day. If he had met a competent German scout he almost certainly would have been shot down. Unable through inexperience to see his opponent circling above; flying a machine far too slow and unmanoeuvrable to escape; and absolutely untrained in the Lewis gun, Horridge would have been nothing more than Fokker fodder.

> The poor old BE2 C just trickles along with the weight it has to carry. Thirty gallons of petrol, two officers, two Lewis guns with 400 rounds of ammunition, two 20lb bombs, wireless with accumulator and a huge camera fitted on the outside of the

machine where it gets all the air resistance. It is just about as much as you can expect the thing to fly with.[43] *Lieutenant Leslie Horridge, 7 Squadron, RFC*

But, if nothing happened, there could be moments of almost serene beauty high above the clouds.

I had a reconnaissance to do yesterday morning. It was still dark when I left the ground but the moon was shining. I went up to 7,500 feet and found that the clouds were too thick. The sun was just beginning to rise and the clouds were about a thousand feet below. They were quite level – except for small waves and it looked like the sea. When I got to them on the way down, it felt as if it would have been quite safe to step out onto them. They were about 2,500 feet thick and when I got through, I hadn't the least idea where I was.[44] *Lieutenant Leslie Horridge, 7 Squadron, RFC*

For the young pilot who survived his first couple of weeks, misplaced confidence was often the next stage of his mental odyssey.

I am beginning to think that you cannot be killed in an ordinary aeroplane smash. I have seen so many, and no-one has been killed, that it seems to be very bad luck if you are ever hurt. If the pilot knows how to fly, flying is as safe as motoring, probably more so, as you never have to worry about being run into. Nearly every smash is caused through carelessness, either in getting off or landing.[45] *Lieutenant Leslie Horridge, 7 Squadron, RFC*

All too soon, Horridge, like so many before him, was an old hand; an experienced campaigner who looked on with pity at the laughable antics of the new replacement pilots.

Some of the new pilots who come out here are very funny when they do their first flights. Our aerodrome is one of the smallest, if not the smallest, in France, which is saying a lot. I had a new pilot today who was inclined to do the 'That's not the way, watch me!' sort of thing. After I had carefully and at great length explained to him how I wanted the thing done, I let him loose solo in the atmosphere in an old machine in case he crashed it. He nearly killed himself when he was getting off and made two shots at getting in before he finally landed. On his subsequent flights he began to see that he had better stop doing fancy turns to get in and afterwards, apart from nearly spoiling a good row of trees when getting off and bending the undercarriage like a bow when landing, he was more or less successful, so I cheered him up by telling him he could practise tomorrow with a dummy passenger in the shape of a 112lb bomb in the front seat. If it goes off he will know that he has made a bad landing.[46] *Lieutenant Leslie Horridge, 7 Squadron, RFC*

The landing was a highly public demonstration of experience and skill – or otherwise . . .

A good landing is a bounce of about 20 feet into the air, and a diminuendo of bounces, like a grasshopper - until you pull up. A fairly bad landing is a bounce of 50 feet and diminuendo. [47] *Second Lieutenant Lessel Hutcheon, 5 Squadron, RFC*

Accidents were frequent with ham-fisted pilots and although the machines were a good deal more robust than they looked, undercarriages frequently gave way under the strain and major damage could be caused to a pilot and his aircraft if they turned over.

Part of the backdrop of the Somme aerial fighting was created by the Pemberton-Billing affair. Noel Pemberton-Billing had served with some distinction in the Royal Naval Air Service, before resigning his commission to fight and win a seat in the House of Commons. Here he took up cudgels against the establishment of the RFC and the Royal Aircraft Factory, claiming that casualties resulting from the perceived inadequacies of service aircraft were due to their criminal negligence. Thus in the House of Commons on 22 March 1916, he made the first in a series of inflammatory statements.

I do not want to touch a dramatic note this afternoon but if I did I would suggest that quite a number of our gallant officers in the Royal Flying Corps have been rather murdered than killed.[48] *Noel Pemberton-Billing MP*

A few days later, on 28 March, he went further with another bald statement in the Commons.

I would like to suggest that it is extremely difficult, even in law, to draw a hard and fast line between murder and manslaughter or between manslaughter and an accident caused by criminal negligence. When this negligence is caused by the official folly of those in high places, coupled with entire ignorance of the techniques which in this case can alone preserve human life, official folly becomes at any rate criminal negligence. When the death of a man ensues, the line between such official folly and murder is purely a matter for a man's conscience.[49] *Noel Pemberton-Billing MP*

He backed this claim up with a series of examples taken from the events of the previous two years. Inevitably a Committee of Inquiry was urgently convened to investigate the whole matter.

One of the periodical air agitations was going on in London. The worst of these agitations was that they were too late to be of any use. It is no use making an agitation for obtaining in a few days' time what it takes a year or more to make. The net result as far as we were concerned I tabulated as follows in my diary on April 8th:

Results of Air Agitation:

A) Positive. Not the hastening of one bolt, turn buckle, or split pin.

B) Negative. 1. General hindering of operations in France.

2. Danger of spread of alarm and despondency among the younger personnel of the RFC.

This last factor was one which never seemed to occur to anyone in England.[50] *Captain Maurice Baring, Headquarters, RFC*

When investigated, the claims for the most part evaporated because of the inherent inaccuracies in the anecdotal evidence that made up the bulk of Pemberton-Billing's sources. Furthermore, many of Pemberton-Billing's complaints were laid against the BE2 C, an aircraft that he considered unsafe for any purpose other than peacetime flying - and then only with great care and supervision. Here he had gone too far - part of the problem with the BE2 C was its stability and overall steadiness as an aircraft.

The Committee entirely dissent from this view, and consider that though somewhat slow, a BE2 C has always been relatively to other machines a safe machine to fly.[51]

In this, the Committee was undoubtedly right. They laid out their findings in an Interim Report with admirable brevity.

To sum up, flying even at home is at present attended with considerable danger. It is imperative that every precaution should be taken to reduce that danger to a minimum. No one could complain if Mr Pemberton-Billing had asked that these cases should be enquired into to ascertain whether the deaths of the men might have been prevented, but to base upon these accidents charges of criminal negligence or murder is an abuse of language and entirely unjustifiable . . . There is one general observation the Committee desire to add to this interim report. There has been an enormous expansion of the Flying Service since the war and all the critics of the Service without exception have borne testimony to the great progress made in its efficiency - a progress which although most noticeable since the beginning of this year is in the opinion of the Committee the result of many months of strenuous work.[52]

The Final Report of the Committee, published much later in the year, investigated the overall charges of inefficiency made against the administration of the RFC. These concerned the alleged lack of foresight in providing the required types of aircraft; an over reliance on the Royal Aircraft Factory at Farnborough in contrast to private manufacturers; insufficient training for pilots and observers; inadequate Home Defence arrangements; a loss of mastery in the air; inadequate airfields and inadequate arming of aircraft. The Committee looked at each charge in considerable detail and overall came to the largely common sense conclusion that in the chaotic circumstances of rapid expansion and a wholly new type of warfare things could, would and did go wrong. Criticisms were made but essentially no-one was to blame. The section relating to the BE2 C perhaps has the most immediate relevance.

But upon the question whether in this war the Royal Aircraft Factory has well served the Royal Flying Corps, the RAF must be judged by its principal achievement, the BE2 C aeroplane combined with the 90hp RAF engine. This is the combination which has been used in far larger numbers than any other, and by it the RAF must, in our judgement, stand or fall. Which is it to do? In answering this question, we bear in mind that at the time the RAF engine was produced, the only possible alternative engine of English design was the Green Engine, for which no one has so far produced a satisfactory aeroplane. There was no inherently stable machine of private design. The BE2 C was strong, the design was aeronautically sound, the drawings were complete. This last circumstance enabled many manufacturers, entirely new to the trade, to build an aeroplane who could not otherwise have done so. Looking at things as they were at the beginning of the war, we adopt the language of one of the witnesses who appeared before us, Mr A E Berriman, the Chief Engineer of the Daimler Company: 'The RAF engine and the BE2 C aeroplane have their defects, but they form a combination that has been instrumental in enabling the Flying Corps to perform invaluable service to the Army in France.'[53]

Various pragmatic suggestions were also made for unifying the purchasing departments of the RFC and RNAS. The research role of the Royal Aircraft Factory was also to be more closely defined. Those who had to fly the benighted BE2 C at the front could easily see these reports as a government whitewash but, however they might complain, it is difficult to see what else could have been done.

It is a pity Pemberton Billing put his case so badly, although they might have given him a fair chance. Most of his complaints have been against the BE2 C and most of the things he said were right. They are the slowest machine out here and do more work than almost any other. They are more or less alright for work this side of the lines, chiefly because the Hun will not come low enough if there are any other machines about. This is the report of the examination of a Bosche prisoner (infantry). "When asked about our aviators he smiled broadly and seemed highly amused at the cheek of our airmen in crossing the lines so low". The majority of the machines will not go any higher! One man asked Pemberton Billing if he had any direct evidence that the Germans had a faster machine than the BE2 C. I would like to take that man across the lines and let him find out for himself. In my opinion if proper attention had been paid to developing machines which are already in existence in England, we should by now have given the Hun airmen such a rotten time that he would be very careful to keep in the background. As an example of what can be done, the machine I am on (BE2 C) takes at least an hour to climb 9,000 feet. We have a few machines here which get to 12,000 in 12 minutes.[54] *Lieutenant Leslie Horridge, 7 Squadron, RFC*

* * * *

The reliable FE2 Bs were at the centre of the fray in their capacity of maids of all work. Fed by the stress of combat, there were serious tensions beneath the surface in several squadron messes. These, not unnaturally, often focussed on the Squadron Leader who had the duty of ordering them into action day after day. In 23 Squadron, rightly or wrongly, many officers questioned the competence of the Squadron Leader, Major Ross Hume.

Adams and Vernon were so rattled by Ross Hume because they had not succeeded in taking the right photographs, that they crossed the lines at 4,000 feet on an impossible day and got them. Why they were not brought down by rifle fire I don't know. The General was furious when he heard about it. Ross Hume has

*FE2 Bs in flight.* IWM Q 67249 / IWM Q 55944

the worst eye for weather I have ever come across - he cannot tell whether clouds are at 500 feet or 1,200 feet.[55] *Captain Harold Wyllie, 23 Squadron, RFC*

After the failure of a morning reconnaissance, Wyllie himself was stung into an ill-considered action when his temper overcame his common sense in the face of provocation from his Squadron Commander.

Went over the lines at 7,000 feet with my engine going badly. I ought to have abandoned the reconnaissance but was so furious at a remark made by Ross Hume the first time I landed, that I carried on against my own judgement. Negative report, which was satisfactory as the staff thought an attack was coming.[56] *Captain Harold Wyllie, 23 Squadron, RFC*

The role of the Squadron Commander could be crucial to establishing the state of morale for the whole squadron. They could provide the kind of personal inspiration that would carry their men joyously into combat; they could provide a secure backdrop of administrative competence - or they could undermine their men by inefficiency and the kind of carping, nit-picking that could destroy a squadron.

When I first joined 5 Squadron, there was a very efficient Squadron Commander there called Major Hearson. He was a regular engineer officer and he wasn't a good pilot but he could fly an aeroplane. But he was very efficient indeed - very particular about the way we entered up our log books and report sheets when we came back from every flight. He saw to it that the morale of the men was good, that the maintenance of the aircraft and engines was well looked after. He was a very good squadron commander and was eventually promoted and became a Wing Commander when he left us. Then we had another man who wasn't nearly so good. He was an ex-gunner and more fond of the drink - rather more lackadaisical and slipshod leaving things to his flight commanders rather than seeing to it himself. He was not nearly so particular about the way that pilots and observers wrote up their reports when they came back from operations. All personnel had to make a report whether they had anything to say or not, even negative reports were better than nothing. Some of them would write a few lines and not expand at all about what had happened during the flight. The Squadron Commander should have seen to it that they made better reports. These reports were sent up to higher authority from which they gained all the information they could and it was all reported in daily orders of the wing. Pilots and observers weren't so punctual to their machines when it was time to take off and there were delays. It might be a question of bad weather coming up and getting the job done before the weather deteriorated, so it was very important that a Squadron Commander should see that his men are punctual. Another way was how people dressed themselves – whether they went about looking sloppy, whether their hair was long or they'd taken the trouble to dress properly for the different meals or if we had visitors. These are little things but they all add up and they all point to whether you've got an efficient and enthusiastic Squadron Commander or not. This had effect on the slackness of all the personnel in the squadron – right the way from the pilots and observer, down to the airmen themselves. I think it most important that the Squadron Commander should be 100% efficient.[57] *Lieutenant Alan Jackson, 5 Squadron, RFC*

Trenchard had banned all his Squadron Commanders from flying over the lines. The experience they had accumulated was just too valuable to lose. Many objected strenuously to what they considered a draconian ruling from RFC Headquarters. On moving to the Somme front Major George Carmichael reported to Trenchard.

*George I Carmichael.* IWM Q 68192

My instructions were brief and my reception could scarcely be termed cordial. My Squadron was allotted to the Cavalry Corps and I was to work with them in readiness to accompany their three Brigades when the breakthrough was effected. He concluded with the words, "You may be one of the most capable officers on the Western Front, but you are too damned cantankerous, you must do what you are told. You are not to fly". I could not think of anything that I had done or said that might justify this outburst. I did not know how to interpret his meaning of the word cantankerous and I doubt whether he did either. Anyway, I was unable to argue and left concerned by the fact that I was to keep on the ground and the effect this might have on the morale of my Squadron. It was typical of 'Boom', as he was called, to give no explanation, but not long after I heard that all Squadron Commanders had been instructed to keep on the ground because of the high rate of casualties.[58] *Major George Carmichael, 18 Squadron, RFC*

This entirely sensible and pragmatic order put many Squadron Commanders in an unenviable position. They henceforth had to order their men up into the hostile skies day after day in all but the roughest weather. Yet they could not share in the inevitable dangers as a combat pilot. Some had already built their reputation and could carry it off without much comment.

Really a Squadron Commander in the Flying Corps can be called a 'soft job' as far as this war is concerned, jolly good pay and no risk (except from over-eating). But I suppose I can claim to have earned it and it certainly carries its worries and responsibilities with it. It is rather hard, sometimes, to order people off on what is obviously a very risky job, but I have a great moral advantage in my little bit of ribbon, it comes better from me than from a Squadron Commander who was never a good flyer and perhaps has never seen active service conditions. Actually, nowadays however, I am glad to say most Squadron Commanders are expert fliers and have seen quite their share of the mill, even colonels know what they are talking about, it is only those higher up still, who unfortunately are chiefly responsible for sending machines out, who have in any way lost touch - or have never been in touch - with modern conditions.[59] *Major Lanoe Hawker VC, 24 Squadron, RFC*

*Lanoe Hawker.* IWM Q 67598

Like Hawker, many of the aggrieved pilots looked higher in the structure of the RFC and found their targets in their senior officers.

Generals (RFC) are the curse of this Corps they have really nothing to do except to annoy and hinder the unfortunate pilots who are doing their best to 'carry on'. And to think that the Hun Flying Corps is run by one Major, and damn well run too judging by results. The result of all these Temporary 'Generals' is that Squadron Commanders, instead of looking after their squadrons are busily engaged in keeping one eye on a 'Temporary' General; and the other on their blessed selves. This works down, causing jealousy and friction between Flight Commanders and Flights as a whole and plays the devil with discipline. Ever since Ross Hume took command of this Squadron I have been obliged to use - or have tried to use - the utmost tact to keep on speaking terms with the other Flight Commanders and their officers. The same thing has occurred with regard to the senior NCOs who have been daggers drawn.[60] *Captain Harold Wyllie, 23 Squadron, RFC*

Feelings were close to boiling point and men in daily action, wracked by their responsibilities to their own flight, could hardly be expected to understand the differing perspective of their seniors.

*FE2 Bs dodging 'Archie'*

Weather too bad. It is extraordinary how little our Wing and Brigade Commanders seem to understand present conditions of work over the other side of the lines. I am given extra and relatively unimportant photographs to take which mean several sharp turns during Reconnaissance. Now this means for an absolute certainty that your formation will get all over the place and the usual thing follows as sure as clockwork i.e. the straggler or stragglers are immediately mobbed and shot down. The Hun has 1,000 rounds on a belt – we 47 in a drum which has got to be changed. I remarked to Murphy that what I was ordered to do would be very difficult to carry out. He said, "Well, you could detach the photograph machine from the formation." Yes, I could and, "One of our machines did not return from Reconnaissance" would appear in the 'Summary' as sure as God made little apples. The responsibility the wretched Flight Commander has to take upon his shoulders on these occasions is very great. Things happen so swiftly and he has got to judge and act in a second or two, wondering whether he is justified in risking the loss of so and so, whom he knows must get out of station on the turn he is making. Add to this the fact that owing to a pilot losing his nerve and begging himself off the Reconnaissance – I am to go over the lines with two pilots who have put in one reconnaissance and one patrol between them. No experience in formation flying or fighting! Sometimes I feel that I simply cannot carry on any more under present conditions. Of course if Ross Hume stuck up for his pilots it would make a big difference - but - he didn't earn his nickname of 'Slippery Sam' in the Corps for nothing.[61] *Captain Harold Wyllie, 23 Squadron, RFC*

In fact most of the senior RFC commanders understood only too well what their pilots were going through - but they had a higher imperative than the safety of their men. They were being leaned on themselves by desperate staff officers and 'real' generals to get the results that might save the lives of thousands of infantry when the offensive finally began. The lives of a few pilots and observers were expendable in the global scheme of things on the Western Front as the timetable hurtled the Fourth Army towards Zero Hour. Both sides had right on their side, but it is difficult not to feel sympathy for Captain Wyllie as he struggled to make sense of his orders in the aerial battlefields.

Air full of Huns. Went on patrol - ordered by Commanding Officer to take up Corporal Porter. Could not send him with Studd, my new pilot, so had to take him myself. At 07.55 we got into hot action with five LVGs over Arras. They had been engaged and thrown into utter confusion by three de Havilland scouts. I never saw such a mix up in the air. They came down for a couple of thousand feet anyhow with the little scouts after them like angry bees. Studd and myself got into the middle of them at 9,000-9,500. Solly put in some good shooting. Unfortunately, Corporal Porter completely lost his head. He had a DCM in his pocket and I gave him some magnificent shots, one dead nose on and the other about 200 feet under. I could not get him to fire. He sat like a sick monkey doing nothing. The air was full of lead and at last I stood up and banged him on the head and yelled, "Fire, you bloody fool!" He woke up then and got off a drum at a machine overhead. My God I was mad. We ought to have got two machines. As it was it is a great wonder we were not shot down. A damned silly way of getting killed too.[62] *Captain Harold Wyllie, 23 Squadron, RFC*

Perhaps Wyllie's fury can be judged by the fact that next day he had a sore throat as a result of him shouting multiple blasphemies at the recalcitrant Porter.

The CO had the grace to say he was sorry he sent him up. He asked me the reason for the state of nerves of so many of the officers and I could not give him the only answer, "A fish rots first at the head!" The Squadron has got demoralised and jumpy simply because officers, in addition to the great strain of the work in the air, have been so hunted and insulted by Ross Hume on the ground that they don't know where they are at.[63] *Captain Harold Wyllie, 23 Squadron, RFC*

The trauma of repeated exposure to aerial combat thousands of feet in the air, far behind German lines and surrounded by a hail of German machine gun bullets could be a devastating experience which could easily break a man's nerve. Second Lieutenant E F Allen who had his observer Lieutenant L C Powell killed in front of him in the clash with five Fokkers on 31 May tried his best to carry on but was found wanting.

Unfortunately Allen completely lost his nerve, and told me today that he could not go on flying. It was a terrible time for him as besides the fact of the engine gradually going worse and worse and finally stopping over the lines, the machine was in a dreadful state, covered with blood.[64] *Captain Harold Wyllie, 23 Squadron, RFC*

\*\*\*\*

The IV Brigade, RFC commanded by Brigadier-General E B Ashmore, was intended to cater to the aerial needs of the Fourth Army: the corps aircraft were provided by 3, 4, 9 and 15 Squadrons who together formed the 3rd (Corps) Wing; the scouts were made up of 22 and 24 Squadrons in 14th (Army) Wing; and No 1 Balloon Squadron provided the kite balloons. The 9th (Headquarters) Wing had also been moved into the Somme area, namely 21, 27, 60 and 70 Squadrons. As required elements of I Brigade (2 and 10 Squadrons), II Brigade (7 and 16 Squadrons) and III Brigade (8, 12 and 13 Squadrons) were made available as required to assist in the bombing offensive designed to paralyse the German railway system. In total the RFC concentrated some 185 aircraft in the Somme area, plus the outside aircraft flying on bombing missions. Of these some 76 were the new scout aircraft. The

French had also concentrated considerable aircraft for the offensive. To face this aerial Armada the Germans could only deploy some 129 aircraft of which only a meagre 19 were scouts. As the British concentrated all their resources for the offensive the Germans were hampered by their equally onerous commitments battling the French Air Service over Verdun. The Allies had achieved a significant aerial superiority over the Somme.

The British kite balloons complemented the services provided by the aircraft. They had many advantages in that they could remain aloft all day and all night, the observers were not distracted by the responsibilities of flying an aircraft and had near perfect communication with the ground by telephones. This meant that if the German batteries suspended fire for the fear of discovery, as they often did when aircraft passed by, then they would be almost permanently out of action or perforce reveal their locations when they opened fire.

The observers went up for spotting purposes, trying to spot enemy gun positions, trenches and anything behind the German lines that they could see was of interest. That carried on every day that we had the balloons up. Two or three times a week, artillery officers, sometimes infantry officers, would go up as an observer with his sketching map and binoculars to spot whatever he could, making notes of it for his own purpose and for recording purposes, which was telephoned to the telephone lorry on the

*RFC balloon section near Fricourt, 1916.*

ground. We had a telephone in the basket which was knotted to the balloon cable. Later we found we were losing a lot of telephone cables and they had new cables made with the telephone wire inserted in the cable itself.[65] *Sergeant Edward Bolt, No 1 Kite Balloon Section, RFC*

In general the balloons were best at reporting the overall situation and locating German batteries firing, but aircraft were far better at ranging the guns directly onto their targets.

As the intensity of the conflict was ratcheted up, it seemed for a long time that the Germans would never break. Then, on 18 June, there occurred an event that marked the end of the supremacy of the Fokker and the beginning of a period of British hegemony above the trenches.

*George McCubbin.* RAFM/RAeC 264

At about 9pm whilst on patrol duty over Loos, three Fokkers were seen behind the lines. Lieutenant McCubbin proceeded over the lines towards them. One Fokker dived away from the other two and left them. The remaining two made for Lens, towards another FE. Lt McCubbin followed them. Whilst one of them was attacking the FE piloted by Second Lieutenant Savage (both machines diving steeply) Lt McCubbin dived towards the attacking machine and fired upon it. Immediately the Fokker turned to the right from the other FE and dived perpendicularly towards the ground. It was seen to crash by 22 Anti-Aircraft Battery. The second Fokker was either above or directly behind Lt McCubbin's machine. After he turned he saw neither the FE nor the two Fokkers.[66] *Major Robert Cherry, 25 Squadron, RFC*

*Remnants of Fokker EIII.* IWM Q 67249

*Max Immelmann.* IWM Q 58026

The crashed Fokker was piloted by none other than the Eagle of Lille – *Leutnant* Max Immelmann. The loss of their inspirational leader was a severe blow to the German Air Service and of course in particular to the other Fokker pilots. To try and guard against any further such disaster, Kaiser Wilhem intervened in person to remove his other champion, Oswald Boelcke, to a place of relative safety by sending him on an inspection tour of the Balkan states and Turkey. This of course removed the other great German pilot from the Western Front and left the advantage with the British as the Fokker menace spluttered out ignominiously.

If a Hun sees a De Hav he runs for his life; they won't come near them. It was only yesterday that one of the fellows came across a Fokker. The Fokker dived followed by the De Hav but the wretched Fokker dived so hard that when he tried to pull his

*Immelmann's Funeral.* IWM Q 63121

machine out his elevator broke and he dived into our Lines; not a shot was fired.[67] *Second Lieutenant Gwilym Lewis, 32 Squadron, RFC*

Hawker in command of 24 Squadron had developed his tactical thinking to a peak of sophistication that encapsulated his personality and the ethos of the RFC.

Tactical Orders by Officer Commanding No. 24 Squadron, Royal Flying Corps:
"ATTACK EVERYTHING."
[67] *Major Lanoe Hawker*

\* \* \* \*

The final battle plans drawn up for 1 July had been the result of considerable wrangling and heart searching between the Commander in Chief, Sir Douglas Haig and General Sir Henry Rawlinson commanding Fourth Army. The Germans had constructed a truly formidable defensive position in the Somme area. Their Front Line was in fact a complete integrated trench system that consisted of three lines stiffened at intervals by extensively fortified villages, linked by communication trenches, provided with plentiful deep dugouts to shelter the garrison troops and protected by two thick belts of tangled barbed wire. Around two miles behind this was a similar Second Line system, built into the reverse slopes of the ridges and beyond the range of the British field artillery. In turn, behind that, a Third Line system was also under construction. Between the lines were more of the heavily fortified villages. Faced with this daunting series of obstacles, not unnaturally, Rawlinson and his staff tended to a cautious approach by limiting their first objectives to the capture of the German front line system, before launching a second phase when the artillery had been moved forward to the Second Line. Haig was more ambitious and sought to capture the whole of the German Second Line as part of the first rush, hopefully while the German defences were still suffering from the confusion inspired by the loss of their First Line. Haig believed that the possibilities inherent in the initial partial successes that had been achieved at both Neuve Chapelle and Loos had been cast away by a failure to exploit them through lack of readily available reserves. He believed that now he had amassed such a gargantuan force it was absolutely vital to maintain the initial momentum of an attack to keep the Germans on the back foot. A pause to allow the artillery to move forward would also give the Germans time to bring up their reserves, plug the gaps and all momentum would be irretrievably lost. Inevitably Haig had his way and Rawlinson's plans were extended accordingly. Both plans relied on massed artillery power to sweep away the German barbed wire and smash down their defences to capture the German front line system.

The artillery orders for the preliminary bombardment called for a six day concentrated barrage along the 25,000 yard front. The work was divided into stages; the first two days would be devoted to wire cutting and registration of targets; during the next three days these targets were to be pounded into destruction; finally on Z Day the guns would provide a supporting bombardment as the troops went over the top. Trenches and strongpoints were to be erased; observation posts and command headquarters put out of action; counter-battery work was to remove the threat of the German guns; any identified rest billets that the long range guns could reach were to be harassed; lines of communications to and from the front line area were to be disrupted every night; finally the wire cutting programme would continue unabated. To carry out this ambitious programme were 1,537 guns and howitzers. This allowed one field gun for every 21 yards of front and one heavy piece for every 57 yards. As the batteries moved into the line gun positions had to be dug, secure observation posts prepared in the

*An 8-inch siege howitzer in a camouflaged position on the Somme, 1916.*

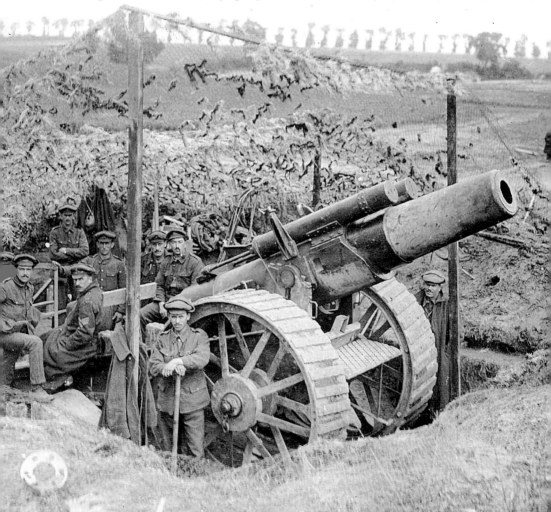

front line, thousands of miles of telephone wire laid and 3,000,000 shells brought up ready for the guns.

Amidst this unprecedented effort it seemed impossible that such a concentration of artillery could fail in whatever task it was set. Yet, in this complacency lay the seeds of many of Fourth Army's subsequent problems. The extension by Haig of the first day objectives, to include the Second Line, meant that the amount of trenches to be destroyed by the British artillery was effectively doubled; yet most of their guns did not have the range to reach the Second Line and direct observation was inevitably made more difficult by their location on reverse slopes. These factors reduced the number and weight of shells falling on the German Front Line system, which meant that the chances of outright failure were correspondingly increased. The intensive nature of the artillery programme also meant that although the importance of counter-battery work had been mentioned in the orders it had unwittingly slipped down the priority lists of the hard-pressed gunners. Insufficient guns were allotted to the purpose and there had been no recognition of the huge number of shells that were required to put a single German battery out of action.

The much-vaunted barrage finally opened on 24 June. And as ever the wry depreciating humour of the young pilots had its own mocking perspective.

> The newspaper stories of the firing in France being heard in Ireland, the north of Scotland and Timbuctoo amuse me greatly. Those people must have 'some' ears.[69] *Second Lieutenant Lessel Hutcheon, 5 Squadron, RFC*

Immediately the air was full of flying heavy metal, which added yet another danger for the British aircraft whose activities of course escalated yet again in a willing response to the orders of their masters on the ground.

> The batteries were being piled in night after night - the roads were roaring with the traffic going up as the guns went into position. This enormous feeling of the build up of a big offensive. The day was peaceful, there wasn't a thing on the road, as soon as dusk came it started and it went right through the night. Our billets were right on the road and one had a tremendous feeling of war and what it meant. When everything was in position they began to build up to the main bombardment which lasted for about a week before the actual offensive took place. We used to go out and photograph and these jobs were among the most terrifying that I ever did in the whole war. By that time we were flying very much lower - down to a 1,000 feet - and when you had to go right over the lines you were mid way between our guns firing and where the shells were falling. The intensity of the

Second Lieutenant Cecil Lewis.

bombardment was such that it was really like a broad swathe of dirty looking cotton wool laid over the ground so close and continual were the shell bursts. When you looked on the other side, particularly in the evening, the whole of the ground beneath the darkening sky was just like a veil of sequins which were flashing and flashing and flashing and each one was a gun. One knew that these things were coming over all the time. The artillery had orders not to fire when an aeroplane was in their sights - they cut it pretty fine you know! One used to fly along the front on those patrols and the aeroplane was flung up with a shell that had just gone underneath and missed you by two or three feet; or flung down when it had gone over the top. This was continuous so the machine was bucketing and jumping as if it was in a gale but it was shells. You didn't see them - they were going much too fast but this was really terrifying. One had the sort of feeling that they were flying at us - it's us they wanted to get - this was extraordinarily ridiculous but quite terrifying. At last having finished the photos and got out of the buffeting I thought, "Well heavens alive I've come through that!" Because so many of the boys and many of my friends were just hit and destroyed by a direct hit by a passing shell.[70] *Second Lieutenant Cecil Lewis, 3 Squadron, RFC*

The howitzers were a particular threat as they lobbed their shells high into the air above the battlefield.

While we are on the subject of howitzers and high trajectory guns, there is an interesting story that wanders the messes about a certain pilot who is supposed to have lost his nerve because one day while he was ranging a howitzer, he saw its shell come up, look at him, and turn at the top of its parabolic path to go down again and blow up the Hun. I have often wondered why the idle gunners chalk ugly faces on the noses of their shell. Now I know.[71] *Lieutenant Robin Rowell, 12 Squadron, RFC*

It may not have been just a rumour, for Cecil Lewis actually caught a brief sight of a shell in flight himself.

Out of the corner of my eye, when I wasn't really looking, I saw something moving like a lump. I didn't really know what the devil it was. It was a mystifying sort of effect. Then I looked again and focused and about a 100 yards ahead there was the business part of a 9 inch howitzer shell right at the top of its trajectory - just about 8,000 feet. It had come up like a lobbed tennis ball and right at the top it was going quite slowly and it was a pretty hefty bit of metal, turning end over end before it gathered speed again and went off down to the ground again. The battery was evidently firing and we saw two or three shells and once you had caught them you could follow them right down to burst.[72] *Second Lieutenant Cecil Lewis, 3 Squadron, RFC*

The Corps machines were in the air for hours on end. Photographing again and again the front line areas so that the effects of the bombardment could be assessed; the artillery observation crews directed the shells onto their targets and coolly recorded the exact locations of many of the German batteries that were forced to try and retaliate. Few German aircraft attempted to interfere with their work and none managed to carry out any meaningful reconnaissance or observation over the British lines.

On 25 June, it was planned to launch simultaneous co-ordinated attacks on every German observation balloon all along the British front. It was intended to try and put out these eyes in the sky during the vital last phase before the offensive began. Thus 20 Squadron was ordered to escort a group of aircraft armed with phosphorus bombs that would be used to set fire to the balloons.

As the first plane moved slowly down the field for the take-off and the second was taxiing into position, there was a blinding flash of flame and the air was suddenly rent asunder. Wham! Went one of the phosphorus bombs on the first machine. It had tripped itself bumping over the rough ground. Wham! Went one on the second plane. Instantly those two ships and all others near them

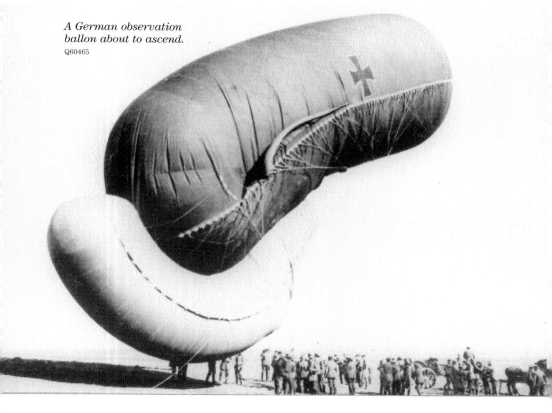

*A German observation ballon about to ascend.*
Q60465

were in the centre of an appalling hurricane of flying phosphorous, streaking every which way, like giant chrysanthemum bursts of rockets. Like a scared rabbit, I dashed for my new ship. Our planes, by a rare chance, were not parked close together. Wham! Went more explosives as the spreading flames and flying phosphorous did their bit for the enemy. When the excitement died down, we counted up the damage - two hangars and five aeroplanes destroyed.[73] *Second Lieutenant Harold Hartney, 20 Squadron, RFC*

When the raid finally got off the ground, low clouds severely hampered the chance of a successful attack on any of the 23 German kite balloons reported to be in the air. Lieutenant Albert Ball took part in the attacks having returned from a period of well-earned home leave.

Oh! It was rotten, for I only just got back. Three of us were sent from this squadron. The first time we did no good, so I asked for another chance. We all set out again. I went for my balloon and set it on fire, but my engine was badly hit, and I had to come back all the eight miles over Hun land, at half speed, and only a few feet up. My machine was hit badly. I have enclosed one of the bullets. This bullet went through my induction pipe, engine bearer plate and three inches of wood. Not so bad, is it? The other chaps were not very successful. One crashed his machine and the other did no good. The other four balloons were brought down by other squadrons. Five were brought down by the RFC. About 100 machines went up for different balloons, so I think five is quite a good average for such a rotten job. You see, we had to get so low.[74] *Second Lieutenant Albert Ball, 11 Squadron, RFC*

On the same day, Lieutenant W Tudor-Hart, flying as observer with his pilot, Lieutenant W A Summers of 22 Squadron, ran into severe trouble that nevertheless illustrated that the morale of some German pilots was close to cracking at last.

We were on patrol from 9 to 12 am and while at 9,000 feet, the clouds being about 7,000 feet, we saw our anti-aircraft guns firing at two flocks at 10,000 feet, one going home from south-west, the other from north-west. We headed off the flock coming from the south-west, consisting of ten machines. They were in formation, three lines of three and one behind. We had climbed to 9,500 feet and they passed over our heads. We turned, and I opened fire on the last machine, which was 200 yards above us and lower than the rest. The rear machines all opened fire and then the whole formation broke up and scattered. A general action ensued and we fought them for 15 minutes. We turned right and left, firing bursts into the machines as they dived at us; several fired down at us from above and on the flanks while we attacked those in front. I would glance round and see a Hun diving at our tail, signal Summers, and he would swing round, and I would put a burst at him, and we would turn again for another. There was a continuous crackling and bang of machine guns the whole time. We held our fire, and only let off at machines that got to ranges of 100 yards or less, as our ammunition consisted of seven drums only of 47 rounds. During the fight the Huns were reinforced by four others, so that we were at one time fighting 14 machines. They all engaged us. At one time a fast Hun biplane that was doing 95 an hour (air speed) came for our tail. Summers at a signal swung round. I covered him to 100 yards and pulled, but a gun stoppage occurred because the bag was choked with empty cartridges. A bullet from the Hun hit the clip on the drum and chipped a bit off the field glasses hung round my neck. Summers acted at once. As soon as he saw what had happened he put our machine's nose down and the Hun bullets whizzed over our heads. The drum shot off overboard and I got another on as we turned to meet another machine. One machine I fired half a drum at went down in a steep nose-dive east of a town we were in front of. I was too busy to follow it and see if it crashed. The Huns broke off the fight one by one and when we had exhausted all our ammunition only two were still fighting us. When all our ammunition was done I signalled to Summers and he put our nose down and we got back across to our lines to the accompaniment of the Hun 'Archies'. We dropped on our way back to 6,000 feet. We are jolly lucky to get back unscratched. There were two bullet holes in the undercarriage – the mechanical petrol pump shot away – holes in the tail, tail boom, main spars and wing, one through the nacelle in front of me. The Huns must have fired over 1,000 rounds at us, perhaps 2,000. It was all the time like being in the 'butts' during the 'mad moment' i.e. rapid fire. The bullets were singing past our heads all the time. It was gloriously exciting and I don't think it can be said the RFC is inferior to the Huns when an FE2 B, a slow machine, fights 14 Huns, who are fought till they have all broken off the fight, and for 15 minutes and their formation scattered. Summers is a star pilot and no mistake.[75] *Lieutenant W O Tudor-Hart, 22 Squadron, RFC*

Tudor-Hart was not the only pilot to recognize and applaud the courage shown by Summers.

Summers is always 'trailing the tail of his coat' over the lines and is constantly coming back with his machine riddled with holes as the result of fights.[76] *Lieutenant Eynon Bowen, 22 Squadron, RFC*

On 27 and 28 June, thick mist enveloped the Somme valley, followed by heavy showery rain from the lowering clouds. Many patrols were cancelled, but Ball managed to get aloft and his old training as a corps pilot was obviously not wasted as he kept his eyes peeled for significant developments on the ground over the German lines.

I was on the 7 o'clock patrol today and on my patrol I saw over the lines a lot of transports. etc., in a wood. I went over the lines in order to have a good look, so that I could report the place, but the old Huns did not like it. They surrounded us with shells from their 'Archie' guns, and at last we were hit. One of my cylinders was smashed off, also the machine got a few through it. One only just missed my leg. However, the engine stopped, but I saw what I went to see, and also managed to get my machine far enough over our lines to prevent the old fools from shelling it. Later on I had a new engine put in and the machine patched up, and it is now safely in the shed. Tomorrow the Major is going to let me have my own back, for he has arranged for a shoot tomorrow, and we will not leave the place until every stone is smashed up. It was really good sport, and so we want them to have a little of the same kind of sport.[77] *Second Lieutenant Albert Ball, 11 Squadron, RFC*

The bad flying and observation weather severely hampered the artillery observation of the RFC. Although the artillery doubled their rate of fire in an effort to compensate this was still a setback. Every hour that was lost was a tremendous boost to the German cause. Due to the bad weather and uncertainty as to the results of the bombardment, it was decided to add two extra days to the preliminary bombardment, which meant the first assault would be made on 1 July.

*FE2 B on line patrol.*

F.E. ON LINE PATROL.
NOTE OBSERVER.

During the last days of June, interdiction bombing raids were stepped up in scale to hit at the rear areas that even the longest-range guns could not reach. As usual, many of the raids were directed against the railheads in an attempt to delay and disrupt the inevitable movement forward of the German reserve divisions once the battle had commenced in earnest. Unfortunately the weather conditions were not conducive to success.

> Left the ground at 08.25 to bomb railhead and do fighting patrol for two hours round Rovay. Got into cloud at 4,000. Climbed through it to 9,000. Gave it up after two hours during which time I hardly saw the ground and only one of the machines. Nearly had a head on collision in a thick white cloud. Studd passed me about ten yards distance. I saw him, or the silhouette of him tear past at 140 miles an hour. He had one wing very much down, which just saved us as his machine was turning.[78] *Captain Harold Wyllie, 23 Squadron, RFC*

On the last couple of days they were ordered to attempt the raids whatever the risks. The gusting westerly wind meant that the FE2 Bs could only reach an air speed of 20mph during their return flight flying right into the teeth of the gale.

> Standing by to drop bombs on railhead. Ordered to attempt it. Wind blowing up from west about 50-55mph, could not climb well on account of extra weight of bombs. Nearly had a bad smash getting off as got a bad bump which stalled the machine and she crashed back on one wheel – a horrid moment with four bombs in the rack. Could only get to 8,500 in $1\frac{1}{2}$ hours. Went across and dropped bombs, on railway at Fampoux. Got heavily shelled coming out. One nearly got us with a direct hit and burst above. No machines hit for a wonder, as 20mph is no speed to dally over 'Archie' with.[79] *Captain Harold Wyllie, 23 Squadron, RFC*

On 30 June, Albert Ball acted as escort on a raid made by some 30 aircraft.

> Yesterday we did two bombing raids. On the first one I had to lead, for the Wing Commander had to land owing to engine trouble. It was great sport as 30 machines went. On the second, it was more sport still. Three Fokkers came for us, but we did the job OK and set the place on fire. However, you will think I am a very bloodthirsty chap just now, but I am not really.[80] *Second Lieutenant Albert Ball, 11 Squadron, RFC*

For the Nieuport scout pilots such as Ball, burdened with both offensive patrols and escort work, the stress was unremitting. Despite his recent leave, Ball began to show the strain in his letters home to his family.

> The three Nieuport machines stand from 2.30am until 9.30 at

night, so you bet we are getting a rotten time just now. However, things are looking good just now, so we might all help and keep things going at any cost. But it is a long day and I am afraid that if it lasts very long, a few of the chaps will be going sick . . . I am OK, but oh! so fagged. However, I shall soon get over that.[81] *Second Lieutenant Albert Ball, 11 Squadron, RFC*

Ball was notified that he had been awarded the Military Cross on 29 June.

During the period of preparation the RFC had been successful in securing both a numerical and qualitative superiority over the disputed battlefields. The RFC had struggled in the early stages of the aerial preparations, but the arrival of the new generation of aircraft, coupled with the determination to follow a cold blooded aggressive air strategy, had left them ready to reap the fruits of aerial supremacy at the very moment it most mattered, when the offensive was finally launched. Although hard pressed staff officers always wanted more, in truth, they had all the photographs they could reasonably expect of the German trenches, reserve lines and strongpoints. Many of the German batteries had been engaged or their position registered, the German reserve troops had been harassed by the bombing of their billets and the crucial rail routes to the battlefield had been disrupted. In the later stages no German aircraft had been able to cross the British front line to expose the details of the offensive preparations to the German High Command. Trenchard could be proud of his men.

The infantry moved up into their 'jumping off' trenches full of a strange mixture of extreme trepidation and hope for the morrow. Throughout the whole army there was a feeling of optimism in the air, for surely this mighty bombardment, this huge army could not fail when it went forward to its destiny?

I expect you have heard about the Virgin of Albert. On

top of the church there was a gilded figure of the Virgin and when most of the church was shelled, this figure was somehow caught as it fell. It now lies in a horizontal position from the top of the tower hanging over the road below. I saw it today from about 10,000 feet with the sun shining on it. It must be an extraordinary sight. The superstition is that the war will end on the day it falls.[82]
*Lieutenant Eynon Bowen, 22 Squadron, RFC*

Many felt that it would fall on 1 July to signal a glorious British victory.

*Eynon Bowen.* RAFM/RAeC 16

1. IWM DOCS: R. Rowell, typed Manuscript
2. IWM SR: C. Lewis, AC 4162
3. L. F. Hutcheon, *'War Flying'*, (London: John Murray, 1917), p81
4. IWM DOCS: R. Rowell, typed Manuscript
5. General Staff Intelligence I Corps, 'Notes on the Interpretation of Aeroplane Photographs', 12/1916
6. IWM SR: A. Jackson, AC 23
7. IWM DOCS: R. Rowell, typed Manuscript
8. IWM SR: A. James, AC 24 (Copyright Churchill College, Cambridge)
9. IWM SR: A. James, AC 24 (Copyright Churchill College, Cambridge)
10. IWM DOCS: T. Hughes, Transcript diary, 1/5/1916
11. IWM DOCS: R. Rowell, typed Manuscript
12. L. F. Hutcheon, *'War Flying'*, (London: John Murray, 1917), p63
13. L. F. Hutcheon, *'War Flying'*, (London: John Murray, 1917), pp71-72
14. IWM DOCS: R. Rowell, typed Manuscript
15. A. J. Evans, *'The Escaping Club'*, (London: John Lane The Bodley Head Ltd, 1921), pp3-4
16. IWM SR: A. James, AC 24 (Copyright Churchill College, Cambridge)
17. RAF MUSEUM: Lt A. Dore, Typescript diary, 27/4/1916
18. RAF MUSEUM: Lt A. Dore, Typescript diary, 29/4/1916
19. RAF MUSEUM: Lt A. Dore, Typescript diary, 1/5/1916
20. RAF MUSEUM: Lt A. Dore, Typescript diary, 16/5/1916
21. IWM DOCS: H.Wyllie, Transcript diary, 31/5/1916
22. IWM DOCS: H.Wyllie, Transcript diary, 8/6/1916
23. IWM DOCS: S. H. B. Harris, *'Lecture on Aerial Tactics from the Point of View of a Two-Seater Pilot and Observer'*, notes attached to papers of Robin Rowell, 85/28/1
24. IWM DOCS: R. Macfarlane, Transcript memoir, p9
25. H. Schroder, *'An Airman Remembers'*, (London: John Hamilton, ca 1939), p229
26. IWM DOCS: S. Attwater, Typescript memoir, p3
27. IWM DOCS: R. Macfarlane, Transcript memoir, p9
28. IWM DOCS: R. Rowell, typed Manuscript
29. B. G. Gray & the DH2 Research Group, *'The Anatomy of an Aeroplane: The de Havilland DH2 Pusher Scout'*, (Cross & Cockade, Vol 22, No. 1), p4
30. IWM DOCS, A. M. Wilkinson typescript memoir
31. F. Immelmann, *'Max Immelmann: Eagle of Lille'*, (London: John Hamilton, ca 1930) p194
32. IWM DOCS: S. E. Cowan, Combat Report, 25/4/1916
33. B. G. Gray & the DH2 Research Group, *'The Anatomy of an Aeroplane: The de Havilland DH2 Pusher Scout'*, (Cross & Cockade, Vol 21, No. 3), p136
34. F. Immelmann, *'Max Immelmann: Eagle of Lille'*, (London: John Hamilton, ca 1930) pp197-198
35. W. A. Briscoe & H. Russell Stannard, *'Captain Ball, VC'*, (London: Herbert Jenkins Ltd, 1918), p150
36. W. A Briscoe & H. Russell Stannard, *'Captain Ball, VC'*, (London: Herbert Jenkins Ltd, 1918), p150
37. W. A. Briscoe & H. Russell Stannard, *'Captain Ball, VC'*, (London: Herbert Jenkins Ltd, 1918), pp156-157
38. RAF MUSEUM: Lt A. Dore, Typescript diary, 11/5/1916
39. RAF MUSEUM: Lt A. Dore, Typescript diary, 12/5/1916
40. IWM SR: A. Jackson, SR 23

41. H. E. Hartney, *'Wings over France'*, (Folkestone: Bailey Brothers, 1974), p34

42. IWM DOCS: L. Horridge, Manuscript letter, 29/5/1916

43. IWM DOCS: L. Horridge, Manuscript letter, 19/7/1916

44. IWM DOCS: L. Horridge, Manuscript letter, 20/6/1916

45. IWM DOCS: L. Horridge, Manuscript letter, 14/7/1916

46. IWM DOCS: L. Horridge, Manuscript letter, 19/7/1916

47. L. F. Hutcheon, *'War Flying'*, (London: John Murray, 1917), p58

48. *'Interim Report of the Committee on the Administration and Command of the Royal Flying Corps'*, (London: HMSO, 1916), p3

49. *'Interim Report of the Committee on the Administration and Command of the Royal Flying Corps'*, (London: HMSO, 1916), p3

50. M. Baring, *'Flying Corps Headquarters'*, (Edinburgh & London: William Blackwood & Sons, 1968), p138

51. *'Interim Report of the Committee on the Administration and Command of the Royal Flying Corps'*, (London: HMSO, 1916), p6

52. *'Interim Report of the Committee on the Administration and Command of the Royal Flying Corps'*, (London: HMSO, 1916), p8

53. *'Final Report of the Committee on the Administration and Command of the Royal Flying Corps'*, (London: HMSO, 1916), p8

54. IWM DOCS L. Horridge, Manuscript letter, 3/7/1916

55. IWM DOCS: H.Wyllie, Transcript diary, 30/4/1916

56. IWM DOCS: H.Wyllie, Transcript diary, 4/5/1916

57. IWM SR: A. Jackson, AC 23

58. RAF MUSEUM: G. I. Carmichael, Typescript memoir, p150

59. T. Hawker, *'Hawker VC'*, (London: Mitre Press, 1965), p145

60. IWM DOCS: H.Wyllie, Transcript diary, 10/6/1916

61. IWM DOCS: H.Wyllie, Transcript diary, 13/6/1916

62. IWM DOCS: H.Wyllie, Transcript diary, 18/6/1916

63. IWM DOCS: H.Wyllie, Transcript diary, 19/6/1916

64. IWM DOCS: H.Wyllie, Transcript diary, 21/6/1916

65. IWM SR: E. Bolt, AC 3

66. RAF MUSEUM: Neal O'Connor Collection, Combat Report, 18/6/1916

67. G. Lewis, *'Wings Over the Somme'*, (Wrexham: Bridge Books, 1994), p33

68. T. M. Hawker, *'Hawker V.C.'*, (London: The Mitre Press,1965), p182

69. L. F. Hutcheon, *'War Flying'*, (London: John Murray, 1917), p92

70. IWM SR: C. Lewis, AC 4162

71. IWM DOCS: R. Rowell, typed Manuscript

72. IWM SR: C. Lewis, AC 4162

73. H. E. Hartney, *'Wings over France'*, (Folkestone: Bailey Brothers, 1974), p38

74. W. A. Briscoe & H. Russell Stannard, *'Captain Ball, VC'*, (London: Herbert Jenkins Ltd, 1918), p170

75. C. H. Cooke, *'Historical Records of the 19th (Service) Battalion Northumberland Fusiliers'*, (Newcastle upon Tyne: Chamber of Commerce, 1920), pp266-267

76. RAF MUSEUM: E.G. A. Bowen, Manuscript Letters, 28/7/1916

77. W. A. Briscoe & H. Russell Stannard, *'Captain Ball, VC'*, (London: Herbert Jenkins Ltd, 1918), p167

78. IWM DOCS: H.Wyllie, Transcript diary, 26/6/1916

79. IWM DOCS: H.Wyllie, Transcript diary, 30/6/1916

80. W. A. Briscoe & H. Russell Stannard, *'Captain Ball, VC'*, (London: Herbert Jenkins Ltd, 1918), p188

81. W. A. Briscoe & H. Russell Stannard, *'Captain Ball, VC'*, (London: Herbert Jenkins Ltd, 1918), pp172-174

82. RAF MUSEUM: E.G. A. Bowen, Manuscript Letters, 31/5/1916

## Chapter Three

# A Perfect Summer Day

On the morning of July 1st when the zero hour was to come I was on the first patrol on the northern part of the salient from Pozières down to Fricourt. They'd put down two enormous mines right on the front line hoping to clear the whole of the front line with this enormous burst. This was what we were looking for. We had our watches synchronised. We were up at about 8,000 feet and really it was a fantastic sight because when the hurricane bombardment started every gun we had, and there were thousands of them, had all been let loose at once. It was wild, you could hear the roar of the guns above the noise of the aircraft like a rain on a pane. Extraordinary this roll of thousands of guns at the same time. Then came the blast when we were looking at the La Boisselle Salient – suddenly the whole earth heaved and up from the ground came great cone shaped lifts of earth up to 3 4, 5,000 feet. A moment later we struck the repercussion wave of the blast which flung us over right away backwards over on one side away from the blast.[1] *Second Lieutenant Cecil Lewis, 3 Squadron, RFC*

Saturday, 1 July 1916, brought the dawning of a perfect summer day. A gentle soothing south-westerly breeze, a clear sky and a temperature that climbed to a balmy 72° Fahrenheit. At 07.30, the officers' whistles blew all along the line and the brave men of Kitchener's Army climbed out of their trenches and began their stumble to destiny across No Man's Land. Their confidence was for the most part high and many thought it would be literally and figuratively a walkover. They were wrong.

The bombardment that had seemed so earth shattering had flattered to deceive. Although millions of shells had been fired; they were fired

*Opposite: Y Sap crater and Lochnagar Crater, blown 1 July 1916.*

*Opposite below: Y Sap crater and behind it the flattened ruins of la Boisselle.*

*Tynside Irish walking towards the German occupied village of la Boisselle and the front line at 0730, 1 July 1916.*

GERMAN FRONT LINE

Y SAP CRATER

LA BOISSELLE

SH FRONT LINE

LOCHNAGAR CRATER

on a front stretching over nearly 20 miles. The number and weight of shells falling per yard of German front to be assaulted was actually less than had been achieved at Neuve Chapelle back in 1915. This diluted the effect of the shells and it needed a far greater concentration to guarantee the outright destruction of the German front line. Furthermore the integral strength of the numerous German strongpoints had not been recognized. The Germans had constructed deep concrete shelters and dugouts – especially in the villages that dotted the area. Cellars had been expanded, reinforced and chained together to make each village a powerful fortress in its own right. It needed the repeated pinpoint accuracy of multiple direct hits by heavy shells to destroy or incapacitate the garrison. For the most part, field artillery shells merely rearranged the bricks of the shattered villages. The gunners were also for the most part new to their trade and the accuracy of their fire onto specific targets was just not adequate to the task. Even when they hit the targets a substantial proportion of the shells failed to explode as standards in munitions manufacture had been lowered to facilitate the rapid increase in production. This is not to say that the barrage was wholly ineffective, for many of the German front line troops had been killed, wounded or buried by direct hits on their trenches and dugouts. But many more had survived. Physically and mentally battered with their ears ringing from the ceaseless crashing detonations, frequently cut off from their headquarters or neighbouring units, nervous and often shell shocked, but they were still alive and ready to do their duty for their country.

For the most part, the absence of a proper creeping barrage meant that the British guns lifted their fire from the German front line and began to pound the rear areas just as their troops went over the top

*The killing ground in front of La Boisselle, No Man's Land is llittered with the dead and wounded.*

across No Man's Land – precisely at the moment when they most needed the shells to be moving towards and across the German front line. The raw British troops were restricted to advancing in waves at a plodding walk, both by the weight of their equipment and the belief that neither they, nor their officers, were sufficiently well trained to use any more sophisticated tactics. Nevertheless, they were confident that numbers and British pluck would win the day.

Went over the top at 7.30 after what seemed an interminable period of terrible apprehension. Our artillery seemed to increase in density and the German guns opened up on No Man's Land. The din was deafening, the fumes choking and visibility limited owing to the dust and clouds caused by exploding shells. It was a veritable inferno. I was momentarily expecting to be blown to pieces. My platoon continued to advance in good order without many casualties and until we had reached nearly half way to the Bosche front line. I saw no sign of life there.[2] *Lieutenant Alfred Bundy, 2nd Battalion, Middlesex Regiment*

Unfortunately, as the British barrage lifted from their front line the Germans had time to emerge from their dugouts and begin to pour rifle and machine-gun fire into their slow moving opponents. They were an easy target.

Suddenly an appalling rifle and machine-gun fire opened against us and my men commenced to fall. I shouted, "Down!" but most of those who were still not hit had already taken what cover they could find. I dropped in a shell hole and occasionally attempted to move to my right and left, but bullets were forming an impenatrable barrier and exposure of the head mean certain death. None of our men were visible but in all directions came

pitiful groans and cries of pain.[3] *Lieutenant Alfred Bundy, 2nd Battalion, Middlesex Regiment*

The carnage was made far worse by the German artillery barrage that redoubled its efforts to sweep the British front line and No Man's Land with a torrent of exploding shells. Despite the best efforts of the Royal Artillery it was apparent that many of the concealed German batteries had survived, and those that had been identified had neither been properly destroyed in advance, nor 'suppressed' by the gunners' programme of counter-battery fire during the crucial moments when British troops were in No Man's Land. In front of them the shells had failed also to clear the wire and in places it was almost untouched.

So it was that above them the contact patrols witnessed tragedy unparalleled in British military history before or since. It was their role to determine the exact progress of troops on the ground. This information was vital to inform the supporting artillery batteries, as it had been found through bitter experience that conventional means of communication frequently broke down when the troops launched themselves across No Man's Land. The German counter-bombardment severed telephone links, killed runners and the advancing waves disappeared into the unknown. As Lieutenant Cecil Lewis flew his Morane Parasol above La Boisselle his eyes were glued to the ground.

We had all our contact patrol technique perfected and we went right down to 3,000 feet to see what was happening. We had a klaxon horn on the undercarriage of the Morane – a great big 12 volt klaxon and I had a button which I used to press out a letter to tell the infantry that we wanted to know where they were. When they heard us hawking at them from above, they had little red Bengal flares, they carried them in their pockets, they would put a match to their flares. All along the line wherever there was a chap there would be a flare and we would note these flares down on the map and Bob's your uncle! It was one thing to practise this

*Morane Parasol.* IWM Q 55974

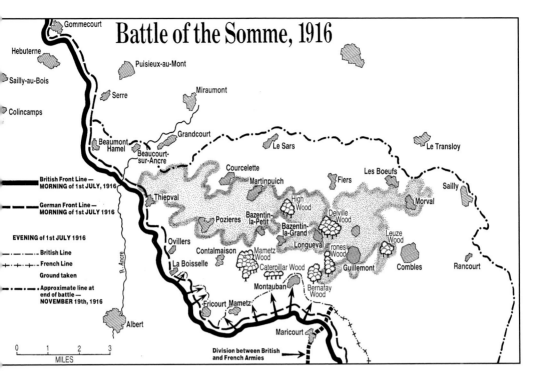

**Battle of the Somme, 1916**

Gommecourt

Hebuterne

Puisieux-au-Mont

Sailly-au-Bois

Serre

Miraumont

Colincamps

Grandcourt

Beaumont Hamel

Beaucourt-sur-Ancre

Le Sars

Le Transloy

Thiepval

Courcelette

Martinpuich

Flers

Les Boeufs

Sailly

High Wood

Morval

Pozieres

Bazentin-la-Petit

Delville Wood

Bazentin-la-Grand

Leuze Wood

Ovillers

Contalmaison

Longueval

Mametz Wood

Trones Wood

La Boiselle

Caterpillar Wood

Guillemont

Combles

Rancourt

R. Ancre

Montauban

Bernafay Wood

Fricourt Mametz

Albert

Maricourt

British Front Line —
MORNING of 1st JULY, 1916

German Front Line —
MORNING of 1st JULY 1916

**EVENING of 1st JULY 1916**

British Line

French Line

Ground taken

Approximate line at
end of battle —
NOVEMBER 19th, 1916

Division between British
and French Armies

0   1   2   3
MILES

but quite another thing for them to really do it when they were under fire and particularly when things began to go a bit badly. Then they jolly well wouldn't light anything and small blame to them because it drew the fire of the enemy on to them at once. So we went down looking for flares and we only got about two flares on the whole front. We were bitterly disappointed because this we hoped was our part to help the infantry and we weren't able to do it.[4] *Second Lieutenant Cecil Lewis, 3 Squadron, RFC*

The attack was launched by the French Army on either side of the Somme; while the British XIII, XV, III, X and VIII Corps of Fourth Army attacked all along the front from Montauban to Serre. North of Serre, VII Corps of Third Army made a diversionary attack on Gommecourt. On this day of failure the French prospered. They succeeded in making an advance of about a mile almost uniformly along the stretch of front attacked. To their left, the XIII and XV Corps attacks were also relatively successful, although at the cost of considerable casualties. All their objectives were achieved in pushing the line forward from Montauban facing Bernafay Wood to Mametz. Although the German garrison of Fricourt held out, advances made on either side left it isolated and it fell the next day. Along the rest of the front, stretching from La Boisselle to Serre and in the attack on Gommecourt, the story was one of almost uniformly pitiful disaster. In the few places where the

*91*

infantry actually managed to reach the German lines, they were soon isolated from their own front line and picked off piecemeal by the German counter-attacks. The human cost was unimaginable: 57,470 casualties, of which 19,240 were dead. The so-called 'Pals Battalion's of Kitchener's Army had made virtue of recruiting friends and work colleagues to the colours. Now the disadvantages were apparent as they fought and died together bringing misery to countless families across the country. All that had been gained was a narrow strip of ground about 3½ miles wide and just a mile deep.

\* \* \* \*

The artillery observation aircraft had been aloft from 04.00, but the early morning mists that marked the birth of a new day meant that they could achieve little until the sun cleared the skies. As the bombardment grew ever stronger they were able to search out targets for the guns and identify the positions of the German batteries that had opened up to such devastating effect. But in a landscape torn by thousands of shell bursts every minute it proved difficult to correct the fall of shot as they could not tell which battery was firing which shells. Throughout the day 22 and 24 Squadrons of 14th (Army) Wing undertook a constant stream of patrols designed to prevent any possible interference with the vital work of the Corps' machines.

When over Curlu with rest of Patrol, I saw a hostile machine over Peronne, and attacked, firing half a drum at about 150 yards. He turned and dived Eastwards. When over Pys about 10 minutes later, I saw 2 H.A. Type A coming West over Bapaume. The other de H's were over Gommecourt. I dived at the hindmost machine and fired half a drum, passed him, and fired the rest of the drum into the other machine. The observer in this machine ceased fire and collapsed into the nacelle, so I climbed up and having changed drums, again attacked the first H.A., which had attacked me from behind. I fired several bursts into him at close range and he suddenly did a side slip tail slide and fell into a cloud, apparently out of control and was seen to crash. About five minutes later, while regaining my height, somewhere over Achiet-le-Grand, I saw another H.A., Type C approaching from the North East. He opened fire at about 400 yards and turned back. I managed to get within about 200 yards and as I was unable to catch him up, fired about 20 rounds. He dived East and I rejoined the patrol.[5] *Lieutenant Sidney Cowan, 24 Squadron, RFC*

Under Brigadier-General E B Ashmore's arrangements 22 Squadron were responsible for the area between Douchy and Miraumont. The FE2 Bs took off in pairs and patrolled over their assigned sector of the line until they were relieved by the next pair. Lieutenants Firstbrook and Burgess took off at 06.30 but were taken by surprise as machine gun bullets ripped through their aircraft.

I left the aerodrome of my Squadron at Bertangles on an FE2 B carrying two 20 lb Hales bombs. When I reached the height of 8,000 feet, I crossed the German lines in the sector between Albert and the Somme. I remember releasing one of the bombs, but do not remember the target. From that moment on I remember nothing until I regained consciousness in a German Field Hospital on July 7th. I was wounded by a machine gun bullet entering my back between the spine and shoulder blade, and it travelled in a downward direction and lodging in the diaphragm. I was unconscious for six days from concussion caused by my machine crashing.[6] *Lieutenant J H Firstbrook, 22 Squadron, RFC*

Lieutenant R Burgess seems to have managed a reasonable crash landing before he succumbed to his wounds. At least Lieutenant Tudor-Hart saw the German aircraft that shot them down.

I was with Captain Webb and we went about 4 or 5 miles over the German lines in his machine on 1st July at 11am. We saw eight German machines approaching from the south-west – they were higher than us, and we flew towards them to attack. Two passed over our heads together about 300 yards or so apart, and I opened fire on one. They both replied together. I gave the signal to Webb to turn so that I could fire at the other machine behind us, but he put the machine's head down. I turned to see what was the matter, and he pointed to his abdomen and collapsed over the 'joy stick'. He died in a few seconds I think, but his last thought was to save his machine. The machine at once began turning towards the German side, and I had to get back to my machine-gun to fire at a machine diving at us. This happened again and again, but my fire would always prevent them finishing the dive. Other machines fired from above all the time. I had only time to get the machine pointing towards our lines when I had to get back to the gun. I never got a chance to pull Webb out of the pilot's seat, so I had to steer with my hand over the windscreen. I didn't expect to get off alive, but tried to put up as good a fight as possible, and tried all the time to keep her towards our lines, but having to man the gun so often made it impossible to make progress, but the erratic course the machine flew probably saved it. At last, still being fired at, I got right down near the ground and proceeded to make a landing, as it was all I could do. I saw a lot of men with rifles, and realised that I might get shot before I could set fire to the machine, so I, at the last minute, put her nose down in order to crash. One wing tip hit first, the whole machine was destroyed, I was hurled out and escaped with a bruised and paralysed side and broken ankle and rib.[7] *Lieutenant W. O. Tudor-Hart, 22 Squadron*

The sacrifice of men like these was justified by the fact that German aircraft were generally fended off and were unable to intervene over the battlefield itself where it actually mattered.

Although many of the aircraft involved belonged to units to the north of the Somme front, the distances of 20 to 30 miles were negligible to an aircraft and redeploying units did not pose the transportation problems the army faced. Thus bombing raids were launched by units of I, II and III Brigades in an attempt to cut the rail lines that would allow the Germans to move in their reserves. Lieutenant Lawrence Wingfield was one of the pilots of III Brigade assisting as part of the aerial concentration on the IV Brigade front. He was ordered to bomb the St Quentin railway station, but there was a catch. To increase the bombing load that could be carried the bombers were to fly without an observer. The BE2 C was often described as defenceless and now it truly was.

I had to go to St Quentin, a large town then about 35 miles on the German side of the lines, there to 'lay' a couple of 'eggs' on the railway station. The 'eggs' to be carried were large ones, weighing 110lbs each full of TNT and I had to carry two. That in a BE2 C meant that all superfluous weight had to be sacrificed. No observer could be carried and even the weight of a machine gun would be an unjustifiable load. I ultimately decided to take a machine gun (Lewis) though it proved to be rather a disadvantage than otherwise. It was fixed in such a position that I could not readily use it, whilst its weight reduced my rate of climb. I had been informed that I was to be escorted all the way and back by a squadron of DH2s, but in fact, the escort failed to materialise. At the appointed time I started off; arrived at the line and awaited the escort. As it did not appear in sight, I gave up waiting and proceeded over the line. The wind was SW, about 30mph. I arrived at St Quentin and dropped my bombs at the railway station. I observed a column of smoke arise to a great height. On the way home, I met a Fokker monoplane and that was the end of the story. It took the Fokker about 15 minutes to shoot me down, but I do not think there was at any time during the encounter much hope of my getting away from him. On my arrival on terra firma which I achieved without personal injury, I found myself on a parade ground. My machine and I were immediately surrounded by German troops, and I found myself amongst gentlemen, who knew Brighton and London well, and who were all questioning me as to the condition of

*Lawrence Wingfield.*
RAFM/RAeC 1781

these places – did I know them? Had they suffered very much through the war? And so on. I was able to reassure them on these points.[8] *Lieutenant Lawrence Wingfield, 12 Squadron, RFC*

Wingfield, or one of the other aircraft that failed to return, had a really significant impact that was only later revealed during the interrogation of a German soldier taken prisoner later in the fighting.

At the end of the month of June the 22nd Reserve Division was at rest in the neighbourhood of St Quentin. On the 1st July the Division was warned to proceed to the Somme front. About 3.30pm the first battalion of the 71st Reserve Regiment and the 11th Reserve Jaeger Battalion were at St Quentin Station ready to entrain, arms were piled and the regimental transport was being loaded onto the train. At this moment English aeroplanes appeared overhead and dropped bombs. One bomb fell on a shed which was filled with ammunition and caused a big explosion. There were 200 wagons of ammunition in the station at the time; 60 of them caught fire and exploded, the remainder were saved with difficulty. The train allotted to the transport of troops and all the equipment which they had placed on the platform were destroyed by fire. The men were panic-stricken and fled in every direction. One hundred and eighty men were either killed or wounded. It was not till several hours later that it was possible to collect the men of 71st Regiment. It was then sent back to billets.[9] *Anon German Prisoner*

Repeated raids were launched on the train system centred on the major rail junctions and railheads at Cambrai, Busigny and St Quentin. The German Headquarters at Bapaume was also repeatedly attacked during the day. It was difficult to achieve direct hits with the primitive bomb aimers available and the load that the bombing force carried was nowhere near enough to flatten a target without a certain amount of luck. Hence results were patchy, but they did achieve some successes.

I saw a train about four miles from Cambrai on the Cambrai-Douai line, going towards Douai. I opened from 7,000 feet at it. When it saw me coming it pulled up and started going backwards to Cambrai; when I was at 1,000 feet I released my bombs. The train pulled up. Suddenly one of my bombs fell 30 yards in front of the rear coach, destroying the line and preventing the train going back to Cambrai. Another bomb fell on the embankment. When about 300 feet from the train I came under heavy machine gun fire. Flying wires, longeron, petrol tank were shot and several holes in the machine.[10] *Lieutenant Scott, 5 Squadron, RFC*

Another notable success was achieved by Lieutenant A L Gordon Kidd of 7 Squadron who, from the height of just 900 feet, scored a direct hit on a train as it passed through a cutting. The train had obviously been carrying ammunition, for his bomb set off a series of explosions and a major fire that was still burning several hours later.

The bulk of 32 Squadron, the DH2 scout squadron of III Brigade, took off at 03.40 to escort the aircraft of 2 and 25 Squadrons on bombing raids on German rail communications. Their Squadron Leader, Major Lionel Rees, ignored the standing orders to stay on the ground and himself took off at 05.35, accompanied by Lieutenant J C Simpson, to patrol over the Loos area North of the Somme area. Simpson and Rees were soon separated and at 06.15, when Rees saw a formation of aircraft above him, he assumed it was one of the British formations returning from their mission. He had begun to climb, intending to help escort them home, when he identified they were German. Rees was utterly undaunted and continued his climb.

As I got nearer, at about Annequin, the second machine turned out of the position and dived towards me firing his guns. I waited until he came within convenient range and fired one drum. After about the 30th round I saw the top of his fuselage splinter between the pilot and the observer. The machine turned round and went home. This machine was marked with a big '3' and a small cross on the fuselage. I then went to attack a second machine. When he saw me he fired red Verey Lights, and three more joined him. They fired an immense amount of ammunition but were so far away that they had no effect. The escort machines swooped down onto their own machine instead of me, and so shot past him and went out of action. When I got to a convenient position, I fired one drum. After about 30 rounds a big cloud of blue haze came out of the nacelle in front of the pilot. The machine turned and wobbled, and I last saw him down over the lines under control. It looked either as if a cylinder was knocked off or else the petrol tank punctured. I then saw five close together. They opened fire at very long range. I closed, and fired one drum at very long range at the centre and the five dispersed in all directions. I then saw the leader and the two second machines going West. I overhauled them rapidly and, when I got near the lowest, he turned sharply to the left and dropped a bomb. He opened fire at long range. I closed, just as I was about to fire, a shot struck me in the leg, putting the leg temporarily out of action. I fired another drum, but not having complete control of the rudder, I swept the machine backwards and forwards. I finished firing about ten yards away, and saw the observer sitting back firing straight up into the air, instead of at me. I grabbed my pistol but dropped it on the floor of the

*Lionel Rees.* IWM Q 68027

*96*

nacelle and could not get it again. I then recovered the use of my leg and saw the leader going towards the lines. I got within long range of him. He was firing an immense amount of ammunition. Just before he reached the lines, I gave him one more drum. Having finished my ammunition, I came home.[11] *Major Lionel Rees, 32 Squadron, RFC*

Rees was badly wounded but he made it back to the airfield where Second Lieutenant Gwilym Lewis saw him land.

*vilym Lewis.* IWM HU 86612

I told you he was the bravest man in the world. He came across them a little later, and the 'Archie's' batteries say they have never seen anything so gallant or comic in their lives. The Huns were in a tight little bunch when he came along – after he had finished they were all scattered in twos and ones all over the sky, not knowing which way to go . . . He landed in the usual manner – taxied in. They got the steps for him to get out of his machine. He got out and sat on the grass, and calmly told the fellows to bring him a tender to take him to hospital. I am afraid he has got a very bad wound, though he is lucky not to have had an artery in his leg shot, as I understand he would never have got back if he had. Of course, everyone knows the Major is mad. I don't think he was ever more happy in his life than attacking those Huns. He said he would have brought them all down one after the other if he could have used his leg![12] *Second Lieutenant Gwilym Lewis, 32 Squadron, RFC*

Major Hawker ordered his DH2s of 24 Squadron to begin a series of daily offensive patrols on 1 July. Four patrols, each of six or seven machines, were made in addition to escort duties. Hawker had been ordered not to fly, but he could not keep

*DH2s of 32 Squadron.* IWM Q 11897

away entirely, and compromised by carrying out a detailed reconnaissance patrol from his DH2 high above the battlefield at 12.30.

No Hostile Aircraft seen. About 12, six horsed vehicles moving south along Artillery Lane towards, and two or three moving East from Beaucourt-sur-Ancre. Two or three vehicles moving both ways along St. Pierre Divion-Grandcourt Road. Big High Explosive shells bursting on our trenches opposite Thiepval. Hostile trenches from Ancre to Thiepval crowded with dark infantry – presumably Germans. Very few men seen in trenches from Thiepval to Albert-Bapaume Road. Crater North of road empty. Crater South of road and communication trench to North East held by us. Many dead lying on Eastern slopes outside this crater. One horsed vehicles moving in Contalmaison. Our men in communication trenches North of Fricourt facing South. Shrapnel bursting on a line Mametz Wood-Montauban. No indication that Ovillers, Contalmaison or La Boisselle had been captured, but enemy apparently contained in Fricourt. Pilot's impression: enemy holding on to the line Thiepval-Ancre while he evacuates his artillery.[13] *Major Lanoe Hawker, 24 Squadron, RFC*

At 20.05, he set off again to check progress.

No Hostile Aircraft seen. Hostile shelling very heavy North and South of Hamel. Hostile batteries very active along road from R21a7-8 to R15c7-4, also active at R1a9-2 and R2a4-7 our shrapnel falling on line Beaucourt-Pozières. White lights fired from second German Trench from Thiepval to Ancre. Our shrapnel falling on line Pozières-Bois de Mametz, and very heavy shelling along ravine from Caterpillar Wood to North of Bois de Bernafay followed by white and red lights along same ravine. Pilot's impression: attack progressing favourably from Montauban but held up at Thiepval though half the village and the first two lines have been carried.[14] *Major Lanoe Hawker, 24 Squadron, RFC*

Captain Wyllie of 23 Squadron, RFC, was assigned to a series of reconnaissance and offensive patrols. The FE2 Bs always seemed to attract trouble and once again he was in the thick of the action.

Went on reconnaissance at 3.15pm to find out whether reinforcements were being sent up road. Ordered to stay over two hours. Unfortunately we had to carry four bombs which spoilt our climbing. Went over lines at 7,500. Dropped bombs as soon as possible and got to 8,000. Shelled heavily going over. Met five Huns at Vaulx. Engaged – they got tired of it after about 15 minutes close action and went down, giving us some parting shots as they went. Solly got in a very good burst at one fellow and he got on his gliding angle at once and didn't appear any more. My flight behaved well and got off their drums. The issue of the fight was never in doubt. Solly was hit in the thigh very early in the fight but did not tell me. Another bullet ripped up one of his boots. The way he worked his gun was splendid – he got off 260 rounds. He had a marvellous escape as one bullet went right through the upper tube of the nacelle not a foot from him, and made a big hole in the top plane. His Verey Light pistol was smashed by another, and his map case cut. We could have followed the enemy down but it would have been too risky to lose much height as it was blowing hard from the West and we were on reconnaissance. We saw three of them land on their aerodrome at Queant. As we were re-crossing the line we saw that Gopsill was in great danger from an Albatross who was coming up behind him. We immediately dived 1,000 feet at him and got off a burst. Two others did the same and after another dive and burst the Hun made off for Plouvain. We were being very badly shelled at the time but managed to get back into some sort of formation and all got over the lines safely but low down. Solly, I am sorry to say, left the Squadron this evening. A very great loss. Gopsill had his radiator shot through by the Albatross, but landed in the aerodrome – poor boy, this is the second time in a few days that he has been shot down.[15] *Captain Harold Wyllie, 23 Squadron, RFC*

Second Lieutenant Morris and Sergeant Glover of 11 Squadron also ran into a group of German aircraft.

Had been patrolling for about half an hour and had turned North from Gommecourt towards Souchez, when we saw some specks over the Hun line coming towards Souchez. I turned the nose of the machine towards Souchez and we gradually saw that eleven machines were coming towards us, all very high. After about five minutes we discovered that they were eleven Huns. We were at 9,000 feet and the lowest Hun was about 9,300 feet so we tackled him. One of the others came up and fired at us but after a few shots from us he sheered off and left us to deal with the first one. The Hun opened fire at about 300 yards but Glover reserved his fire until we were within about 30 yards of him and then gave him a burst of about ten shots. He then circled and we followed and got in two more bursts of tracer both of which I saw were well into him. He then put his nose down and I saw some pieces of stuff flying off him. He went right down and disappeared through a bank of clouds. We then had time to look around and I discovered that our engine was going badly and we couldn't climb at all and as the rest of the Huns were almost out of sight we decided to come home. When we got home we discovered that our machine had been hit in several places. There was a hole through the front of the

*nel Morris*
M/RAeC 2334

nacelle and several through the planes, while the engine had gone dud owing to a cylinder having been hit. 'Archie' reported that the Hun we hit went right down and probably crashed. We were awfully bucked of course.[16] *Second Lieutenant Lionel Morris, 11 Squadron, RFC*

There was tension for those left behind on the ground as the pilots flew off on their life or death missions.

After luncheon, with Waldron and Smith-Barry, I saw the pilots start, and then one waited and waited . . . Who would come back? Who would not come back? At 4.30 Ferdy Waldron came back with his machine riddled with bullets. I went home at 4.30 and reported to the General, and then went back again at six, and stayed till 6.30. This time I saw a lot of pilots hot from the fighting and in a high state of exhilaration as they had had a grand day.[17] *Captain Maurice Baring, Headquarters, RFC*

Victorious on the ground, it was apparent that the Germans had been roundly defeated in the air. Over the battlefield it was estimated that some 110 pilots were in the air for some 108 hours and there were only nine combats. The British had harvested the fruits of the RFC aerial supremacy, but they could not counter-balance the miscalculations and tactical naivety that was fully exposed on the ground. They could fly freely over ground that unsilenced German gun batteries and machine guns made it impossible to cross on foot.

1 IWM SR: C. Lewis, AC 4162

2. IWM DOCS: A. Bundy

3. IWM DOCS: A. Bundy

4. IWM SR: C. Lewis, AC 4162

5. IWM DOCS: S. E. Cowan, Combat report, 1/07/1916

6. W. F. J. Harvey, *Pi in the Sky* (privately published)

7. W. O. Tudor-Hart quoted in C. Cole *'RFC Communiques, 1915-1916'*, (London: Kimber, 1969), pp298-299

8. L. Wingfield, *Journal of the Institution of Engineers*, 1926

9. M. Baring, *'Flying Corps Headquarters'*, (Edinburgh & London: William Blackwood & Sons, 1968), p155

10. M. Baring, *'Flying Corps Headquarters'*, (Edinburgh & London: William Blackwood & Sons, 1968), pp153-154

11. W. Alister Williams, *'Against the Odds; The Life of Group Captain Lionel Rees VC'*, (Wrexham: Bridge Books, 1989), p90

12. G. H. Lewis, *'Wings over the Somme'*, (Wrexham: Bridge Books, 1994), pp47-48

13. B. G. Gray & the DH2 Research Group, *'The Anatomy of an Aeroplane: The de Havilland DH2 Pusher Scout'*, (Cross & Cockade, Vol 21, No. 3), p16

14. B. G. Gray & the DH2 Research Group, *'The Anatomy of an Aeroplane: The de Havilland DH2 Pusher Scout'*, (Cross & Cockade, Vol 21, No. 3), p16

15. IWM DOCS: H. Wyllie, Transcript diary, 1/7/1916

16. RAF MUSEUM: L. Morris, Manuscript diary, 1/7/1916

17. M. Baring, *'Flying Corps Headquarters'*, (Edinburgh & London: William Blackwood & Sons, 1968), p153

# Chapter Four

# July: Masters of the Air

The people to be pitied are the infantry – the poor fellows who get all the shelling and all the discomforts of war and who have all the hard work to do. The people who can be pitied in the RFC are the people on BE2 Cs and such machines who float about at 6,000 feet and sit over 'Archies' all day while they are doing artillery work or photography – and who can be attacked by anybody – if they are brave enough – on account of their slow speed – necessarily slow be it added on account of the nature of their work. We, the lords of creation, who float about at 10-12,000 feet should not be pitied.[1] *Second Lieutenant Edmund Lewis, 32 Squadron, RFC*

The overwhelming disaster of the first day did not, could not, stop the British offensive. Sir Douglas Haig decided to reinforce success by directing Sir Henry Rawlinson to concentrate on the right flank, where a sizable advance of around a mile had been made to seize the villages of Montauban and Mametz amidst the overall gloom and despondency. This success offered several clues to the future: more attention had been paid to the concept of a creeping barrage, many of the troops had on the initiative of local commanders been moved forward into No Man's Land under the cover of the bombardment to reduce the amount of time they were exposed when Zero Hour came; no attempt had been made to breach the German Second Line; the German defensive system was altogether less well developed and backed by far fewer artillery batteries in this sector. Together within this jumble of cause and effect lay the clues to a viable future tactical doctrine for attacks.

Rawlinson was ordered to push home any advantage that existed on his right flank between the junction with the French and La Boisselle. To allow him to concentrate on this task, Rawlinson was further directed to hand the reins of command in the northern sector over to Sir Hubert Gough, whose Reserve Army took over the X and VIII Corps covering the front from La Boisselle to Serre. The German Second Line still lay inviolate far in front of them on the high ground of the Bazentin Ridge. The next stage resolved itself into a series of bitter battles to capture the tactical staging posts which would allow a full scale assault on the German Second Line in mid-July. There was to be much hard fighting to secure the capture of Bernafay Wood, Mametz Wood, Trones Wood, Contalmaison and La Boisselle. The pattern of assaults was totally uncoordinated, with most of the attacks taking place on a narrow front and involving only a couple of battalions. Thus these insignificant names on the map came to have an awful significance in the home-towns of those battalions unfortunate enough to be ordered into the attack on a particularly contested small wood or village. With inadequate artillery support, attacking strong German positions, raked by machine-gun fire and pounded by artillery fire, many of the attacks made little or no progress in the face of crippling casualties. Yet, some gains were made amid the carnage and slowly the British line inched forward.

Above them the RFC carried on its work exactly as before. There was a slight morbidity in evidence, as in the guilty desire to view the aftermath of a train crash.

> Visit yesterday on early patrol to scene of British attack. From aloft an inspiring sight. Great clouds of smoke rolled over the stricken ground, creeping along the valleys like clouds of fleecy whiteness. Around Gommecourt the ground was pitted and pock-marked, but all was still. I could see the shrapnel bursting in little white puffs towards the Somme. Far behind the lines at 5am the white of the anti-aircraft shells showed that our aeroplanes were busy. Apart from this the sun cast long shadows and a yellow radiance over a deserted world. Yesterday I was told that you could see blood in the craters formed by the shells.[2] *Lieutenant Alan Dore, 13 Squadron, RFC*

Some of the pilots made the effort to visit the front lines on the ground to try and get a closer look at what was going on.

*Area around Gommecourt, 1 July 1916.*

I've been up and had a look at the various bits of war-on-the-ground on days when the weather's been dud. Our fellows were splendid, but the Hun was very tenacious in one or two places. We examined some of their trenches and they were a sight, beautifully deep and tidy at one time I suppose, but now all blown to pieces and the dugouts in a horrid mess.[3] *Major Lanoe Hawker, 24 Squadron, RFC*

The RFC continued to exercise their dominance over the battlefield. But, the Germans did not always give way easily and many British pilots were still fighting in frankly inadequate aircraft. This was exemplified by the plight of 60 Squadron of 9 Wing who were still flying the obsolete Morane Biplanes and Morane Bullets. Neither had the benefit of synchronized machine guns, relying instead on the old system of a fixed Lewis gun firing through the propeller fitted with a metal deflector to prevent it being shot through. The Bullet in particular lacked engine power and its pilots complained that it had the gliding angle of a brick and was dangerously prone to stalling. As such these aircraft were inadequate for service over the Western Front and their pilots were sadly exposed. On 3 July, 'A' Flight of 60 Squadron set out on a dawn patrol in their Morane Bullets. With them was their Squadron Leader 'Ferdy' Waldron who, despite his clear orders, insisted in trying to personally accomplish at least one mission a day over the lines with his men. He was accompanied by Captain Robert Smith-Barry, Lieutenant Armstrong, Lieutenant Simpson and an 18 year-old novice, Second Lieutenant Harold Balfour.

Both Armstrong and Simpson fell out, through engine trouble, before we reached Arras. Waldron led the remaining two along the Arras-Cambrai road. We crossed at about 8,000 feet, and just before reaching Cambrai we were about 9,000 feet, when I suddenly saw a large formation of machines about our height coming from the sun towards us. There must have been at least 12. They were two-seaters led by one Fokker (monoplane) and followed by two others. I am sure they were not contemplating 'war' at all, but 'Ferdy' pointed us towards them and led us straight in. My next impressions were rather mixed. I seemed to be surrounded by Huns in two-seaters. I remember diving on one, pulling out of the dive, and then swerving as another came for me. I can recollect also looking down and seeing a Morane about 800 feet below me going down in a slow spiral, with a Fokker hovering above it following every turn. I dived on the Fokker, who swallowed the bait and came after me, but unsuccessfully, as I had taken care to pull out of my dive while still above him. The Morane I watched gliding down under control, doing perfect turns, to about 2,000 feet, when I lost sight of it. I thought he must have been hit in the engine. After an indecisive combat with the Fokker I turned home. Smith-Barry I never saw from start to finish of the fight. I landed at Vert Galant and reported that 'Ferdy' had "gone down under control".[4] *Second Lieutenant Harold Balfour, 60 Squadron, RFC*

In fact, Waldron had been mortally wounded and, although he survived the crash landing, he died that night. Afterwards Balfour was haunted by his role in the fight. Unable to accept that he had been helpless to change Waldron's fate, aware too of the inferior nature of his aircraft, he in effect lost all confidence in his own abilities.

The fight in which our Commanding Officer was killed affected me severely, for I felt that I might have done more, and kept worrying and questioning myself as to what I should have done other than that which I did. So much did this disturb my mental balance that I found myself hesitating on entering a fight, which hesitation rapidly developed into nothing short of a dislike to standing up to the enemy, and a strong inclination to turn tail with a dive homewards. One day I did this when out on patrol with another Morane. We were attacked by two Fokkers and my opponent could obviously out-manoeuvre me in every way. So I acted the complete funk, and turned my nose downwards and in the direction of our lines. My companion was fighting about two miles South of me. I told myself that it was up to me to look after myself, and up to him to look after himself, and with those temporarily comforting sentiments I regained safety. My companion never returned, and when I looked back from the sanctuary of our lines I saw a small streak of flame falling earthwards, which I knew must have been his Morane, on fire defeated by the attacking Fokkers.[5] *Second Lieutenant Harold Balfour, 60 Squadron, RFC*

Balfour was struggling with the combined effects of his youth, inexperience and the paralysing effect of misplaced guilt. Once fear had been allowed out of the Pandora's box of his psyche, it could not easily be re-imprisoned.

Balfour was not alone in this. Many pilots wrestled with their natural terrors.

The heat of the long summer days was terrific, and our flying hours were many. All these facts assisted to play upon the temperaments of those who were flying in France for the first time, and had not got confidence either in their ability or in their aeroplanes. I can remember my bedroom companion in the farmhouse in which we were billeted, felt as I did, and how each of us lay awake in the darkness, not telling the other that sleep would not come, listening to the incessant roar of the guns, and thinking of the dawn patrol next morning. At last we could bear it no longer, and calling out to each other admitted a mutual feeling of terror and foreboding. We lit the candles to hide the dark, and after that felt a bit better, and somehow got through that night as we had to get through the next day.[6] *Second Lieutenant Harold Balfour, 60 Squadron, RFC*

He managed to survive, until a farcical accident ended his first ignominious tour of duty.

I took a deckchair on the aerodrome, sat down, moved it to a more comfortable position and again put my weight upon it. The chair collapsed, and crushed the tips of the middle fingers of both my hands. This sent me to hospital, and kept me off flying for some days. Smith-Barry took advantage of the opportunity, and without any fuss or bother arranged that I should go back to England. Everybody in the Squadron was very charming, and nobody said anything about the brief and inglorious part which I had played. There was no question of being sent home in official disgrace, but purely that at that time I was of no real use to the unit and therefore was better out of the way.[7] *Second Lieutenant Harold Balfour, 60 Squadron, RFC*

Balfour had enough moral fibre to return a little older and a great deal wiser in 1917. By the time the war finished in 1918, he had been credited with shooting down nine German aircraft.

The scout pilots continued to endure the punishing schedule that was essential if they were to protect the vital corps machines.

For a long period we did three patrols a day – two of the flights were down for three shows a day, and the third was on standby for Headquarters. I think we were the first Squadron to do this, as a Squadron, though Ball and one or two others worked individually. A system of alarms was arranged. A bell ringing both at the Squadron office and the mess – and how vividly we all remember those bells – which generally seemed to ring about two minutes before one's relief came, for we stood by ready to leave the ground immediately the alarm rang. With the Mono engine, no time was wasted in starting or warming up and quite frequently, machines were in the air well within one minute of the alarm bell ringing. I well remember the general alarm sounding on one occasion, on a rather dud day, when most people were in the mess. (A general alarm sounded if more than 10 machines were reported.) On this occasion in one minute, machines were streaming out of the hangar and twelve machines were off the ground in under two minutes. We never found anything at all and we all supposed afterwards that 'Archie' had been seeing things.

It was probably six machines which passed four times over a gap in the clouds. To save time a large board was placed outside the Squadron office with the area and number of Hostile Aircraft on it, and as one took off, one glanced at the board to see what one's task was. This was, like most of our other gadgets, Major Hawker's idea . . . Three and sometimes even four shows a day (I have done the latter myself in extreme cases when an attack was on) and throughout it all a great spirit of responsibility and unselfishness ran right through the Squadron. The work done by some of the mechanics was at times tremendous – again and again work having to be continued all night to enable us to keep machines serviceable. Speaking of my own flight – which was representative – the men at that time were really wonderful. No holidays, no leave and all work, but never a grumble. I had on more than one occasion to order men to bed in the daytime, or otherwise I knew they would collapse and break down.[8] *Lieutenant A M Wilkinson, 24 Squadron, RFC*

Later in the month, Hawker ordered offensive patrols across the front lines to strafe the German troops on the ground while every DH2 was also to carry a drum of Buckingham trace ammunition in readiness for any opportunity to attack the German observation balloons peering behind the British lines. The stress on Hawker's pilots was incredible and he was not the kind of leader to take advantage of official disapproval of squadron commanders flying. Without any fuss, Hawker often ignored his orders and flew missions in the place of pilots rendered more nervous than usual on the approach of their long anticipated leave. This was not just a kindness, as Hawker believed that he needed to experience at first hand the problems and trials his pilots underwent on a daily basis.

Such a schedule was a strain even to the bravest of the brave. Those that managed to survive were kept going by a muddled mixture of motives in which a sense of duty mingled with the desire not to let down their comrades or expose themselves to ridicule. As the pressure mounted their youthful resilience was tested to the absolute limit. Yet, very few translated their fears into any kind of virulent hatred for their German opposite numbers.

I am feeling a poo-poo crock today. I went up this morning after three Huns and managed to get underneath them, but could not get nearer than 3,000 feet owing to my engine. Am spending remainder of the day trying to get it right. You ask me to let the devils have it when I fight. Yes, I always let them have all I can, but really I don't think them devils. I only scrap because it is my duty, but I do not think anything bad about the Hun. He is just a good chap with very little guts, trying to do his best. Nothing

*lbert Ball.*

makes me feel more rotten than to see them go down, but you see it is either them or me, so I must do my best to make it a case of them.[9] *Second Lieutenant Albert Ball, 11 Squadron, RFC*

Compared to the infantry, casualties were slight. But in a small unit a casualty a day would soon wipe out the original personnel of a squadron. Although squadrons were ceaselessly regenerated by replacements, it did not require much perception to work out that the odds of surviving a prolonged tour of duty in action were minimal.

Really one has only just time to button up one's tunic. I am having a poo-poo time, but most interesting. On the 6th, three topping chaps went off and never returned. Yesterday, four of my best pals went off and today one of our new chaps has gone over, so you can guess we are always having to get used to new faces . . . Yesterday I was up at 5am and during the day had twelve flights, but at last nature is asking to have its own way. However, I am not done yet. I shall get at them again soon.[10] *Second Lieutenant Albert Ball, 11 Squadron, RFC*

Ball was clearly suffering under the strain and although he had recently had a period of leave he put in a direct request to his Squadron Leader for more rest. This was bold in the extreme and Brigadier General J F A Higgins commanding 3rd Brigade, RFC could not grant the request, as it would inevitably set a dangerous precedent if every exhausted pilot could take rest as they pleased.

The day before yesterday we had a big day. At night I was feeling very rotten, and my nerves were poo-poo. Naturally, I cannot keep on for ever, so at night I went to see the C.O., and asked him if I could have a short rest, and not fly for a few days. He said he would do his best. What has taken place has been that I have been sent to No. 8 Squadron, back on to BE2 Cs. Oh, I am feeling in the dumps.[11] *Second Lieutenant Albert Ball, 11 Squadron, RFC*

For the moment his career as a scout pilot was stalled.

For the Corps' pilots there continued the ceaseless grind of photographic reconnaissance and artillery observation work. As the battlefield changed beneath them so the photos had to be taken and retaken to allow the staff to monitor and interpret the slightest change in the German defence works. The roar of the guns never ceased along the line.

When the battle had started the counter-battery work became our main task. It was wonderfully exciting and interesting. Nothing can give a more solid feeling of satisfaction than when, after seeing the shells from the battery you are directing fall closer and closer to the target, you finally see a great explosion in

a German gunpit and with a clear conscience can signal, "OK"![12]
*Lieutenant A J Evans, 3 Squadron, RFC*

As usual humans are variable beasts and what was food for one was another's poison.

> The work I dislike most is artillery cooperation. You have to pilot the machine, watch the target for the burst and work the wireless, all at the same time while 'Archie' is probably at work also. The aeroplane signals to the battery by wireless and the battery signals to the aeroplane by strips of white cloth on the ground. It is a common fallacy to think that you can see everything from an aeroplane. It is often very hard to make out details. When ranging with shrapnel it is quite easy to see the burst, but with high explosive it is quite difficult. Unless you are watching the place where the shell bursts at the right moment you will miss it as the smoke is brown and cannot be seen against the ground and all you can see is the earth thrown up which of course falls back in a second. You are usually at a height of about 8,000 feet although some days you have to come much lower. All the time you have to be on the lookout for Huns.[13] *Lieutenant Leslie Horridge, 7 Squadron, RFC*

The bursting shells of the German anti-aircraft fire were a backdrop as always and in a BE2 D, Lieutenant Tomson and Captain Jefferd found to their cost that 'Archie' was not always toothless.

> There was a good bit of 'Archie' about, but it was not fearfully good. Then, at about 2.30 we got practically a direct hit. It stopped the engine and cut both the rudder and elevator controls. The machine at once started to spin rapidly to earth. I of course experimented with the one bit of control I had and I found that by one movement I could temporarily slow up the progress. Then I waited – not very long – until the earth was unpleasantly near and then made the movement.[14] *Lieutenant W J Martin Tomson, 9 Squadron, RFC*

They crashed just over the German lines just north of Bazentin-le-Grand Wood

> The first thing that I remember was waking up and finding myself walking along a trench with my Observer, Captain Jefferd being conducted by a German. My Observer was still concussed and kept asking me if I was sure I knew the way back to No. 9 (our squadron). I told him, at first, the position of affairs, but soon realised that he could not take it in, so replied, "Yes, rather – this is allright." Every now and then, Jefferd would wander off amongst the shell shingled trees and our little German would run back and put him on the path again.[15] *Lieutenant W J Martin Tomson, 9 Squadron, RFC*

The Corps' aircraft were of course benefiting from the fruits of aerial dominance. The artillery observation aircraft were almost immune from the attentions of the German scouts pinned back miles behind their own lines by the British offensive patrols.

German aeroplanes were remarkably scarce and never interfered with us at our work. If one wished to find a German plane, it was necessary to go ten miles over the German lines and alone. Even under these conditions the Germans avoided a fight if they could.[16] *Lieutenant A J Evans, 3 Squadron, RFC*

The battlefield that lay beneath them was theirs to explore as they willed.

Went up with Sheridan to have a look at the fighting on the Somme. Clouds 3,000 feet with occasional rainstorms. Passed Gommecourt – the Wood being nothing more than a splintered wreckage. Over Hebuterne glimpses of old trenches looked rather battered. Then on to Thiepval where the shrapnel was bursting. A string of our kite balloons made it necessary to steer carefully lest we ran into the cable. I picked out Mametz Wood where the white puffs of our shrapnel bursting on the Eastern edge showed that we had now gained the whole of it. Contalmaison was covered with smoke where the HE were bursting. A number of our aeroplanes were about, some flying low over the new line which I could just discern.[17] *Lieutenant Alan Dore, 13 Squadron, RFC*

*The splintered wreckage of Gommecourt wood.*

For those lucky enough to be within sight of the end of their tour of duty at the front, there were mixed emotions that were perhaps inevitable after such a shared experience. Dore, an experienced observer, was to return home to qualify as a pilot.

> Powell comes to me with the information that I am to go home on the 21st. I don't know whether to be glad or sorry. Glad I am to go home to learn to fly, but sorry to leave some of the best fellows in the world, amongst whom I have spent some of the happiest moments of my life.[18] *Lieutenant Alan Dore, 13 Squadron, RFC*

As the piecemeal attacks continued on the ground, so contact patrols continued to be flown to try to give the Generals some idea of how their troops had progressed.

> The principle is for the pilot or observer to get to know the trench system of his own and the enemy area, by direct observation and by the careful study of maps made from photographs, so that he had merely to look at the ground and know it by heart. When the battle is being waged the observer or pilot will watch our troops from above and report their progress or otherwise by message bag to Headquarters . . . To start with it was found that the staff were somewhat disbelieving, but after a time they learnt to trust us and we were often sent back to make further observations on important points.[19] *Lieutenant E J D Routh, 34 Squadron, RFC*

Considerable thought was being given to the vexed problem of establishing contact between the low flying contact patrol aircraft and the infantry caught up in the heat of battle.

> Flares can be easily seen and distinguished from the air and proved their value on may occasions for defining the positions reached by the infantry. From the observer's point of view they were not lit in sufficient numbers. This was no doubt partly due to a shortage in the supply, only a proportion of the men carrying them in consequence. Some of our men seem to think that the flares draw shell fire. If judiciously placed, however, they can easily be screened from the enemy's view altogether. The Germans use Verey Lights and rockets freely, although they are more likely to draw fire than are our flares. On July 1st pieces of tin on the mens' backs were clearly seen in the XIII Corps attack. Once an attack become confused however, mirrors are unsuitable because there are so many shining objects on the ground that observations become unreliable. Lamps have been used with success both by day and night, especially by No. 9 Squadron working with XIII

MORANE PARASOL
No 3 Sqd. R.F.C

Corps. The Aldis pattern with the pistol grip is the best, as it is light (apart from the accumulators) and can be held and worked in one hand. It is moreover easy to direct. The Hucks Lamp is also light and easy to work but gives more wind resistance. The capture of Bernafay Wood was signalled to an aeroplane by means of a lamp and was know at Corps Headquarters nine minutes afterwards. Signalling panels have been considerably used and can be easily seen, but difficulty has been experienced by the aeroplane in knowing when a ground station wants to signal to it, and by the ground station in knowing when its message has been received. In the case of both lamp and panel signals the following points are of great importance:

1) Signallers must send slowly and with an even cadence.
2) Signallers with ground stations must have patience and continue sending until their signals are acknowledged.
3) Messages should as far as possible be confined to the authorised code. The aeroplane observer has a great many units to attend to.

The system used to indicate any point to which it was necessary to refer was that of map square and coordinates. It is for consideration whether the clock code as used in artillery work would not provide a better method. It is difficult for those on the ground to give the co-ordinates of the place whence fire is coming, but it would be easy to indicate it by clock code with respect to their own position. The Clock Code, however, necessitates a knowledge of where the North lies, and this might prove a difficulty. Wireless has been used to a certain extent for transmitting messages received by the infantry to Corps Headquarters, but most of the information has been given by dropping message bags. All observers agree that most information as to the position of our own and the enemy's troops can be obtained by direct observation flying low. Our own men can be distinguished from the enemy by the difference in colour of the uniforms up to 600-700 feet, while it is possible to see whether trenches are occupied from 1,500 to 2,000 feet in a good light. The steel helmet, if uncovered, is confusing as it shews black like the German helmet. In cases where it was uncertain which side, if either, occupied a trench, machines have on several occasions come down low to see whether they drew fire. In order to observe troops when not moving it is necessary to come down to 500 feet. As was foreseen, flying has proved possible during a battle at very much lower altitudes than during ordinary periods of trench warfare and much of the contact patrol work has been done from between 500 and 1,000 feet, while a height of between

1,500 and 2,500 has been normal. Below 2,000 feet musketry and machine gun fire begins, while under 1,000 feet it is usually very heavy, rifle fire being experienced even when the troops are actually fighting. No machines have been brought down through this low flying, with the exception of one which received a direct hit from a shell thought to be our own, and the casualties to personnel have been few; but some machines have been so riddled with bullets as to make it necessary to dismantle and reconstruct them. When it is necessary to clear up a situation, and required information cannot otherwise be obtained, low flying is essential, but the various systems of signalling, which enable machines to fly normally at reasonable heights, should be developed and should be employed whenever they meet the necessities of the case. One Army called the attention of its formations to the necessity of weighing the importance of the information likely to be gained before issuing orders which will necessitate flying at very low altitudes, pointing out the difficulty of replacing at short notice good observers with a detailed knowledge of the ground. This should always be borne in mind.[20] *Major General Trenchard, Headquarters, RFC*

However not everyone came up with sensible suggestions and the more cynical junior officers had many opportunities to direct their spleen at the more misguided or farcical suggestions.

Major Lumsden of the V Corps also arrived with a couple of ordinary umbrellas, painted half white, in sections. His idea was that the infantry should indicate their position to an aeroplane by opening and shutting their umbrellas. I think he was rather offended when I laughed. I did not gather whether it would be the Colonel who would leap over the parapet with a joyous shout and lead the charge brandishing his umbrella.[21] *Recording Officer Lieutenant Thomas Hughes, 1 Squadron, RFC*

Day after day, raids were launched on the German airfields, as the RFC sought to destroy the power of their counterparts. Well-placed bombs could destroy aircraft at their most vulnerable whilst they lay immobile on the ground; they killed highly trained ground personnel, destroyed hangars and technical equipment, harassed the already exhausted pilots and of course disrupted the crucial repair and maintenance work that had to be undertaken every day by the mechanics.

Standing by to bomb Douai aerodrome at 4.45pm. Seven machines left the ground at 7.20. Went over the lines at 9,000 steering by compass over cloud. Hit off the aerodrome exactly. Dropped twenty eight 20 pounder bombs through a gap in the clouds. Nearly all bursts observed, and position of A.A. guns on aerodrome which opened on us. Returned over clouds steering by compass. Some A.A. fire through gaps. My machine hit. Near Arras observed Fokker coming up through clouds to cut off Firbank whose engine was going badly. Formation very bad. Turned myself therefore, dived and opened at Fokker who immediately turned away and disappeared into the clouds. The formation was so bad that I was relieved not to have met a fighting patrol of Huns.[22] *Captain Harold Wyllie, 23 Squadron, RFC*

The main railway towns and junctions were still prime targets. As such targets were by definition well behind the German lines it was increasingly important to ensure that aircraft kept formation or the stragglers would be picked off by the German scouts. The latter hesitated to attack a well drilled formation acting in concert and bristling with machine guns, but fell on isolated lone aircraft with ruthless precision.

We turned south just beside Cambrai and found our mark, Marcoing station. I let my bomb go and had to turn off quickly to dodge a bomb from another youth who was above me. I saw his bomb go down. Several lit on the tracks in the station yards, and probably ruined them. As soon as our bombs were dropped we turned and lit out for home, devil take the hindmost. He did, as poor old Hewson was picked off by a bunch of Huns, who attacked us from behind and fired at us and went away.[23] *Lieutenant Don Brophy, 21 Squadron, RFC*

Stung by casualties he considered unnecessary, their Wing Commander, Colonel Hugh Dowding decided to show how it should be done. He therefore successfully requested permission to break the rule barring senior officers from crossing the front lines and went up, taking his adjutant with him as his observer.

The Colonel decided he'd lead us to show us how. He was to lead and Captain Carr and I were next, four others in pairs behind and nine scouts. At 6,000 we met thick clouds and when I came through I couldn't see anyone anywhere, so I just flew around and finally sighted three machines. I went over and found Carr and the Colonel and two scouts, so I got into place and the Colonel went over to the lines, and kept circling to get higher for half an hour, right over the lines. I thought this was a foolish stunt, as I knew the Huns could see us and would be waiting for us. I was very surprised that they didn't shell us, but there was a battle on and they were probably too busy. We were right over Albert, as I recognised two huge mine craters that had been sprung July 1st. When we did cross over with only two scouts, we hadn't been over more than a couple of minutes before I saw three Fokkers coming towards us and a couple of LVGs climbing up to us. Another Fokker was up above me and behind, between our two scouts. I knew he was going to dive at one of us, but expected the scouts to see him and attack him, so I didn't bother about him, but began to get the stop-watch time of my bomb-sight to set it for dropping. While I was doing this I suddenly heard the pop-pop-pop's of machine guns and knew the Huns had arrived. I looked and saw them diving in amongst us and firing. There were seven LVGs and three Fokkers as far as I could make out, but they went so fast I could hardly watch them. Our scouts went for them and I saw the Colonel turn about. My gun being behind me I couldn't get in a shot and turned round after Carr and the Colonel. They fired some more as we went back but didn't hit me. The Colonel was hit and so the show was over. He had about a dozen bullets in his machine and was hit in the hand. His gun was shot through and his observer hit in the face. He probably won't try to lead us again.[24]

*Lieutenant Don Brophy, 21 Squadron, RFC*

In fact, Dowding's hand had only been grazed as the Fokker's bullets shattered his cockpit instruments. Blasted fragments of the Lewis gun mechanism had also caused bloody, but only superficial wounds, to his observer. Although senior officers railed against the ban on them flying, an incident such as this exemplified the very real reasons that lay behind Trenchard's eddict. Dowding was out of practice and unused to the prevailing realities of aerial combat. He was therefore not a great deal of use in the air and in fact as *de facto* novices he and his adjutant were easy meat. But his hard won administrative skills were invaluable on terra firma in a fledgling service such as the RFC with no great reservoir of experienced officers.

*Hugh Dowding.* IWM HU 866

On the ground the intensity of the conflict boiled up once again. On Friday, 14 July, a general attack which was to be known as the Battle of Bazentin Wood took place all along the right sector of the line stretching from Longueval facing Delville Wood on the right to Bazentin-le-Petit Wood. Although it would be going too far to claim that the tactical mistakes of the previous two weeks had been fully recognized and digested, there were some hopeful signs for the future. The artillery was dealing with a frontage of only 6,000 yards and also not dissipating so much of their efforts on the German trench systems lying behind what had been the German Second Line. It was still an enormous gathering of artillery strength – some 1,000 guns – that generated five times the amount of shells on every yard of trench attacked than had been achieved in the bombardment that preceeded 1 July. The barbed wire would be cut by a preliminary bombardment and the assault was to be made in the darkness before dawn following a five-minute hurricane of artillery fire on the German front line. In a further tactical innovation the troops moved out into No Man's Land in the dark and crept forward ready to attack the moment the barrage ceased. When the attack came at 03.25 it caught the Germans by surprise. The whole German Second Line fell with little resistance and the troops pushed through to attack the support lines. The artillery had done its job and the German front line was a mass of shell holes and general devastation. The new line ran around Trones Wood, up to the edge of Delville Wood and along the ridge taking in Longueval, Bazentin le Grand and Bazentin le Petit. The next target lay not so very far in front of them in High Wood and the German Switch Line that ran through it. Optimism for a while was high

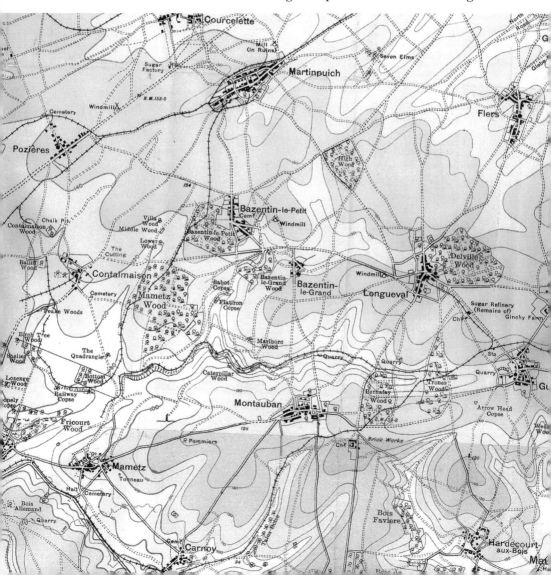

and the cavalry were indeed moved forward ready to exploit any opportunities that might arise. Although their participation was not the disaster it might well have been, they were not able to achieve any kind of breakthrough and were soon withdrawn. The infantry were belatedly launched into an attack on High Wood in the early evening but it was too late. They were thwarted by the arrival of German reserves and the inevitable counter-attacks that stabilized the German position. On 15 July, Lieutenant Cave took off in his BE2 C and flew across the benighted battlefield.

At 4.00pm I went up with Duke. There was practically nothing doing. Martinpuich was in flames and Pozières was very heavily bombarded. They were both fine sights. We were 'Archied' a lot, but very few really came near us. We had one hole through one plane. We have captured Ovillers, High Wood, Bazentin-le-Grand and I believe Longueval. I believe we are trying to get the cavalry through.[25] *Lieutenant Francis Cave, 4 Squadron, RFC*

*Francis Cave.* RAFM/RAeC 28

For the rest of the month vicious fighting contnued back and forth in High Wood and Delville Wood. The terrible nature of the conflict in these woods has added their names to the folklore of suffering on the Somme.

Haig realized his dreams of a breakthrough were unlikely to be realised in the short term, and he came to see the fighting in July and August as an attritional period whereby the strength of the German Army would be worn down ready for another major offensive in mid-September. Many of the operations undertaken were of a relatively small scale designed to straighten the line and thus improve the position from which the ultimate attacks would have to be made on the original German Third Line in front of the village of Flers. Identified German strongpoints that would inevitably cause trouble were to be tackled before the event. The Germans, of course, could not allow the British to steadily gain the advantage and they were drawn into a murderous circle of counter-attacks that raised their own casualty lists to a frightening degree. For the infantry on the ground these attacks seemed terrifyingly dangerous and completely without point. Thousands of lives were sacrificed to capture, recapture and capture again, features that no longer had any resemblance to their designation on the map. Villages were marked only by the red dust of pounded bricks, copses reduced to a tangled mass of shell holes and splintered wood. Formal trench structures began to disappear under the deluge of shells to be replaced with a more informal structure of linked craters. The Somme battlefield became hell on earth for all who served there. The Generals were not fools, they knew what they were doing, but they were demanding unprecedented sacrifices from their men. Perhaps they asked too much.

* * * *

As the fighting raged on the ground, aerial reconnaissance missions were vital to track the movements of rail and road traffic behind the German lines in an attempt to piece together the movement of German reserves. Lieutenant A J Evans and his observer Lieutenant H O Long (who had dropped an RFC wreath on the death of Immelmann) were sent to carry out a series of reconnaissances from Bapaume to Cambrai. At first all went well and they were even successful in shooting down a German aircraft.

After a manoeuvring fight lasting about ten minutes, the end of this fight came when, for perhaps twenty seconds, we flew side by side, and at the same time as Long shot down our opponent, he riddled us with bullets, and I was very lucky to get home without the machine catching fire.[26] *Lieutenant A J Evans, 3 Squadron, RFC*

They were re-equipped with a replacement Morane LA and were sent out again on 16 July. At this point their luck ran out as their new aircraft let them down in the most drastic fashion.

The engine suddenly stopped dead at 4,000 feet. I can only attribute the failure of the engine to a bullet in the magneto or petrol tank, probably the former. We must have been just North East of Bapaume, ten miles over the line, at the time, and I turned her head for home and did all I could; but there is very little one can do if the engine stops. After coming down a couple of thousand feet I began to look about for a landing place away from houses and near a wood if possible, and told Long to get out matches. Just at that moment the fiery rocket battery near the one sausage balloon, which remained to the Germans after the anti-balloon offensive of 4 July, opened fire on us, and I had to dodge to avoid the rockets. By the time they had stopped firing at us we were about 500 feet from the ground, and I heard a good deal of rifle fire, apparently at us. As my engine showed no signs of coming to life again, I picked out an open field where I thought we should have time to set fire to the machine in comfort before the Germans came up. I was only up about 200 feet or less when I found we were landing almost on top of a German battery, of whose existence I had no idea. I don't think the position of this battery was known to our people, but I may be wrong, as I temporarily lost my bearings while dodging those infernal rockets. As soldiers from the battery could be seen running out with rifles in their hands towards the spot where we obviously had to land, and as I much doubted whether we should have time to fire the machine, I determined when I was about 50 feet from the ground to crash the machine on landing. This I managed pretty successfully by ramming her nose into the ground instead of holding her off, and we had a bad crash. I found myself hanging upside down by my belt. I was a bit shaken but unhurt and got out quickly. Long was staggering about in a very dazed condition near the machine and the Germans were about 50 yards away. I got a matchbox from him and crawled under the machine again, but found, firstly, that I could not reach the petrol tap and in spite of the machine being upside down there was no petrol dripping anywhere; and, secondly, that Long in his dazed condition had handed me a box without any matches in it. The Germans were now only about 25 yards off, and I thought of trying to set the thing on fire with the Lewis gun and tracer bullets, but I could not find the gun. I think Long must have thrown it overboard as we came down. We were then surrounded by soldiers – they were a filthy crowd, but showed no signs of unpleasantness.[27] *Lieutenant A J Evans, 3 Squadron, RFC*

Although Evans failed to set the Morane alight, it was severely damaged by his deliberate crash landing with a broken propeller, crumpled wing and undercarriage. His observer had been severely shaken up by the impact.

Long was thoroughly shaken, and walked and talked like a drunken man. He kept on asking questions, which he reiterated in the most maddening way – poor chap – but to be asked every two minutes if you have been captured, when you are surrounded by a crowd of beastly Huns! I own I was feeling pretty irritable at the time, and perhaps a bit shaken. It took Long several days to become anything like normal and I don't think he was completely right in his mind again for weeks. He was obviously suffering from concussion.[28] *Lieutenant A J Evans, 3 Squadron, RFC*

Although treated well, just for a moment the eternal problems of captured airmen were soon evident. Infantry generally, not unnaturally, took exception to people throwing bombs and machine gunning from the heavens. Their opportunities for revenge were normally limited – now they had their chance.

A crowd of orderlies learnt that we were officer aviators. They collected round us and assumed rather a threatening attitude, accusing us of having thrown bombs onto a hospital train a few days before. This was unfortunately true as far as Long was concerned, but as the train had no Red Cross on it, and was used to bring up troops as well as to take away wounded, we had a perfect right to bomb it, and anyhow could not possibly have told it was a hospital train. However, this was not the time for complicated explanations, so I lied hard for a very uncomfortable ten minutes. Just when things were looking really nasty an officer came up and took us off.[29] *Lieutenant A J Evans, 3 Squadron, RFC*

They had been saved but then Evans faced a new dilemma.

An officer, whose face I disliked, came up and, saluting very correctly, asked me to hand over all my papers and maps. Rather than be searched, I turned out my own and Long's pockets for him. In doing so, I found to my horror that I had my diary on me! Why, I can't think, as I was always most careful to go up without any paper of importance and particularly without my diary. However, I managed to keep it from the Germans and got rid of it about an hour later without being detected.[30] *Lieutenant A J Evans, 3 Squadron, RFC*

The Germans brought in more aircraft, desperate as they were to claw back some semblance of parity in the skies. Their air strength was raised to some 164 aircraft and from this point they continually deployed every aircraft they could spare into the Somme skies. The results became apparent to the British in the ever-increasing severity of aerial clashes. This was illustrated on 20 July, when a routine morning patrol by four DH2, flown by Captain R E A W Hughes-Chamberlain, Lieutenant Charles Chapman and Second Lieutenants Alfred McKay and Henry Evans of 24 Squadron, escalated into one of the first real 'dogfights' as numerous aircraft twirled in anarchic symmetry across the skies. In such a clash a man's survival depended on uncanny anticipation, lightning reactions and a large slice of pure luck. The action was summarized in Major Hawker's laconic squadron report.

The eight machines (five LVGs and three Rolands) flying South were joined over Bapaume by three Fokkers, and Captain Chamberlain led his patrol to the attack. Diving at an LVG which immediately dived East, Captain Chamberlain saw a Fokker underneath, attacked it, and fired half a drum. The Fokker went down in a nose-dive, but flattened out very low down. Attacked from behind by a Roland, Captain Chamberlain, turning on a climb outmanoeuvred and attacked it, firing the remainder of his drum. The Roland went down, but Captain Chamberlain was too busy changing drums to see what became of it. Meanwhile Lt Evans closed with a Roland, and fired half a drum at a range of only 25 yards. The Roland went straight down apparently out of control, and Lt Evans was attacked from behind by two Fokkers, but these nearly collided and Lt Evans escaped them and attacked an LVG firing the remaining half of his drum. Lt Chapman attacked an LVG which turned off, he was attacked from behind, but he escaped the Hostile Aircraft (HA) by turning sharply and attacking another machine. A Fokker and an LVG attacked Lt

Evans, whose gun jammed, but were driven off by Lt Chapman. Lt Evans cleared the jam and attacked an LVG which dived East. Lt McKay's engine was running badly and he could only reach 8,500 feet at which height he followed under the patrol. A Roland dived at him from in front, but Lt McKay outmanoeuvred it and attacked, firing the remainder of his drum. The Roland ceased fire and fell in a spinning nose-dive. Lt McKay was now attacked by a Fokker, which he could not out-manoeuvre owing to his engine being shot, so to escape its fire, he descended in a steep spiral. Lt Chapman observing this, dived to the rescue and attacked the Fokker at 1,000 feet over High Wood. The Fokker fell in a spinning nose-dive, hit the ground and burst into flames. Captain Chamberlain was attacked by a Fokker which dived straight at him firing continuously from 400 yards. Captain Chamberlain flew straight at it, firing from 100 yards till it passed just over his head. The Fokker went down, but Captain Chamberlain did not see what happened to it, as he immediately attacked an LVG. Meanwhile Lt Evans attacked and drove off an LVG and a Fokker. All HA had now been driven off retiring down East, except for one Fokker, which tried to manoeuvre onto Captain Chamberlain's tail. Captain Chamberlain, however, climbed in a spiral to attack and the Fokker climbed away East. Captain Chamberlain and Lt Evans remained on patrol for another quarter of an hour, but did not see any more HA. The AA batteries reported one de Havilland and three HA driven down. The de Havilland was Lt McKay, but he managed to return low down though his engine was badly shot about. An observer of 9 Squadron, who saw the fight, reports three HA were shot down and crashed, one of them bursting into flames. Probably the following were responsible for the three HA brought down:-

OH! BEWARE.
DH₂ DIVING TO ATT

1.) Lt Evans, who fired half a drum into a Roland from 25 yards.
2.) Lt McKay, who attacked a Roland which ceased to fire and was seen to fall in a spinning nose-dive by several pilots.
3.) Lt Chapman, who attacked a Fokker, and saw it crash and burst into flames.
4.) Capt. Chamberlain. One Roland or one Fokker, or perhaps both seen to fall out of control by observer on the ground.[31] *Major Lanoe Hawker, 24 Squadron, RFC*

The observers in the corps aircraft that witnessed the dogfight were

Lieutenants Coller and Scaife in a humble BE2 C.

When doing artillery observation over Ginchy several machines were seen fighting at 8,000 feet. We made off in the direction of the machines, and the pilot opened fire from the rear mounting on the Type F machine just above. This machine got on to the tail of a de Havilland, which apparently could not get rid of him. We followed the hostile machine down and with the third drum, tracers appeared to enter him and smoke was seen. He side-slipped and left the de Havilland apparently going East. The hostile machine went down in flames soon afterwards on the Bazentin le Petit railway. A second enemy machine was seen crashed East of Bazentin le Petit and a third in flames South East of Martinpuich.[32] *Lieutenant Bernard Coller, 9 Squadron, RFC*

The discrepancies in the collated accounts are obvious and are usually explained by the sheer confusion of the dogfight coupled with a natural buoyant optimism as to the results of one's own interventions in the affray. Together 24 Squadron made tentative claims to five victims whilst Lieutenant Coller makes his own claim for a Fokker and actually attributes only two crashed aircraft to 24 Squadron. Throughout the war, British pilots would invariably claim more 'victories' than the German records show were suffered at the time. This was not generally the result of deliberate egotistical inflation of 'scores'; rather it should be remembered that the RFC did most of their fighting on the German side of the lines and confirmation was difficult in many cases. An aircraft plunging seemingly out of control in a spinning nose-dive could be merely escaping from a conflict or destined for destruction. Without confirmation from the ground it was difficult to be sure.

The bombing raids continued relentlessly. One new British machine used for bombing was the Martinsyde Elephant, a single-seater biplane with a 120hp Beardmore engine that had come into service with 27 Squadron. They had been intended as a long range scout, but had been overtaken by the fast moving pace of technological advances in aerial warfare. Although reasonably quick, it was hampered by a sluggish response to its controls that meant it was ill suited to combat. Consequently, it was increasingly used for bombing missions as it could carry a worthwhile bomb load. Day after day, 27 Squadron raided the German villages behind the line where they hit the resting German troops and the store depots.

Our Martinsydes had no proper bomb-sights, except for a wire contraption fixed to the right side of the cockpit. It was almost impossible to fly straight and level and at the same time peer sideways over the edge. So I got my rigger to make a hole in the floor of the cockpit through which I could try to pick out a target. But accuracy was impossible unless one was flying low and many of our bombs must have fallen ineffectively. High explosive bombs were not the only weapons used against the Boche by the Squadron. Periodically a tender was sent into the nearest town and returned having denuded the shops of rolls of Bromo and as many china articles as could be found. Over our target the Bromo rolls were hurled out – to descend fluttering to earth as the paper unrolled – and followed by a 'jerry' which we fondly hoped would fall on the head of an unsuspecting enemy, gazing up at our paper streamers. Other lethal weapons in the shape of broken gramophone records, soda-water bottles and other rubbish were likewise cast overboard.[33] *Lieutenant Hugh Chance, 27 Squadron, RFC*

The Martinsydes found that the attentions of the Germans were not the only thing that they had to endure. At the instigation of Trenchard, Baring seems to have written an amusing reprimand to Major Smith Barry commanding 60 Squadron, after one of his pilots attacked a Martinsyde of 27 Squadron in a case of mistaken identity.

Bullets there be that can't abide
The fighting bombing Martinsyde

*Martinsyde Elephant.* IWM Q 57579

Without the slightest rhyme or reason
They strafe him in and out of season
This elephant is not the Hun
It must not be attacked for fun
It isn't very hard to see
The crosses on an LVG
On Martinsydes the British rings
Are clearly painted on the wings
An elephant (not very large)
Is painted on the fuselage
The G.O.C. complains this act
Displays a grievous want of tact
And recommends that you should shoot
Your bullets at a hostile brute
Please warn your pilots, every one
We're out to fight the bloody Hun.[34]

*Captain Maurice Baring, Headquarters, RFC*

Throughout July, the unmistakeable, ever-faithful FE2 Bs were kept as busy as ever.

Yesterday we went and bombed a town over the lines and heavily 'Archied', one shell burst just behind my tail and later another just underneath – the concussion caused a big bump. Today if it clears we are going out again, but at present it is rather cloudy.[35] *Second Lieutenant Don Macaskie, 23 Squadron, RFC*

*Donald Macaskie* RAFM/RAeC 1788

They did indeed go out again and Macaskie's log book reported that he went up at 18.00 with Second Lieutenant Sandys-Thomas. Ninety minutes or so into the flight, they encountered a Fokker. Both their petrol tanks were hit and Macaskie was wounded in his right leg and arm, forcing them to crash behind the German lines. Macaskie and Sandys-Thomas were POWs, but Macaskie was able to escape reaching Switzerland in December 1916. He finally returned to his relieved family in September 1917 and could at last complete his flying logbook entry for 20 July.

Another FE2 B crew were surprised right in the middle of a photographic reconnaissance the same day.

I and my observer, a really useful lad named Mansell, had the luck to bring down a Boche which attacked us while we were doing photographs. It really was very lucky, as he only saw him just as he was on top of us. However, my observer kept his head and I got the machine into a decent position for shooting and he peppered him in great style. We had a regular field day, as another man in the Squadron got another Boche that evening, and the scout squadron of our Wing got at least six in the 24 hours. The one I brought down was a new type; I wish we could have got it down in our lines, as it would have been very interesting to see it. However our gunners shelled it, so it won't be any more use to the Huns.[36] *Lieutenant Eynon Bowen, 22 Squadron, RFC*

Many flights were fairly uneventful and a typical routine report makes for dull reading, but at the same time it clearly demonstrates the multifarious nature of their work.

At 10.45 dropped four bombs on MT vehicle parked at U.11a4.1 by railway. Dumps observed on railway at O.16b and at O.23c-O29a. One dump at O.16b; there are five stacks of timber at U.10a7.7; between the forked roads there are three long sheds built in a triangle. These are partially disguised and may be an ammo store. A light railway runs from Beaucamps and Haubourdin crossing the Wavrin-Erquinghem railway at O.29b0.4. The above dumps appeared to be in use recently. Saw small trench at M36d3.7 on North side of small building. This trench appeared to be recently dug and was very conspicuous. Average height: 6,500 feet.[37] *Captain Joseph Callaghan, 18 Squadron, RFC*

*Joseph Callaghan.* RAFM/RAeC

Even when the Fokkers broke through the RFC scout screen to get at the corps aircraft, they did not seem to pose the same deadly menace. On 27 July, Lieutenant Horridge was engaged in a difficult artillery observation mission, which entailed crossing the German lines to a greater extent than was usual.

I had a bit of excitement this afternoon. Today was the first fine day we have had for about a week and I went up to range a big gun on a town about seven miles over the lines. It was rather a nasty bit of work and I had another machine to escort me. As usually happens on these occasions I got separated from the escort and had to go over alone. I went over pretty low at 5,000 feet and when we got to the target an LVG which I had been watching for a few minutes came for us . . . I tried to call my observer's attention to him but he did not see it until it opened fire. The LVG soon turned off and went to a Fokker which had arrived on the scene. We returned to our target and saw no more of the LVG. In a few minutes I saw four machines in front of us. I wasn't certain what they were and as they did not appear to be taking much notice of us we carried on with the shoot. I watched two of them which were straight in front of us. The next thing I knew was a tapping sound from behind. At first I thought it was a bit of my tail which had been hit by 'Archie' flapping in the wind, but when I looked round it was a Fokker diving on us between us and the lines. He was three or four hundred yards away and gaining on us quickly. I turned the machine round and he followed. My observer got his gun going, shooting over my head and over the tail. All the time I could hear the Hun machine gun getting louder and louder. The Hun gun fires a belt of I believe 150 rounds. Our Lewis gun fires a drum of 47 rounds before being changed. The Hun was firing almost continuously and getting quite close while my observer was firing in bursts of about five. When our drum was finished my observer could not get at the others owing to the machine being new and no accommodation, within easy reach, for drums. I thought my number was up and I was thinking who was most likely to get hit first, my observer who was standing up or myself, when the Hun stopped firing and turned off. He was then about 150 feet away. The other three Fokkers had disappeared. By that time we were nearly over the lines. If he had not opened fire so early, but dived close first, he would have had us stiff as the observer was watching the target and I was watching the machines in front, who were of course acting as a decoy. Also if he had gone on firing for ten seconds longer than he did he would have been so close that he couldn't miss while we could not fire back. It shows what the Hun airmen are like. There were four Fokkers in that particular bit of sky, but only one of them attacked a BE2 C. Afterwards we picked up the escort and finished the shoot without trouble.[38] *Lieutenant Leslie Horridge, 7 Squadron, RFC*

By this time the DH2 pilots had entirely mastered their machines. What once had been regarded with caution and even outright fear as a dangerous beast, was now regarded with considerable affection.

I must say the DHs are wonderful machines. I don't suppose there are any scouts quite as stable. This morning I glided down from 12,000 feet at a nice even pace without touching the controls except the rudder. It is a glorious sensation having your hands free. The other day I tested what she would do if you stalled her. If you hold the stick right back she climbs steeper and steeper until stalling point is reached when she puts her nose down level. Then she gains speed, climbs and repeats the process all the time you are holding the stick back.[39] *Second Lieutenant Edmund Lewis, 32 Squadron, RFC*

There was a period, before fatigue and nerves took their toll, when scout pilots realized that they had managed to master the basic elements of their trade and for a while they positively relished the fights that lay ahead of them.

We should be looked upon, as the Army Service Corps, as the wise men who have chosen an easy job during a nasty war. We

*DH2 takes off at Vert Galand Aerodrome. Note the flag on the strut on right of the plane, indicating Flight Commander's machine.*

have comfortable billets, plenty of rest, quite a slack time, and have speed and climb enough to be equal to any of the enemy. What is there to mourn over in a fight on equal terms? If only the infantry could fight the Hun on equal terms without any artillery or machine guns – just bayonets. If we get picked off it is our own fault and we fall to one more skilled than ourselves – the rule of every branch of life.[40] *Second Lieutenant Edmund Lewis, 32 Squadron, RFC*

Of course such confidence often presaged a sad fall from grace as the realities of aerial warfare imposed themselves. Thus on 28 July, Edmund Lewis was wounded.

I've gone and been and done it once again and am now for the second time occupying a bed in hospital. Please don't get startled as I am as fit as rain, and don't feel that I deserve to come home. I had a scrap with about six Huns, I got off about two drums of ammunition at them when they got a lucky burst in and got me in the leg. The bullet has missed all bones and all I feel is as if I had strained my ankle rather badly. The bullet came out the other side and just missed my anklebone. I am afraid I did not bring any Huns down. There were too many of them to really concentrate on one Hun. They shot away two rudder controls for me, but luckily they are duplicated.[41] *Second Lieutenant Edmund Lewis, 32 Squadron, RFC*

By late July, there were serious battles in the air as the reinforced German scout formations fought hard to prevent successful raids on their vital rail junctions. On 30 July, a raid was carried out by seven Martinsydes of 27 Squadron, escorted by four of the Sopwith 1½ Strutters of 70 Squadron, on the junction at Marcoing.

> The patrol seemed to break up just as we were crossing the lines. As I didn't see any signals to return and as I still had a Sopwith with me I went on to Marcoing and dropped my bombs both of which fell in the village – I turned quickly round and almost ran into an LVG, I gave him a drum and he went down underneath me, I saw the Sopwith take him on and whilst I was changing drums I was attacked again in front by a Roland, gave him a drum and at the same time I heard a machine-gun behind me, looked round and I saw three Rolands on my tail. I was hit in the leg almost immediately, but managed to give them a drum of my side gun and they went away, my engine started spluttering and I saw a hole in my petrol tank – my engine stopped so I started gliding down thinking I should have to land – petrol was flowing all over my left leg so I put my left knee over the hole in the petrol tank. It struck me that by pumping I might be able to get a little pressure, by this time I was about 200 feet up – the engine started and I was then about 15 miles from our lines, I kept pumping hard all the time and managed to just keep enough engine to keep going – I thought I should have to land three or four times, once I had actually flattened out to land but my engine just picked up in time. I came back to the lines for about 15 miles at an average height of 50 feet. During the time that I was flying so low I was subject to a lot of rifle and machine-gun fire. I had lost myself and was so low that I could see very little of the country, I then picked up with a 'Horace' French biplane that was flying low and followed him and eventually landed at Moreuil aerodrome – crashing the machine on landing. I was feeling very weak as I had lost a lot of blood and was exhausted by having to pump so long.[42] *Second Lieutenant R H C Usher, 27 Squadron, RFC*

Although expensive in men and machines the long-range raids were successful in causing significant damage behind the German lines. Trenchard pursued his bombing offensive throughout July. The inevitable death toll led some to resent what they considered to be a simplistic and brutal approach.

> Trenchard follows the good military principal of repeating any tactics that have not been actually disastrous – and often those

that have – again and again, regardless of the fact that the enemy will probably think out some very good reply, until they really are so disastrous that they have to be abandoned.[43] *Recording Officer Lieutenant Thomas Hughes, 1 Squadron, RFC*

Whatever the truth of these sardonic observations, simplicity also has many virtues, and the Germans were undoubtedly forced to surrender all semblance of initiative and concentrate their resources instead on defensive patrols irrelevant to the requirements of their troops in the main battle being fought on the ground. The German infantry were not amused and one soldier billeted at Ligny-Tilloy vented his spleen in a letter home.

Now just a word about our own aeroplanes. Really, one must be almost too ashamed to write about them; it is simply scandalous. They fly up to this village, but no further, whereas the English are always flying over our lines, directing artillery shoots, whereby getting all their shells, even those of heavy calibre, right into our trenches. Our artillery can only shoot by the map as they have no observation. I wonder if they have any idea where the enemy's line is, or even ever hit it. It was just the same at Lille. There they were sitting in the theatre, covered with medals, but never to be seen in the air.[44] *Anon German Soldier, 24 Infantry Division*

A few days later this disgruntled soldier moved up into the front line.

And what a bad position this is! You have to stay in your hole all day and must not stand up in the trench because there is always a crowd of English over us. Always hiding from aircraft, always, with about eight or ten English machines overhead, but no-one sees any of ours. If German machines go up at all, they are only up for five minutes and then retire in double-quick time. Our airmen are a rotten lot.[45] *Anon German Soldier, 24 Infantry Division*

Unfair comment perhaps, but these men were really suffering from the full might of the British artillery and they could see the 'eyes' in the sky peering down to expose them to ever more accurate bombardments that were more than flesh and blood could stand.

The bombardment never ceases for one second. It is one continuous whistle and scream through the air and the crash and thunder of the exploding missile. We each lie in our little hole in the ground . . . Everybody is wishing for rain or at least bad weather so that one may have some degree of safety from the English aviators. One daren't leave one's hole all day.[46] *Anon German Soldier, 28th Infantry Regiment*

The German High Command were only too aware of their situation.

The beginning and the first weeks of the Somme battle were

marked by a complete inferiority of our own air forces. The enemy's aeroplanes enjoyed complete freedom in carrying out distant reconnaissances. With the aid of aeroplane observation, the hostile artillery neutralised our guns and was able to range with the most extreme accuracy on the trenches occupied by our infantry; the required data for this was provided by undisturbed trench reconnaissance and photography. By means of bombing and machine-gun attacks from a low height against infantry, battery positions and marching columns, the enemy's aircraft inspired our troops with a feeling of defencelessness against the enemy's mastery of the air. On the other hand, our own aeroplanes only succeeded in quite exceptional cases in breaking through the hostile patrol barrage and carrying out distant reconnaissances; our artillery machines were driven off whenever they attempted to carry out registration for their own batteries. Photographic reconnaissance could not fulfil the demands made upon it. Thus, at decisive moments, the infantry frequently lacked the support of the German artillery either in counter-battery work or in barrage on the enemy's infantry massing for attack.[47] *General Fritz von Below, Headquarters German First Army*

There is no greater praise than the grudging admiration of one's enemies.

*Aeroplane observation enabled the artillery to range with increasing accuracy on the trenches of the Germans.*

1. G. H. Lewis, 'Wings over the Somme', (Wrexham: Bridge Books, 1994), p183
2. RAF MUSEUM: Lt Dore, Typescript diary, 4/7/1916
3. T. M. Hawker, 'Hawker V.C.', (London: The Mitre Press,1965), p186
4. A. J. L. Scott, 'Sixty Squadron, RAF: A History of the Squadron, 1916-1919', (London: Greenhill Books, 1990), pp11-12
5. H. H. Balfour, 'An Airman Marches', (London: Hutchinson & Co, 1933), p46
6. H. H. Balfour, 'An Airman Marches', (London: Hutchinson & Co, 1933), p47
7. H. H. Balfour, 'An Airman Marches', (London: Hutchinson & Co, 1933), p59
8. IWM DOCS: A. M. Wilkinson, typescript memoir, 'The Somme Battle'
9. W. A. Briscoe & H. Russell Stannard, 'Captain Ball, VC', (London: Herbert Jenkins Ltd, 1918), pp179-180
10. W. A. Briscoe & H. Russell Stannard, 'Captain Ball, VC', (London: Herbert Jenkins Ltd, 1918), pp178-184
11. W. A. Briscoe & H. Russell Stannard, 'Captain Ball, VC', (London: Herbert Jenkins Ltd, 1918), p185
12. A. J. Evans, 'The Escaping Club', (London: John Lane The Bodley Head Ltd, 1921), p4
13. IWM DOCS: L. Horridge, Manuscript letter, 3/7/1916 & 7/7/1916
14. IWM DOCS: W. J. Martin Tomson, Letter, 17/7/1916
15. IWM DOCS: W. J. Martin Tomson, Typescript memoir, 'The Englishman Laughs', p12
16. A. J. Evans, 'The Escaping Club', (London: John Lane The Bodley Head Ltd, 1921), p4
17. RAF MUSEUM: Lt Dore, Typescript diary, 12/7/1916
18. RAF MUSEUM: Lt Dore, Typescript diary, 16/7/1916
19. IWM DOCS: E. J. D. Routh, Typescript Memoir, p2
20. IWM DOCS: Typescript Report, Advanced Headquarters, RFC, 30/7/1916 (contained in Quinell Papers 83/17/1)
21. IWM DOCS: T. Hughes, Trancscript diary, 4/7/1916
22. IWM DOCS: H. Wyllie, Transcript diary, 6/7/1916
23. J. B. Brophy quoted in S. F. Wise, 'Canadian Airmen and the First World War: The Official History of the Royal Canadian Air Force Volume I', (Toronto, University of Toronto Press), p375
24. J. B. Brophy quoted in S. F. Wise, 'Canadian Airmen and the First World War: The Official History of the Royal Canadian Air Force Volume I', (Toronto, University of Toronto Press), pp376-377
25. IWM DOCS: F. O. Cave, Manuscript diary, 15/7/1916
26. A. J. Evans, 'The Escaping Club', (London: John Lane The Bodley Head Ltd, 1921), pp4-5
27. A. J. Evans, 'The Escaping Club', (London: John Lane The Bodley Head Ltd, 1921), pp5-6
28. A. J. Evans, 'The Escaping Club', (London: John Lane The Bodley Head Ltd, 1921), pp5-6
29. A. J. Evans, 'The Escaping Club', (London: John Lane The Bodley Head Ltd, 1921), pp7-8
30. A. J. Evans, 'The Escaping Club', (London: John Lane The Bodley Head Ltd, 1921), pp7-8
31. IWM DOCS: 24 Squadron, RFC Combat Report, 20/7/1916
32. B. T. Coller, RFC Combat Report, 20/7/1916
33. IWM DOCS: H. Chance, typescript memoir, 'Subaltern's Saga', pp12-13
34. IWM DOCS: contained in Quinell Papers 83/17/1
35. IWM DOCS: D. S. C. Macaskie, Manuscript Letter, 20/7/1916
36. RAF MUSEUM: E.G. A. Bowen, Manuscript Letters, 22/7/1916
37. RAF MUSEUM: J. C. Callaghan, Manuscript Log Book, 31/7/1916
38. IWM DOCS: L. Horridge, Manuscript letter, 27/7/1916
39. G. H. Lewis, Wings over the Somme, (Wrexham: Bridge Books, 1994), p184
40. G. H. Lewis, Wings over the Somme, (Wrexham: Bridge Books, 1994), pp183-4
41. G. H. Lewis, Wings over the Somme, (Wrexham: Bridge Books, 1994), p187
42. H. A. Jones, 'Official History of the War: The War in the Air, Being the Story of the part played in the Great War by the Royal Air Force, Volume II', p253-254
43. IWM DOCS: T. Hughes, Transcript diary, 2/7/1916
44. Anon, 'Extracts from German Documents and Correspondence', (SS 473), p3
45. Anon, 'Extracts from German Documents and Correspondence', (SS 473), p4
46. Anon, 'Extracts No 2 from German Documents and Correspondence', (SS 515), p1
47. F. von Below, quoted in H. A. Jones, 'Official History of the War: The War in the Air, Being the Story of the part played in the Great War by the Royal Air Force', (Oxford: Clarendon Press, 1922-1937)Vol. II, pp270-271

Chapter Five

# August: The Fight Goes On

The pattern of fighting which had been established in mid July, continued right through August: desperate attacks by just a few British battalions to gain some tactically significant feature, their desperate efforts to consolidate any gains and the equally determined German counter-attacks. Names that even now cause a shiver of communal recognition were at the centre of these battles: Delville Wood, Longueval, Trones Wood, Ovillers, High Wood and Pozières. These battles have since been cruelly satirized as nothing more than the deaths of thousands of men in futile attempts to move their General's cocktail cabinet a few yards nearer to Berlin. But in fact the aim was simple – to gain the best possible jumping-off point for the next major attack in September. This would make the main assault a lot easier and hopefully reduce the overall toll of casualties. In all this fighting the RFC continued to play its part. It was absolutely central to the detailed planning of the attacks for the contact patrols to determine

*Officer observing from the ruins of Longueval Church. The shattered remains of Delville Wood in the background.*

where the troops had got to, while the aerial photography exposed the exact location of hitherto unseen trench lines, machine gun posts and trench mortars. The Royal Artillery had come to recognize with almost complete equanimity the idea of the RFC 'amateurs' in their artillery observation aircraft and kite balloons directing the precious guns; and the bombing raids were steadily growing in scale. The fighting was bitter and costly and the truly awful panoply of modern war unfolded beneath the Corps' pilots.

There was an intense bombardment going on while I was there before but I think it was almost worse this time. Shells were going past like rifle bullets – every now and then you could see them whizzing by and as often hear them above the noise of the engine. We were down to 2,000 feet so were right in it. Flares were scarce and did not show any increase of territory on our part. Battalion Headquarters, with three exceptions, did not show themselves, I think they had too bad a time. Longueval was getting it in the neck and consequently our men. I saw liquid fire being used or what appeared to be such from above. It appeared as though many hundreds of white Verey lights were being shot forward. It was horrid. On the left by Thiepval the Germans loosed off gas which crossed the main road South West of Pozières getting thicker and higher as it went. Intense shelling was taking place in it, so I imagined they were going to attack. I hope they got it in the neck.[1]
*Lieutenant E J D Routh, 34 Squadron, RFC*

Some of the ethical problems of aerial bombing were slowly seeping through to the more sensitive pilots.

Dropped 20lb bombs on Lille from 6,500 feet. It was quite usual to drop bombs on any target at random, and accuracy was almost nil. Thus I was content to merely drop my two small bombs on the large city of Lille, regardless of where they actually fell. I shudder to think of the innocent French civilians that must have been hit during the war, as it was an accepted thing throughout the Flying Corps to bomb in this casual way.[2] *Lieutenant Ewart Garland, 10 Squadron, RFC*

Night bombing had become increasingly recognised as a means of hitting targets whilst minimising the risk of being caught by the German scouts. However the natural dangers of flying were massively increased in pitch darkness.

I went night bombing yesterday – rather an Irish way of putting it, though! I went up after dinner and as it was a bit misty I signalled down 'bad mist'. They signalled to me to come down, but I wasn't having any and turned my blind eye to 'em and beetled off. You see, from the ground it didn't look misty and so, as I

*Pilots examining a map before starting on a raid.* IWM Q11862

didn't want any doubts on the subject, I sloped off towards the lines. I soon lost sight of the flares and then became absolutely and completely lost. Everything was inky black and I could only see an occasional thing directly below me. My mapboard was in the way of my compass, so I pulled the map off, chucked the board over the side and then flew due East for about quarter of an hour, when I saw some lights fired. I crossed the lines about 4,000 feet up and tried to find my objective, but it was no go. I went about four miles over and then came down to 2,000 feet with my engine throttled down, but could not even recognise what part I was over, owing to the mist. Then, to my surprise, the Huns loosed off some 'Archie' nowhere near me, so I expect they couldn't see me; but it looked ripping. They got a searchlight going and flashed it all round, passing always over the top of me. Then some more flares went up from the lines, and I could see the ground there beautifully, as clear as day, and some deep craters, but it did not show me sufficient to enable me to recognise what part of the lines I was over. Deciding it was hopeless, I set out for home, flying due West by my compass. It seemed ages before I picked up the aerodrome lights again, and I was afraid I might have drifted away sideways, but I spotted them all right, and just as I was nearing them, passed another of our machines by about 200 yards in the darkness. He was a wee bit lower than I was, and as he passed I could see his instrument lights in his little cabin. I then

*FE2b night bomber. Pilot and observer watch a mechanic fuse a bomb under the aircraft. Flares can be seen beneath the FE's wings.*

switched on some little lights I had on the wing tips, and flashed my pocket lamp and then gave an exhibition of spiralling and banking in the dark. They said it looked topping from the ground. Then I signalled down, 'N.B.G.' and came in, perched (with all my bombs on, of course), and made a perfect dream of a landing. Altogether, I had really enjoyed myself, and would rather do night bombing than day bombing. The only thing that annoyed me was that I couldn't find my target, 'cos the bombs would have looked so pretty exploding in the darkness.[3] *Second Lieutenant Lessel Hutcheon, 5 Squadron, RFC*

A few nights later he had better luck.

I found my way quite well, crossed the lines, picked up the road I was to follow and finally reached the place I was to bomb. Here I ran into clouds and had to come down to between 1,000 and 2,000 feet. I dropped my bombs all right, and saw them explode – as good as a Brock's firework display. Moreover, I heard the bangs from them, and felt the machine bumped by the rush of air caused by the explosions. Flying back by compass, I soon picked out some flares which I headed for. Realising that I was over the wrong aerodrome, I looked round, spotted ours, got there, did a good landing, reported and went to bed.[4] *Second Lieutenant Lessel Hutcheon, 5 Squadron, RFC*

Just as the bomber pilots gained in experience so the German night anti-aircraft fire began to improve as yet another new area of warfare began to be opened up.

There were some wonderfully near shots and the machine was

badly shaken by one which made a most appalling crash just behind the tail. I was horribly scared, of course. I looked round, saw the tail was still there, said, 'Remarkable!' and went on. The Hun aerodrome was a very nice looking place. It had two landing 'T's out – great white strips of sheet and there was a machine on the ground. I dropped several bombs there, one landing on the road beside the 'drome and one by the landing 'T'. I don't know if I hit any of the sheds or not, as it was rather cloudy and I could not see the effect of all my bombs. When I had finished I came back with the wind, nose down, at some pace, and hardly got any 'Archie' at all. I was jolly pleased when it was over.[5] *Second Lieutenant Lessel Hutcheon, 5 Squadron, RFC*

In their turn the RFC pilots worked out an effective ruse to confuse the Germans.

There are many dodges for the night flyer – in fact so many that it would be a waste of time to start telling them. But perhaps the most well known is the 'throttle stunt'. If you are approaching a target that you know will be well defended by searchlights and AA guns and you are particularly anxious to damage it, you may find the 'throttle stunt' will work admirably, as it has done so hundreds of times in days gone by. When you are some distance off you will see the lights go out if there are any, shortly after which you will see the searchlights light up and begin their search of the sky, probably in your direction. Now while you are still unobserved, close your engines down very, very slowly, until they are just turning over, and you will notice that the searchlights will wander all over the sky and possibly some of them will go out. From the ground it sounds exactly as if you had gone away home again. Plane down to a height at which you can make sure of the target, but don't open up your engines until you have let go your bombs. You then find your way home as best you can. Your chances of escape are good.[6] *Lieutenant Robin Rowell, 12 Squadron, RFC*

As the intensity of the war in the air continued undiminished some of the pilots who had been out for a long tour of duty found that they were beginning to show the tell-tail signs of stress. Close escapes, that once were an occasion for jubilation or another splendid yarn in the mess, became just part of a countdown to almost inevitable dissolution.

I went up with Duke at 11.30 am, my machine to shoot on 'F.73', but just as we got over High Wood, an 'Archie' burst practically on us. I turned and found both main spars and inner struts on right bottom plane were smashed and the wing riddled. I got a nasty bruise on my fingers but got safely back.[7] *Lieutenant Francis Cave, 4 Squadron, RFC*

Cave went straight back up in another machine.

> Had a shoot on 'F.73' but had our main spar and landing wire shot through, so returned. The Major was very bucked with us going up again and complimented us and said he would tell the Colonel. The Colonel happened to turn up just after and he didn't know what to say, but felt he had to compliment us. I have managed to keep a few small pieces of the 'Archie'. I have had the wind up and a bad headache for the rest of the day.[8] *Lieutenant Francis Cave, 4 Squadron, RFC*

Next day, still suffering from a violent headache he was sent off on a reconnaissance mission over Pys.

> I went off with Duke and we had two de Havilland Scouts to escort us. I took about 12 photos, then clouds came and I only managed to take another five. Apparently all the batteries round Pys are holding up our advance, so they want photos of them. Duke reconnoitred it and found several positions. Quite a lot of 'Archie' but very bad (from his point of view). Some of my photos have come out fairly well, but I have left a small gap undone. Have got frightful wind up and don't feel at all well tonight.[9] *Lieutenant Francis Cave, 4 Squadron, RFC*

As the number of German aircraft disputing the battlefield increased the DH2s found that they had their work cut out.

> At 11.15, I noticed that our anti-aircraft guns were firing over Grandcourt. I went towards them and saw four type 'A' hostile machines turning back towards Bapaume. I dived, firing a drum at one at about 200 yards range. They all dived steeply and I was not able to catch them up. At 11.45, four Rolands were circling over Bapaume climbing. As they were climbing faster, I went towards them. When they reached my height of 13,000 feet they all attacked, and I closed with one, firing a drum in bursts at 75-50 yards. I then attacked another after changing drums. After firing two bursts,

*Lewis gun deployed on anti-aircraft mounting*

my aileron control was shot away and my engine stopped. I saw that petrol was running out of the petrol safety bag, so turned on the emergency supply. The engine picked up but the machine having no aileron control, I could only fly in small circles, firing a few shots when the gun passed in the direction of any of the Hostile Aircraft. There were three of them still around me, but they turned East and dived. I noticed that petrol was running over the floor of the nacelle so immediately switched off. The machine gradually straightened up and I was able to glide with the wind and land at Bazieux.[10] *Second Lieutenant Henry Evans, 24 Squadron, RFC*

His machine had been fairly riddled with bullets, but Evans was unscathed at least for the moment. The raison d'être of the scouts was to protect the Corps' machines and the ethos that Lanoe Hawker, Lionel Rees and others had developed meant that they would accept any odds to perform their duty. Their reward was made manifest only in the continuation of the routine reconnaissance and artillery observation flights. Thus poor Lieutenant Cave had yet another brush with death that he only evaded thanks to two unsung DH2 pilots.

We went and took five photos of Pys, but there were too many clouds, and 'Archie' was too hot, so we waited half an hour and then went over again. I got 16 photos altogether, the camera jamming once. I was just going to take another couple when 'Archie' hit our sump; at the same moment, we saw three Huns above us. They were engaged by a couple of de Havillands and driven off to Bapaume.[11] *Lieutenant Francis Cave, 4 Squadron, RFC*

It was in such nondescript reports that the scouts' true worth to the war effort can be determined. Cave got back with his photographs – without the intervention of the DH2s he could well have been shot down and the possibly vital intelligence lurking in the photographs would have been lost, obliging another pilot to risk his life to retake them. The Corps' aircraft operated behind the invisible screen provided by the offensive patrols of the scouts. But the cost to the scout squadrons was a constant drip, drip of casualties which slowly raked backwards and forwards through the ranks until few of their original personnel remained. Pilots became experienced veterans in just a couple of weeks – if they survived. The new pilots found the sheer sang-froid demonstrated by all personnel – in public at least – almost as unnerving as the Germans.

I arrived at Bertangles in the early hours of the morning and went to bed in comfortable quarters. I was awakened by a batman who said, 'A fine morning, Sir, and Mr 'A' has been shot down and Mr 'B' crashed in flames in the village.' I think 'A' was Hughes-Chamberlain and 'B' came from another squadron. I inherited 'A's' flying coat. I was sent up by Hawker to demonstrate that I could fly. I gave him of my best. When I landed I was ticked off for showing off and told that I would have to learn to do my turns without losing height. I had arrived in a squadron of veterans. I felt very inexperienced, the more so as I had never seen a Lewis gun.[12] *Second Lieutenant Robert Capon, 24 Squadron, RFC*

Such a newcomer had a lot to learn before he could make a useful contribution in the air. Although they knew how to fly, such novices had little conception of the formation flying that was becoming ever more essential.

*Robert Capon.* RAFM/RAeC

A Pilot of course must be able to fly properly. Now a man may be a good horseman, but that does not of necessity mean that he is a good Cavalry Soldier, and the same applies in my opinion to Aerial Fighting – in fact I have noticed myself cases where Pilots who were expert in handling their machines at home became quite at sea when they went overseas and began to manoeuvre with and against other machines, and unless they made a study of the points of the game they remained at sea, while those who gave thought to the matter, and only those, have been successful and have developed into experts. Start by simply following one another in turn. It will be found that unexpected things occur in the first endeavours to keep station. The machine in front may seem suddenly to ascend vertically while keeping its normal flying position, and the rear Pilot will find it hard to realise that by a slight forward pressure on the stick he has unconsciously caused this. Formation flying will develop his judgment for manoeuvres in relation to other machines in the air, and should be constantly carried out – this is as necessary to two-seaters as it is to Scouts. Both small and large formations should be practised from two to six machines, and when the Pilot can, without undue effort keep proper station for any length of time, he has accomplished a lot.[13] *Lieutenant John Simpson, 60 Squadron, RFC*

Once formation flying had been grasped, then the simple rules of air fighting had to be hammered in. Such advice was the distilled wisdom of men who had learnt it all the hard way. Air fighting was a new genre and the rules had to be made up and learnt as they went along. A single mistake would, or at least could, be fatal.

Before going over the lines there are certain things which you should note. Direction of wind is very important, because it limits your range of action. Take the Western Front. A westerly wind gives you a very short range of action over the lines for the simple reason that even if you are manoeuvring around another machine you are drifting very rapidly from your own lines and you have a long way to come back. I am speaking of air distance, flying against a head wind. It is absolutely essential of all things, to keep a good look-out in every direction. It is probably the most necessary of all, because there is not a machine made that has not a blind side and if you fly with that side blind or that direction blind for any length of time, it gives an enemy machine an opportunity to approach you unseen and gives the enemy the chance of surprise which of course is the great factor in air fighting as in fighting of all kinds. Never fly straight for any length of time. That of course works in with keeping a good look-out because if you are keeping a good look-out in every direction you cannot be flying in a straight line, you must swing. Another reason is that enemy anti-aircraft guns get the range, deflection etc., and put a shot straight at you without a ranging shot to warn you. Scouts have flown a good deal in formation, this summer. In the beginning of course the scout's work was simply a single-handed job. One had an expert pilot and a machine in which he could take up and fight in his own way. Later on scout flights came. It was necessary, in order that they should all arrive at a given point together, that they should go together, and the best way of going together was some sort of a formation with a leader. Formations were also used for reasons of defence. Usually there were 3, 4, or 6 machines – sometimes more. On going over the lines treat every machine you see as hostile until you are absolutely satisfied it is otherwise. You will always be able to satisfy yourself before you get within striking distance but until then always treat it as a hostile machine and you will be on the safe side. The scout is essentially an offensive machine and the only thing they have to do is to attack. It is your whole job, and when you do see a hostile machine, go for it. In attack your main object is to get to close quarters. It is quite useless to open fire at long range under present conditions. Later on probably we shall be able to. It is absolutely essential to get to close quarters under the best possible conditions for yourself. Therefore when you see an enemy machine in the distance decide in your own mind at once the type of machine it is, and the way you are going to attack it considering the type of enemy machine you have to deal with. It has a blind side. It has also a side that is probably not blind, though it may be hard for it to see, and therefore take all such things into consideration and go at him. Make up your mind right away, bearing in mind of course the whole time that surprise is one of your strongest weapons. A man can never act as well if he is surprised as he can in cold blood. Take full advantage of all the natural conditions, such as clouds, sun, haze, etc. Approach the enemy machine with the sun behind you, and if there are clouds about above, you can possibly use them to reach him from above, which is an advantage to you. You can make tremendous use of these natural conditions. Probably a lot of you have seen your own shadow on the clouds with a rainbow effect round it. If you keep this on the hostile machine he cannot see you at all. He is quite blind to your approach, because you are right bang in the eye of the sun. You want to work all these things out for yourself and take them into consideration, and to think of them right away before you attack. Of course you have to do it quickly. Always consider and remember that height means speed, particularly in scouting, for then you can dive. When you see a machine underneath you, if you have height, even if he is faster you can dive and overtake him. Particularly in machines using rotary engines always have your engine well in hand. Don't allow it to choke in a dive, because it will probably mean that you will arrive beside the enemy machine and then lose your chance simply through having a choked engine and will not be able to manoeuvre quickly enough. Don't expect a hostile machine to allow itself to be shot down easily. Expect something to happen suddenly when you open fire or are seen. He may loop or zoom, and then you must have your engine to keep to his tail. Always remember then to have your engine well in hand. Never jam your throttle open in stationary engines. You will either choke or starve your engine. Don't open fire more than 200 yards away. Under present conditions it is practically impossible to do any effective firing from more than that distance. It is only a waste of ammunition and you are simply warning the enemy of your approach. Always reserve your main burst of fire until you are quite close – say 50 yards – and, if possible, closer still. Always make your attack vigorous. Don't hesitate. Go right in and don't give him any rest. If the first burst fails get your gun ready again and get at him, without giving him a chance of recovery. Of course your defence in a scout is simply your speed and manoeuvring power. If you have a gun jam, breaking off the action, is the only way out you have. If you are up against a faster machine your manoeuvring power is your only defence. If you are the faster machine, breaking off is easy.[14] *Lieutenant John Simpson, 60 Squadron, RFC*

The novice who had joined the experienced pilots of 24 Squadron, Lieutenant Robert Capon, lasted just two weeks before he was wounded on 31 August.

As August passed by, not only were there more of the German scouts, but reports were increasingly coming in of new types with a vastly superior performance. Once again Lieutenant Cave was in action.

Duke and I had a patrol from 12.30 to 3.30. About 2.45 we saw three Huns 4,000 feet below us near Martinpuich. As we dived towards them I saw another three near Le Sars. Of the former, one was hit and last seen gliding over Flers and another was seen gliding towards the Somme. We then turned to a third one. When a fourth one came across our nose. We exchanged shots. The next moment I saw a Fokker biplane coming towards us. It gained on us so quick and was so infinitely superior that I made for a cloud and got to it just in time. Scott also met some, but had them on his tail and only just got to Contalmaison in time. Don't know where the de Havillands had got to.[15] *Lieutenant Francis Cave, 4 Squadron, RFC*

The aside concerning the absence of the DH2s showed that many pilots did not understand that the whole principle of Trenchard's air offensive relied on the scouts not being tied to the Corps' machines. They often were there, but their prime job was to seek out and destroy the German aircraft wherever they may be and preferably well behind the German lines. They were not to play policeman patrolling a beat. In these circumstances it was inevitable that sometimes the German scouts would get through, but the overall effect was working. Of course it was unreasonable to expect Lieutenant Cave to have this overall cost benefit analysis uppermost in his mind, as he had his own personal safety to consider when the German scouts appeared all around him. In general however, most RFC personnel approved of the overall policy adopted.

Offensive patrols are well worthwhile, but for the comfort of those directly concerned they are rather too exciting. When friends are below during an air duel a pilot is warmly conscious that should he or his machine be crippled he can break away and land, and there's an end of it. But if a pilot be wounded in a scrap far away from home, before he can land he must fly for many miles, under shellfire and probably pursued by enemies. He must conquer the blighting faintness which accompanies loss of blood, keep clear-headed enough to deal instantaneously with adverse emergency, and make an unwilling brain command unwilling hands and feet to control a delicate apparatus. Worst of all, if his engine be put out of action at a spot beyond gliding distance of the lines, there is nothing for it but to descend and tamely surrender.[16] *Lieutenant Alan Bott, 70 Squadron, RFC*

Lieutenant Bott was speaking at least in part from experience, as had encountered almost every problem a masochistic aviator could wish for during an offensive patrol as observer with Lieutenant A M Vaucour in their Sopwith 1½ Strutter on 24 August. Above Bois d'Havrincourt they sighted three German aircraft.

Two thousand feet below three biplanes were approaching the

*Sopwith 1½ Strutter in flight.*

wood from the South. Black crosses showed up plainly on their grey-white wings. We dropped into a dive towards the strangers. As we dived, I estimated the angle at which we might cross the Boche trio, watched for a change of direction on their part, slewed round the gun-mounting to the most effective setting for what would probably be my arc of fire, and fingered the movable backsight. At first the Huns held to their course as though quite unconcerned. Later, they began to lose height. Their downward line of flight became steeper and steeper, and so did ours. Just as our leading bus arrived within range and began to spit bullets through the propeller, a signal rocket streaked from the first Boche Biplane, and the trio dived almost vertically, honking the while on Klaxon horns.[17] *Lieutenant Alan Bott, 70 Squadron, RFC*

It was a trap. The biplanes had achieved their purpose in tempting the four British Sopwiths down to some 6,000 feet and well within range of a powerful concentration of German anti-aricraft guns.

"Wouff! Wouff! Wouff! Wouff! Wouff!" said 'Archie' . . . The ugly puffs encircled us and it seemed unlikely that an aeroplane could get away without being caught in a patch of hurtling high explosive. Yet nobody was hit. The only redeeming feature of the villain 'Archibald' is that his deeds are less terrible than his noise, and even this is too flat to be truly frightful . . . Very suddenly a line of fiery rectangles shot up and curved towards us when they had reached three-quarters of their maximum height. They rose and fell within 30 yards of our tail. These were 'onions', the flaming rockets which the Boche keeps for any hostile aircraft that can be lured to a height between 4,000 and 6,000 feet. I yelled to Vaucour, my pilot that we should have to dodge. We side-slipped and swerved to the left. A minute later the stream of 'onions' had disappeared, greatly to my relief, for the prospect of fire in the air inspires in me a mortal funk. Soon we were to pass from the unpleasant possibility to the far more unpleasant reality.[18] *Lieutenant Alan Bott, 70 Squadron, RFC*

They continued their patrol.

Some little distance ahead, and not far below, was a group of five Albatross two-seaters. Vaucour pointed our machine at them, in the wake of the flight commander's 'bus'. Next instant the fuselage shivered. I looked along the inside of it and found that a burning shell fragment was lodged in a longeron, half-way between my cockpit and the tail-plane. A little flame zigzagged over the fabric, all but died away, but, being fanned by the wind as we lost height, recovered and licked its way towards the tail. I was two far away to reach the flame with my hands, and the fire extinguisher was by the pilot's seat. I called for it into the speaking-tube. The pilot made no move. Once more I shouted. Again no answer. Vaucour's ear-piece had slipped from under his cap. A thrill of acute fear passed through me as I stood up, forced my arm through the rush of wind and grabbed Vaucour's shoulder. "Fuselage burning! Pass the fire extinguisher!" I yelled. My words were drowned in the engine's roar; and the pilot, intent on getting near the Boches, thought I had asked which one we were to attack. "Look out for those two Huns on the left", he called over his shoulder. "Pass the fire extinguisher!" "Get ready to shoot, blast you!" "Fire extinguisher, you ruddy fool!" A backward glance told me that the fire was nearing the tail-plane at the one end and my box of ammunition at the other, and was too serious for treatment by the extinguisher unless I could get it at once. Desperately I tried to force myself through the bracing-struts and cross-wires behind my seat. To my surprise head and shoulders and one arm got to the other side – a curious circumstance, as afterwards I tried repeatedly to repeat this contortionist trick on the ground, but failed every time. There I stuck, for it was impossible to wriggle farther. However, I could now reach part of the fire, and at it I beat with gloved hands. Within half a minute most of the fire was crushed to death. But a thin streak of flame, outside the radius of my arm, still flickered towards the tail. I tore off one of my gauntlets and swung it furiously on to the burning strip. The flame lessened, rose again when I raised the glove, but died out altogether after I had hit it twice more. The load of fear left me, and I discovered an intense discomfort, wedged in as I was between the two crossed bracing-struts. Five minutes passed before I was able, with many a heave and gasp, to withdraw back to my seat. By now we were at close grips with the enemy, and our machine and another converged on a Hun. Vaucour was firing industriously. As we turned, he glared at me, and knowing nothing of the fire, shouted: "Why the hell haven't you fired yet?" I caught sight of a Boche 'bus' below us, aimed at it and emptied a drum in short bursts. It swept away, but not before two of the German observer's bullets had plugged our petrol tank from underneath. The pressure went and with it the petrol supply. The needle on the rev counter quivered to the left as the revolutions dropped and the engine missed on first one, then two cylinders. Vaucour turned us round and with nose down, headed the machine for the trenches. Just then the engine ceased work altogether and we began to glide down.[19] *Lieutenant Alan Bott, 70 Squadron, RFC*

Flying at 9,000 feet and nearly 10 miles behind the German lines they were in desperate straits when their engine stopped. There was nothing for it but to begin the long glide back, all the while desperately calculating whether they could make it across the Allied front line to safety.

Could we do it? I prayed to the Gods and trusted to the pilot. Through my mind there flitted impossible plans to be tried if we landed in Boche territory. After setting fire to the machine we would attempt to hide, and then, at night time, creep along a communication trench to the enemy front line, jump across it in a gap between the sentries, and chance getting by the barbed wire and across No Man's Land. Or we would steal to the Somme, float downstream and somehow or other pass the entanglements placed across the river by the enemy. "Wouff! Wouff!" 'Archie' was complicating the odds.[20] *Lieutenant Alan Bott, 70 Squadron, RFC*

The final straw came as another German aircraft attacked seeking an easy victory.

Taking advantage of our plight, its pilot dived steeply from a point slightly behind us. We could not afford to lose any distance by dodging, so Vaucour did the only thing possible – he kept straight on. I raised my gun, aimed at the wicked-looking nose of the attacking craft, and met it with a barrage of bullets. These must have worried the Boche, for he swerved aside when a hundred and fifty yards distant, and did not flatten out until he was beneath the tail of our machine. Afterwards he climbed away from us, turned, and dived once more. For a second time we escaped, owing either to some lucky shots from my gun or to the lack of judgement by the Hun pilot. The scout pulled up and passed ahead of us. It rose and manoeuvred as if to dive from the front and bar the way. Meanwhile, four specks, approaching from the West, had grown larger and larger, until they were revealed as of the F.E. type – the British "pusher" two-seater. The Boche saw them, and hesitated as they bore down on him. Finding himself in the position of a lion attacked by hunters when about to pounce on a tethered goat, he decided not to destroy, for in so doing he would have laid himself open to destruction. When I last saw him he was racing North-East.[21] *Lieutenant Alan Bott, 70 Squadron, RFC*

All that was left was for Bott and Vaucour to avoid being shot down by

*FE2B*  RAF MUSEUM PC 72/83/10

ground fire as they glided across No Man's Land.

> As we went lower, the torn ground showed up plainly. From 2,000 feet I could almost count the shell holes . . . When slightly behind the trenches a confused chatter from below told us that machine guns were trained on the machine. By way of retaliation, I leaned over and shot at what looked like an emplacement. Then came the Bosch front line, ragged and unkempt. I fired along an open trench. Although far from fearless as a rule, I was not in the least afraid during the eventful glide. My state of intense 'wind up' while the fuselage was burning had apparently exhausted my stock of nervousness.[22] *Lieutenant Alan Bott, 70 Squadron, RFC*

They finally landed without further damage just behind the French lines.

> We climbed out, relieved but cantankerous. Vaucour, still ignorant of the fire, wanted to know why my gun was silent during our first fight; and I wanted to know why he hadn't shut off the engine and listened when I shouted for the fire extinguisher. Some French gunners ran to meet us. The sight that met them must have seemed novel, even to a soldier of two and a half years' understanding . . . What they found was one almost complete aeroplane and two leather coated figures, who cursed each other heartily as they stood side by side, and performed a certain natural function which is publicly represented in Brussels by a famous little statue.[23] *Lieutenant Alan Bott, 70 Squadron, RFC*

Throughout early August, Second Lieutenant Albert Ball served his penance on 'punishment' posting with 8 Squadron. From a modern perspective, it seems that Brigadier-General Higgins was cutting off his nose to spite his face. Ball had asked for a rest and instead had been condemned – perhaps the right word – to a return to flying BE2 Cs. The RFC had lost the services of one of their very best and most inspirational scout pilots and put him in a role where he faced as much risk without employing his talents. But in reality, Higgins may well have hit on the right course of action. Ball undoubtedly found the regular routine of artillery observation and bombing flights far less stressful than the pell-mell life of a scout pilot and he was able to recover much of his early zest for the fray. He played his full part in the day to day work of the squadron but, once he had recovered, it is perhaps fair to say that Ball was not as other BE2 C pilots! He was looking for opportunities to put himself forward and get sent back to the scouts. On one occasion he volunteered to land a spy at night on the German side of the lines.

We got over the lines and after a few seconds three Fokkers came after us. We had no gun, for the machine could not carry his luggage etc and guns, so we had to dodge the beasts. At last it was so dark they could not see us, so they went down. The 'Archie' guns started, also rockets were sent up to try and set us on fire. Oh! It was nice. I really did think that the end had come. The planes were lit up with the flashes. However, at last we found a landing place and we started down. Naturally everything had to be done quickly or we would have been caught. But we got down! Picture my temper when we landed. The damned spy would not get out. The Fokkers had frightened him and he would not risk it. There was nothing to do but get off again before the Huns came along and stopped us, so off we went. I went down three times again after this, but the rotter refused to do his part. So we had to return.[24] *Second Lieutenant Albert Ball, 8 Squadron, RFC*

It can be imagined that the circumstances of the flight that had rattled even Ball, might drive a relatively normal spy into a state of abject terror! He also launched an attack on a pair of German observation balloons.

On Wednesday, August 9th, I attacked a balloon with a BE, and forced the observer to jump out. On the way back from this job, my main spar and wing tip was crashed, but we got back to the aerodrome. Lieutenant Hervey was my observer . . .[25] *Second Lieutenant Albert Ball, 8 Squadron, RFC*

During this 'balloon busting' exploit, Ball and Hervey were accompanied by the BE2 C of their Flight Commander, Captain G A Parker.

As soon as we poked our nose across No Man's Land the ever

*146*

watchful anti-aircraft guns started up. I looked across the five miles or so between us and Parker's machine. It was easy to spot. Parker was lower than we were and making for his target, as always, like a bull at a gate. His machine was surrounded by the rather innocent-looking white puffs of shrapnel and by the very much more vicious and noisy black bursts of high explosives. Meanwhile the gunners were putting up a spectacular display around our machine. It had been hit a number of times by stray fragments but the damage was superficial. We saw the balloon starting to descend and soon it was going down at an astonishing rate, swaying drunkenly under the pull of the winch cable. Ball started to dive and the next moments were a confused jumble of sights and sounds. Men running as we fired down on the balloon, machine gunning from emplacements round the winch site, a glimpse of the balloon observer floating down by parachute, a exploding shell knocking off a chunk of our port lower wingtip and fracturing a main spar. Ball was yelling at me to keep my eyes skinned for Huns as I switched the Lewis gun onto the rear mounting and we started for home. Fortunately, the sky was empty of aircraft.[26] *Second Lieutenant Tim Hervey, 8 Squadron, RFC*

Finally Ball had his wish and was returned to 11 Squadron on 14 August. His experience of air fighting had been broadened considerably but it was immediately apparent that he had not abandoned his attacking philosophy one iota.

You will be surprised to hear that I have started with luck. I went up this morning and attacked five Hun machines. One I got and two I forced down. After this I had to run, for all my ammunition was used. However, I got back OK, with only two hits on my machine.[27] *Lieutenant Albert Ball, 11 Squadron, RFC*

Thus did he immediately resume his former career, flying his Nieuport in ceaseless patrols across the German lines and seeking out trouble wherever he could find it. He became the epitome of Trenchard's offensive spirit that no odds were too great for him to cock a snoot at. On 22 August, Ball took off as an escort to an FE2 B bombing mission. He ran into a large formation of German aircraft.

Met 12 Huns. No. 1 fight. I attacked and fired two drums, bringing the machine down just outside a village. All crashed up. No. 2 fight. I attacked and got under machine, putting in two drums. Hun went down in flames. No. 3 fight. I attacked and put in one drum. Machine went down and crashed on a housetop. All these fights were seen and reported by other machines that saw them go down. I only got hit 11 times in the planes, so I returned and got more ammunition. This time luck was not all on the spot.

> I was met by about 14 Huns, about 15 miles over their side. My windscreen was hit in four places, mirror broken, the spar of the left plane broken, also engine ran out of petrol. But I had good sport and good luck, but only just, for I was brought down about one mile over our side.[28] *Lieutenant Albert Ball, 11 Squadron, RFC*

There is no doubt that Ball was phenomenally lucky. Seemingly he could fly into a hail of bullets time and time again, to emerge with his aircraft shot to pieces but he himself unscathed. Luck is difficult to quantify objectively, but there is no doubt that whatever it was, Ball had it!

\* \* \* \*

At RFC Headquarters it had become apparent that the day of multi-function squadron had gone. The obvious advantages of having homogeneous squadrons all flying the same aircraft for the administrative convenience of supplying the appropriate trained pilots, mechanics and spares had always been a telling argument. However, as the pace and scale of the air war grew it was essential that more scout squadrons should be created and maintained if they were to be able to meet the German scouts in sufficient numbers. One problem was that they had to be the right kind of scouts. In August, 19 Squadron had made its debut flying the new scout, the BE12, produced under the auspices of the Royal Aircraft Factory. In essence this was a single-seater version of the BE2 C.

> Our machines are the latest production of the R.A.F. and are supposed to do over 100 miles an hour and climb 6,000 feet in 10 minutes. The machine gun fires through the propeller the same as the 'Fokkers', so they ought to be very nice machines to fight. They are also absolutely stable and will fly hands-off, they are fitted with bomb-racks, wireless, cameras and every sort of gadget.[29] *Captain Cecil Tidswell, 19 Squadron, RFC*

These were not the specialist highly manoeuvrable scouts that were required. Nevertheless, as they were all that was available, they were thrown into the fray.

> We went out on an offensive patrol after tea and got properly straffed over Bapaume. I had gone over there to drop some 'letters' and was wondering why we were not being 'Archied' at all, the reason being that there were a lot of their own machines up which came for us. I first saw one of ours having a scrap down below me and was diving down to lend a hand when I heard a machine gun quite close to me. For some time I couldn't make out where he was and then suddenly spotted a biplane about 200 yards off to my right with the observer having a nice pot shot at me. As soon as I turned towards them they went off with me in full

pursuit. I had him well on the sights of my gun and got about 50 rounds in before he disappeared under my machine. I don't think they fired a shot at me once I went for them, so I hope I may have done in the observer, as he was sitting behind, so ought to have had a splendid chance of getting a shot at me when I was chasing them. My engine again showed signs of giving out, so I went quickest the best for the lines, and after waiting about for the others a bit, came home. When I landed I found one carburettor had been smashed by a bullet, so the engine did rather well to get me home; there was also a bullet through the back of my seat, which had torn a very big hole in the cushion I have in the small of my back, and another in the one I was sitting on. Of the other three machines, two got very much knocked about by 'Archie' and are still under repair, and the other has not returned.[30] *Captain Cecil Tidswell, 19 Squadron, RFC*

The BE12 pilots needed to operate and work in formations.

It's rather a fine sight when they're all starting off one after the other. You have to fly round at a certain height, usually 5,000 feet, before you get the signal to start; the latest idea is that before going off you fly over the camera-obscura, when they photograph the formation and have a print ready to show you by the time you get back, so that you can see whether it was good or not. I like being leader much the best as you then don't have to bother about

*BE12.* RAF MUSEUM P10343

keeping in the right position, but are entirely responsible for finding the way, everyone else having to conform to you.[31] *Captain Cecil Tidswell, 19 Squadron, RFC*

Even flying in formation, it was soon obvious that the BE12s were not 'scouts' in any real sense of the term and they were increasingly moved onto a bombing role. The failure of the BE12 made it even more essential that the RFC make the best possible use of the scouts that they did possess. The importance of scouts operating in formations was clear, and from a modern perspective obvious, but at the time considerable controversy was aroused when the principle of gathering like with like, was extended to gather all the available scouts up into specialist 'scout' squadrons.

Whitaker rang up about 6.30pm to say that we had got to give up our scouts and furthermore to send three scout pilots with them. All the Nieuport scouts are being collected into a scout squadron so as to minimise their usefulness. They are of immense value in a Corps' squadron where they can go up at any moment in conjunction with our other machines, also they are in touch with the front line and can watch for Huns coming over and judge for themselves (i.e. the pilots can) when it is worthwhile to go up. In an Army Squadron like No. 29 (The de Havillands at Abeele) they are too far back to watch for Huns crossing the lines and if they are wanted to help some of the other machines it involves applying for them through 2nd Wing to 2nd Brigade, and thence down again through 11th Wing – in a word, 'Through the usual channels' – and by the time their use had been authorised, the emergency would have passed. However, this sort of grouping into bunches without any thought as to the use of the arrangement appeals to the military mind.[32] *Lieutenant Thomas Hughes, 1 Squadron, RFC*

On 24 August, as part of this reorganization, Lieutenant Albert Ball was posted to 60 Squadron where he was given command of a flight. There was increasing interest in examining the secret of Ball's success to see if it could be duplicated in action by his contemporaries. Ball quickly summed up his method.

When I get to close quarters I generally pretend that I am going to attack from above. The Hun gets ready to fire up at me as I pass over, and then I suddenly dive under his machine and if I am lucky I empty a drum into his petrol tank and down he goes.[33] *Lieutenant Albert Ball, 60 Squadron, RFC*

Ball had developed a combat method perfectly adjusted to himself and the Nieuport. But his individualized tactics were beyond duplication by pilots who lacked his skills and suicidal bravery.

To surprise his enemy he made clever use of the Lewis gun mounting on the Nieuport scout. There was a curved rail down which the gun had to be run to change drums. By exerting pressure on one side of the stock of the gun, he held it rigid when nearly down and pointing upwards about 80-degrees. By skilful manoeuvre – and incidentally by pluck and determination – he was able to zoom up beneath his intended victim; then, by a slight oscillation of the control stick to cause his gun to rake the target fore and aft, at a range of 30 feet or so . . . I found that my own efforts to emulate Ball in reaching a favourable position beneath a Hun so irritated it that a mêlée ensued in which I soon lost any idea of what was its 'underneath' and what was its 'top'. To say that Ball fought with his head is almost superfluous. He was evidently the offspring of a vixen and a lion. He would sight a formation of as many as 12 Huns afar off, would rise into the sun, fly above them and fire off a burst or two. This would invariably shake the formation's nerve and cause it to open slightly. One pilot, a little more nervous or less disciplined than the rest, would lose his station. In a flash Ball would be on him, and almost as soon the deadly shooting would send him up in flames.[34] *Second Lieutenant Roderic Hill, 60 Squadron, RFC*

Ball's willingness to attack large formations was not unique, but the sheer ferocity of his approach seemed to intimidate the German pilots. Many would be lacking in experience themselves and the 'berserker' approach undoubtedly bred confusion amongst them. The advice Ball gave for those scout pilots wishing to follow his example was simple, but it cannot have reassured inexperienced pilots such as Lieutenant Hill.

NOTE RE ATTACKING FORMATION WITH A LEWIS GUN AND FOSTER MOUNTING. If a scout attacks a large formation of HA, [Hostile Aircraft] I think it is best to attack from above and dive in amongst them, getting under the nearest machine. Pull gun down and fire up into HA. If you get it, a number of HA will put their noses down and make off. Don't run after them, but wait for the HA that don't run, and again take the nearest machine. If they all run wait for a bit and look out for a straggler. One is nearly always left behind. Go for that and give it a drum, at the same time keeping your eyes as much as possible on the other machines, as they may get together and get round you. If fighting on the Boche's side (as you mostly are), never use your last drum, unless forced to do so. Keep it to help you on your way back. A Hun can always tell when you are out of ammunition and he at once closes with you, and if they are in formation, you stand no chance. Keep this last drum and when you want to get back, manoeuvre for a chance to break away, and if they follow you, as they mostly do, keep turning on them and firing a few rounds at long range. When this is done they nearly always turn and run. This gives you a chance to get on the way home.[35] *Lieutenant Albert Ball, 60 Squadron, RFC*

Ball's total commitment can be best judged by his advice as to what to do in the event of the Lewis gun jamming in action.

I do not think it advisable to give up a scrap on account of a small jam. If you are faster than H.A. and he is a scout like yourself, and you have a small jam, don't give up the fight, but try to keep on his blind side, and at the same time correct your jam. You don't get a chance for a Hun every day so don't give in when the slightest bit of trouble arises. He won't know you have a jam, but will think you are holding fire to get a better position or a better chance. If you cannot correct jam, then, naturally, you must break away, but don't break away at once. Manoeuvre until you get a favourable chance.[36] *Lieutenant Albert Ball, 60 Squadron, RFC*

Albert Ball was undoubtedly a skilful pilot, a brilliant marksman and a brave man who daily conquered his natural fears, which only really emerge in his letters home. But he did rely on his luck; fighting the way he did, it was just a matter of time before he was killed. And yet he went from victory to victory. But, Ball was not the only inspirational figure, one officer, who had already lost a leg, showed the same kind of spirit in his determination to carry on the fight.

Gordon now came out in his true colours. When an observer appeared to be a bit shaken in nerves, he persuaded him to change jobs with him and he became an observer. He had two wooden legs. One was one of those life-like representations with a foot, but the other was a peg-leg. He much preferred the peg. Moreover the peg pulled out of its socket just below the knee and fitted alternatively the socket of the passenger's joystick. When therefore he took to the air, he left the passenger's joystick behind and put his peg in the clip ready for use. When the passenger had to use the Lewis gun he had to kneel on the seat and fire aft. This involved having one leg on the floor and one on the seat and when one was changing the direction of fire, one's legs sometimes got in one another's way. Not so Gordon's. His peg was in the clip – out of the way. He had one leg the right length for the seat and one for the floor. He had actually turned his disability to account on the credit side. He was the nippiest observer in the Squadron. Thus the Doctors were defeated. Gordon was once again a combatant officer.[37] *Lieutenant Robert Archer, 42 Squadron, RFC*

At the back of their minds all airmen were aware that, for all the risks that they took, they were in a relatively privileged position compared to their comrades in the infantry slogging forward a yard at a time in a welter of mud and blood. The key point was that unlike the poor bloody infantry, at least they could get away from danger when their day's flying was done.

We enjoyed a Battle of Waterloo sort of life, active flying being interspersed with riding, tennis, visits to Bethune for teas, dinners, drinking etc. Our mess life was at this period also of a Waterloo flavour, with meals, correct wines, including port circulated in a correct and proper manner. Liqueurs with coffee were de rigueur. This 'officer and gentleman' kind of life did not last long, and before many weeks had passed war conditions set in and life became much less pleasant with a growing fear of death seldom far off.[38] *Lieutenant Ewart Garland, 10 Squadron, RFC*

The war could seem a long way away.

We are under canvass and have our mess in the open in a small wood. It is very nice when the weather is as hot as it has been lately. Although we are within range of the shellfire from big guns at present you would not know there was a war. I am sitting in a wood out of the sun. The wind is blowing the wrong way to hear the guns and the only things to be heard are a machine gun shooting away in the distance and the mess gramophone.[39] *Lieutenant Leslie Horridge, 7 Squadron, RFC*

The messes varied according to circumstances, but usually they were eventually found a billet indoors away from the vagaries of the weather.

The messes were right out in the country, usually on the outskirts of quiet villages. Sometimes we lived in huts, sometimes farmhouses in the village. Old simple, whitewashed rooms with terrible old furniture and the food good, but rough. Lamps hanging on strings from the ceiling, thick with dead flies and a general rudimentary primitive sort of life. Sometimes, an old upright piano in the mess with keys so yellow they looked as if the keyboard had been smoking for about 50 years! And we had one chap who played the piano and he'd sit down in the evenings and there were two or three notes missing, it was out of tune and it was a terrible piano – but it didn't matter. He'd play the tunes of the time, the revues on in town, the things we knew by heart, we used to sing in chorus. Occasionally a bit of Chopin or something like that on the nights when we felt

*153*

that that sort of thing was appropriate. All very easy and go as you please. Usually after that turning in fairly early and going to bed because one might be up on the dawn patrol the day after perhaps up at 4 o' clock or more in the morning and wanting to get some sleep in. It was a quiet life really on the airfields themselves. It was only in the town that the binges occurred when the Squadron had perhaps a particularly bad time, or a particularly good time – either was an excuse to go in and whoop it up a bit. We used to take a tender and go off to the nearest town. There we'd find some sort of an estaminet or restaurant, probably a girl or two around the place . . . We'd begin to have a drink or two and start singing songs and enjoying ourselves. Whooping it up to say midnight, and then get into the tender and come back to the airfield again. One mustn't think of it entirely as being 'lived up' because people were being killed every day. My best friend was there one evening, and he wasn't there next day at lunch and this was going on all the time. Because people were killed too frequently the spirit in the mess was usually quiet – not frightfully gay – just workmanlike, professional in a sense. Once you are out of the air it was quiet, but it was safe! You see you were 15 or 20 miles behind the lines, you had a comfortable bed, you had sheets. You didn't have this terrible strain that could occur if you never could get out of gunfire, out of the possibility of being hit even when you were asleep. So we lived, as it were, always in the stretch or the sag of nerves. We were either in deadly danger or we were in no danger at all. This conflict had a great effect on us all. It produced a certain strain, probably because of the change.[40] *Lieutenant Cecil Lewis, 3 Squadron, RFC*

Ball relaxed by taking an interest in gardening and he was not alone in this peccadillo.

There has been a craze here for gardening recently, and people are sowing seeds sent over from England and building rockeries and what not. A counter-craze of dugout digging was started by our Commanding Officer so as to provide a place of retreat if over-enthusiastic Huns come over some day to bomb us. The dugout was almost finished when the rain came and converted it into a swimming bath. The dugout mania has now ceased.[41] *Second Lieutenant Lessel Hutcheon, 5 Squadron, RFC*

Life in the mess could indeed be simple fun as the young pilots in the prime of life revelled in their relative freedom.

Thanks ever so much for the pastries and the cake. They were ripping. But really, though, you mustn't trouble so much over me in the food line, for we have to pinch ourselves and tell each other, "There is a war on", sometimes when we get some unusual delicacies. By the same post I got a pound of lovely nut chocolate from 'S'. We had a tremendous scrap in the Mess over it when I discovered what it was, and it ended up with the box of chocolate in the floor, with me on top of it, and five people on top of me. When they discovered that the more people there were on top of me the further off became the chocolate, they got up and I handed it round in the usual civilised manner! It was great fun though and the chocolate being in a tin did not suffer.[42] *Second Lieutenant Lessel Hutcheon, 5 Squadron, RFC*

All in all messlife could be most convivial.

We had a cheery Mess – particularly when clouds made flying impossible or when all pilots had returned safely from a raid. Captain Maurice Baring – Trenchard's ADC – came to visit us from time to time and was adept in keeping us amused with various parlour tricks such as balancing a liqueur glass on his bald pate while reciting doggerel verse. Writer and poet, he had the knack of keeping up our spirits and advising his Master about the morale of his Squadrons.[43] *Lieutenant Hugh Chance, 27 Squadron, RFC*

True, many officers drank a little more than was good for them, but then most men did when away from civilizing influences. Pilots knew their responsibilities and with occasional exceptions they took a reasonably sensible attitude to drinking. When the mood took them, they sang the popular songs of the day and ludicrous, but strangely touching parodies.

*The bold aviator lay dying, (Chorus) Lay Dying...*
*And as mid the wreckage he lay, (Chorus) He lay...*
*To the swearing mechanics around him (Chorus) Around him...*
*These last dying words he did say, (Chorus) He did say...*
*Take the cylinders out of my kidneys, (Chorus) Of his Kidneys...*
*The connecting rods out of my brain, (Chorus) Of his brain...*
*The cam box from under my backbone, (Chorus) His Backbone*
*And assemble the engine again (Chorus) Again...*

For, at the back of the jolly japes and jokes, lay the ever-present fear of death which each one of them had to come to terms with in their own way.

What was the great difference between trench life and this life? In the trenches you faced death every second not knowing when it would come to you, but in the Flying Corps you could certainly say between flights that you had so many more hours to live, on the other hand, in the air, you could see death coming to you if your machine caught fire at a good height, with no parachute, you knew that it was the end, you could either stay in the machine or jump – but either way death was coming to you.[44] *Sergeant Harold Taylor, 25 Squadron, RFC*

Yet, despite it all, it is noticeable that they still did not hate their German opposite numbers.

The use of the word 'Hun' for enemy aircraft persisted throughout but was never meant to be derogatory nor derisory. I would go so far as to say that flying men on both sides felt less personal antagonism towards their antagonists than, say, footballers in the heat and excitement of play.[45] *Lieutenant Ewart Garland, 10 Squadron, RFC*

1. IWM DOCS: E. J. D. Routh, Manuscript diary, 18/8/1916
2. IWM DOCS: E. Garland, typescript diary, 13/8/1916
3. L. F. Hutcheon, *'War Flying'*, (London: John Murray, 1917), pp99-101
4. L. F. Hutcheon, *'War Flying'*, (London: John Murray, 1917), pp104-105
5. L. F. Hutcheon, *'War Flying'*, (London: John Murray, 1917), p99
6. IWM DOCS: R. Rowell, typed Manuscript
7. IWM DOCS: F. O. Cave, Manuscript diary, 5/8/1916
8. IWM DOCS: F. O. Cave, Manuscript diary, 5/8/1916
9. IWM DOCS: F. O. Cave, Manuscript diary, 6/8/1916
10. B. G. Gray & the DH2 Research Group, *'The Anatomy of an Aeroplane: The de Havilland DH2 Pusher Scout'*, (Cross & Cockade, Vol 22,), pp195-196
11. IWM DOCS: F. O. Cave, Manuscript diary, 16/8/1916
12. R. S. Capon quoted in T. M. Hawker, 'Hawker VC', (London, The Mitre Press, 1965), p203
13. IWM DOCS: J. H. Simpson, *'Aerial Fighting Hints in Training Methods'*, notes attached to papers of R.Rowell, 85/28/1
14. IWM DOCS: J. H. Simpson, *'Lecture on Aerial Tactics from the Point of View of a Single Seater Pilot'*, notes attached to papers of R Rowell, 85/28/1
15. IWM DOCS: F. O. Cave, Manuscript diary, 22/8/1916
16. A. Bott, *'Cavalry of the Clouds'*, (New York: Doubleday Page & Company, 1918), p50
17. A. Bott, *'Cavalry of the Clouds'*, (New York: Doubleday Page & Company, 1918), pp54-55
18. A. Bott, *'Cavalry of the Clouds'*, (New York: Doubleday Page & Company, 1918), pp56-57
19. A. Bott, *'Cavalry of the Clouds'*, (New York: Doubleday Page & Company, 1918), pp57-60
20. A. Bott, *'Cavalry of the Clouds'*, (New York: Doubleday Page & Company, 1918), pp61-62
21. A. Bott, *'Cavalry of the Clouds'*, (New York: Doubleday Page & Company, 1918), pp62-63
22. A. Bott, *'Cavalry of the Clouds'*, (New York: Doubleday Page & Company, 1918), pp63-64
23. A. Bott, *'Cavalry of the Clouds'*, (New York: Doubleday Page & Company, 1918), p65
24. R. H. Kiernan, *'Captain Albert Ball'*, (London: Aviation Book Club, 1939), pp88-89
25. W. A. Briscoe & H Russell Stannard, *'Captain Ball, VC'*, (London: Herbert Jenkins Ltd, 1918), p197
26 T. Hervey, quoted in Chaz Bowyer, *'Albert Ball, VC'*, (Wrexham: Bridge Books, , 1994), p66
27. R. H. Kiernan, *'Captain Albert Ball'*, (London: Aviation Book Club, 1939), p91
28. W. A. Briscoe & H Russell Stannard, *'Captain Ball, VC'*, (London: Herbert Jenkins Ltd, 1918), p202
29. C. R. Tidswell, *'Letters from Cecil Robert Tidswell'*, (Privately published), p30
30. C. R. Tidswell, *'Letters from Cecil Robert Tidswell'*, (Privately published), p32
31. C. R. Tidswell, *'Letters from Cecil Robert Tidswell'*, (Privately published), p33
32. IWM DOCS: T. Hughes, Transcript diary, 15/8/1916
33. W. A. Briscoe & H. Russell Stannard, *'Captain Ball, VC'*, (London: Herbert Jenkins Ltd, 1918), p210
34. R. Hill, quoted in Chaz Bowyer, *'Albert Ball, VC'*, (Wrexham: Bridge Books, 1994), p81
35. A. Ball, Comments by Captain Ball on a lecture on Aerial Tactics from the point of view of a single-seater pilot, notes attached to papers of Robin Rowell, IWM Doc, 85/28/1
36. A. Ball, Comments by Captain Ball on a lecture on Aerial Tactics from the point of view of a single-seater pilot, notes attached to papers of Robin Rowell, IWM Doc, 85/28/1
37. IWM DOCS: R. A. Archer, Manuscript memoir, *'Third Tour of Duty in France'*, 8/1916-3/1917
38. IWM DOCS: E. Garland, typescript diary, 26/7/1916
39. IWM DOCS: L. Horridge, Manuscript letter, 7/8/1916
40. IWM SR: C. Lewis. AC 4162
41. L. F. Hutcheon, *'War Flying'*, (London: John Murray, 1917), pp59-60
42. L. F. Hutcheon, *'War Flying'*, (London: John Murray, 1917), p78
43 IWM DOCS: H. Chance, typescript memoir, *'Subaltern's Saga'*, p13
44. IWM DOCS: H. Taylor, typescript memoir, p11
45. IWM DOCS: E. Garland, typescript diary, 9/8/1916

# Chapter Six

# September: The Tide Turns

British efforts towards the end of the summer were increasingly dominated by the preparations for the next major attack planned to take place on 15 September which would come to be known as the Battle of Flers-Courcelette. The continuous small scale attacks over the previous two months had moved the British line forward less than a mile, on a front just three miles wide, at a cost of some 82,000 casualties – which was in itself worse than the results achieved on 1 July. Now there was to be an all-out assault coordinated with an attack by the French to the south. The intention was a decisive breakthrough to exploit the painful 'wearing out' process. Once again reconnaissance was vital, although some of the observers rather amusingly exchanged their results!

> When you went on reconnaissance you had to watch for new trenches, trains going in any direction, movement of artillery or movement of troops. When we went into the reports room when we got back the joke was that we'd exchange what we'd seen. For instance if I'd seen three trains and my friend had only got one train I used to 'hand' him two trains as well. That meant that everybody had a decent report.[1] *Sergeant Harold Taylor, 25 Squadron, RFC*

*wald Boelcke.*
Q 58027 1639

Unfortunately the RFC preparations for the offensive coincided with the return to the Western Front of the incomparable Oswald Boelcke. On 27 August, he arrived back from his tour of the East to form his own scout squadron, Jasta 2, based at Bertincourt. Boelcke was no fool and had thought deeply about the theory and practice of aerial warfare.

> Boelcke then spent several days with my staff in order to co-operate closely with our experts in establishing the basic principles of scout flying and making preparations for the further development of this new arm. At my request he drew up the following summary of the principles which should govern every air fight; briefly composed and simply expressed, they were also to serve as a source of success for the younger scouts. These principles established by Boelcke remained in force until the end of the war.[2] *Colonel Thomsen, German Air Service*

*157*

The principles have been recorded in slightly varying forms, but in essence they were as follows:

1. Try to secure advantages before attacking. If possible keep the sun behind you.

2. Always carry through an attack when you have started it.

3. Fire only at close range and only when your opponent is properly in your sights.

4. Always keep your eye on your opponent and never let yourself be deceived by ruses.

5. In any form of attack it is essential to assail your opponent from behind.

6. If your opponent dives on you, do not try to evade his onslaught, but fly to meet it.

7. When over the enemy's lines never forget your own line of retreat.

8. For the Staffel: attack on principle in groups of four or six. When the fight breaks up into a series of single combats, take care that several do not go for one opponent.

These rules were a code for effective air fighting with an emphasis on achieving the best possible results and living to fight another day. Even in 1916, they were not earth shatteringly original and they can be compared with the advice given to British pilots in the previous chapter. Nevertheless, as a distillation of Boelcke's experience in combat, intended primarily for the novice, they achieved their purpose admirably.

Slowly the Jasta 2 pilots arrived. Amongst the fledglings was one Manfred von Richthofen. Born in 1892, of an aristocratic family, Richthofen had a keen interest in hunting which he was soon to take to new heights. Early in the war he served as a cavalryman, before in 1915 a desire for excitement caused him to gravitate into the German Air Service, initially as an observer on the Eastern Front. He then served on the Western Front where he managed to shoot down a French two-seater although the 'victory' was not claimed as it fell on the French side of the lines. After a chance meeting with Boelcke, he determined to learn to fly with the aim of becoming a Fokker pilot and qualified late in 1915. He fought in the skies above Verdun and again had a claim that also did not feature in his list of victims. In June, his unit was moved to the Eastern Front. It was here that he again met Boelcke, who had called in to visit the unit on his way back from his inspection tour of Turkey. Boelcke obviously saw potential in the young aristocratic sportsman because

*Manfred von Richthofen.*

he invited him to join his new squadron – and thus Richthofen joined Jasta 2.

On 2 September, Boelcke took off for a test flight in one of the new Fokker DIIIs Biplanes. Although initially peaceably minded, he was unerringly drawn into battle. He attached himself to a group of LVG and Roland two-seaters but they were attacked by two DH2 pilots – Second Lieutenant A S G Knight and Captain A M Wilkinson of Hawker's 24 Squadron.

An LVG escorted by a small brown single-seater machine came over Grevillers at 11,000 feet. The de Havillands were somewhat lower, so commenced to climb, the Hostile Aircraft (HA) flying North towards Arras. Ten minutes later they returned and Lieutenant Knight, who was now at 12,500 and higher than the HA, engaged them NE of Le Sars. The LVG at once dived away and Lieutenant Knight attacked the other machine, diving and firing a few rounds at close range. The HA went down gently and commenced to spiral, the de Havilland following, firing a few short bursts. The HA turned underneath Lieutenant Knight who dived almost vertically and fired the remainder of a drum at about five yards range, almost colliding with the enemy machine. The HA went down in a nose-dive, falling into cloud apparently out of control.[3] *Captain A M Wilkinson, 24 Squadron, RFC*

Wilkinson and Knight had been deceived as Boelcke had survived the clash unscathed, although perhaps a little chastened by the apparent ring-rustiness probably caused by his two month lay off. If so, he was soon to exact his revenge.

I saw shell bursts West of Bapaume. There I found a BE, followed by three Vickers single-seaters, i.e. an artillery plane with its escort. I went for the BE. But the other three interrupted me in the middle of my work, and so I beat a hasty retreat. One of those fellows thought he could catch me and gave chase.[4] *Captain Oswald Boelcke, Jasta 2, German Air Service*

The escort was supplied by the DH2s of 32 Squadron and Captain Robert Wilson was the man who unwisely pursued the German ace.

I saw a German scout intending to polish off one of our slow old BEs and came just in time to rescue it. After I loosed off a couple of shots at the German, he went into a turn and flew home. I was fool enough to chase him and failed to spot that he only wanted to lure me further on to his territory. When I had followed him about 15 miles behind the German lines, he turned round and attacked me by climbing above me at a fabulous speed – he flew a machine I never saw before, and I had no idea of its speed and climbing capacity.[5] *Captain Robert Wilson, 32 Squadron, RFC*

When Boelcke had Wilson exactly where he wanted him, he duly went for the 'kill'.

> When I had lured him somewhat away from the others, I gave battle and soon got to grips with him. I did not let him go again; he did not get another shot in. When he went down, his machine was wobbling badly.[6] *Captain Oswald Boelcke, Jasta 2, German Air Service*

Wilson had no chance and soon his sole remaining priority was survival.

> I hardly let off a couple of shots before my gun jammed, so that I could not fire a single round more. Under these circumstances, I did the only thing left to me and fled to get out of the way of a better machine and a superior pilot. I tried to shake him off by all sorts of tricks, but he followed all my movements magnificently and sat on my neck the whole time. He shot away all my controls, with the exception of two that were jammed, shot holes in my machine, shot the throttle away when I had my hand on it; then he put some holes in my tank and a couple in my coat when it was soaked with petrol. Naturally I lost all control over my machine, which whizzed down in a nose-dive – a most uncomfortable sensation! I sat there, pretty dizzy and waiting for the crash when I hit the ground below, but when about 50 feet up I made a desperate tug at the stick and somehow obtained enough control at the last moment to dodge the crash and bring off some sort of landing, which however set the machine and my coat on fire. I managed to jump out and pull my coat off without getting burnt.[7] *Captain Robert Wilson, 32 Squadron, RFC*

*Robert Wilson and Oswald Boelcke.*

Wilson had escaped with his life and was courteously entertained by Boelcke in his squadron mess.

It should not be imagined that the return of Boelcke marked an immediate end to the British aerial domination. His squadron had not yet been equipped with aircraft and his pilots were for the most part novices, hand picked, but novices nonetheless. He himself made occasional sorties but the British continued to ply their trade with relative impunity. Thus, on 6 September, 27 Squadron, RFC carried out an effective raid on a railway station far behind the German lines.

We had a good show the other day, eight 112lb and thirty six 20lb, or thereabouts on a big station about 50 miles behind the lines. We came down to about 500 feet and fairly buggered the place up. Trains flying miles in the air. One chap dropped his 112 on a turntable and all the slates on the engine sheds round it leapt about 6ft into the air. Huns bolted out of the station like rabbits, they exceeded all speed limits and had colossal vertical breeze. We got machine-gun and rifle fire, but no damage done and all got back safely.[8] *Lieutenant Hugh Chance, 27 Squadron, RFC*

However, those unlucky enough to meet Boelcke often suffered the consequences of his single-handed attempt to stem the British tide. One such was Lieutenant Eynon Bowen who took off on 8 September with his observer Lieutenant R M Stalker to carry out a photographic reconnaissance. He did not come back and his Commanding Officer wrote to his grieving family.

He was out on photographic duty and was attacked by some hostile machines. The machine appeared to go down under control at first, but later was seen to be falling. I fear there is very little hope. We all feel very much his loss, as he was such a splendid fellow and so popular. He was a very valuable officer both on account of his extensive knowledge of flying and also the manner in which he always performed his duties. He was an officer in whom I had complete confidence and feel his going very much.[9] *Major R Barry Martyn, 22 Squadron, RFC*

There was to be no reprieve for Bowen's family. Boelcke had claimed his 21st victory.

I got to grips over Flers. The fight did not last long, as these machines are almost defenceless against a skilled single-seater. I got on to the Vickers obliquely from behind (that is the best position; if you attack him directly from behind, his engine protects him like a thick armour belt); he tried in vain to wriggle out of the situation. Soon his machine took fire. My attack had brought me so near to him that his explosion splashed my machine with the oil that ran out. The machine then went down in spirals, throwing its occupant out, and was completely consumed by the flames.[10] *Captain Oswald Boelcke, Jasta 2, German Air Service*

On that same day some 50 miles to the north, a young British pilot whose experience belied his years, was engaged in a close encounter with a Fokker. Sergeant James McCudden had a considerable pedigree as a pre-war mechanic of the RFC who had graduated naturally as first an observer and then a scout pilot flying DH2s with 29 Squadron.

At about 14,000 feet over Gheluvelt I saw a monoplane West of us coming towards us from the direction of Ypres... I fired a red light to draw the attention of the rest of the patrol and then turned nose-on to the Fokker. We both opened fire together at about 300 yards range. After firing about three shots my gun stopped, and whilst I was trying to rectify the stoppage the Fokker turned round behind me and had again opened fire. I now did a silly thing. Instead of revving round and waiting for the other two DH2's to help me, I put my engine off and dived, but not straight. The Fokker followed, shooting as opportunity offered, and I could hear his bullets coming far too close to be healthy. At one time I glanced up and saw him just a hundred feet above me following my S turns. We got down to about 8,000 feet like this when I managed to get my gun going, so I put my engine on, and zoomed. The Fokker zoomed also, but passed above and in front of me. Now was my opportunity, which I seized with alacrity. I elevated my gun and fired a few shots at him from under his fuselage, but my gun again stopped. The Fokker, whose pilot apparently had lost sight of me, dived steeply towards Houthem, and I followed feeling very brave. Again I got my gun to function, but the Fokker had easily out-dived me . . . My lucky star undoubtedly shone again on this day, for the Fokker had only managed to put two bullets through my machine, so I was indeed thankful, for if the German had only been a little skilful I think he would have got me. But still, this was all very good experience for me, and if one gets out of such tight corners it increases one's confidence enormously.[11] *Flight Sergeant James McCudden, 29 Squadron RFC*

McCudden learnt from each and every such experience to such an extent that he became one of the most lethal pilots the RFC possessed.

Whatever happened in the air, the guns below them had to be serviced and the unsung heroes in the BE2 C crews had to keep going day after day. The importance of spotting German batteries and accurately directing the counter-battery fire had now been fully

*BE2 C of 4 Squadron RFC.* RAF MUSEUM P3087

realised and there was no chance of either aircraft or guns assigned to the task being distracted.

Your first and chief duty is the destruction of enemy guns by ranging our artillery. To do this effectively you must be certain that if your work is interfered with by an enemy machine you can deal with him effectively. This result you can arrive at by close co-operation with your observer, by both of you having a thorough knowledge of your weapon and of aerial tactics as it affects you, and by testing your gun on the ground to ensure that it shoots straight. You are an artillery machine until attacked when, by your own and your observer's efforts, you may change into a most effective fighting aeroplane.[12] *Captain H C Hinchin, RFC*

On 12 September, Lieutenant Horridge and Second Lieutenant Scutt were engaged in vital artillery observation above Pozières when they were surprised by a German scout. Although the BE2 C could never be called an effective fighting aeroplane, they managed a notable triumph against all the odds.

I had a little excitement yesterday morning and my identity disc nearly came in useful. I was doing artillery work just this side of the lines at about 2,000 feet. My observer, Scutt, was doing his first shoot and was just sending down a message when a Hun came from behind a cloud about 100 yards away at the same height and began firing at us. We were broadside on and he was slightly behind us. I could not make out where the sound was coming from for a second or two and when I saw him I dived steeply, at the same time Scutt turned round and opened fire over the tail. It was the first time he had fired from an aeroplane and he was awfully good. About ten seconds after the scrap began Scutt got him with his third burst and brought him down in flames. We were then 700 feet up about a mile this side of the lines. He dropped like a stone, blazing. I have never been so frightened in my life before. I could not see the Hun and when he stopped firing I thought that he had had enough and was going back, but Scutt's face suddenly brightened up and he pointed behind. I looked back just in time to see the machine flare up after it had crashed. Some excitement![13] *Lieutenant Leslie Horridge, 7 Squadron, RFC*

Horridge and Scutt had not escaped unscathed for the doomed German pilot had put two bullets through their engine and they had problems during the return flight. It was the first German aircraft shot down by 7 Squadron on the British side of the lines and they were eager to examine the burnt out remnants and see if they could find some souvenirs. The machine had crashed near Pozières.

I got a tender and with Scutt and my flight commander we went

to look at the machine. We found it about 1,000 yards behind the lines. The machine was still hot although it had been down about an hour and was quite unrecognisable. We collected the machine gun, the magneto and one or two smaller fittings. The engine was a six cylinder stationary one, half buried in the ground. We left it. We thought before that it was a two-seater, but there was only one body, a horrible sight. I think he was shot as well as burned.[14]
*Lieutenant Leslie Horridge, 7 Squadron, RFC*

Later, Horridge believed that he found a photograph of the crash in the *Daily Mirror*.

In the *Daily Mirror* for Monday there is a photograph of what is supposed to be a Fokker brought down by the Canadians. I believe it is the machine I brought down. I cannot make much out of the photo but what I can see is like mine. The official photographer was on the spot where I was.[15] *Lieutenant Leslie Horridge, 7 Squadron, RFC*

This was later confirmed.

The picture in the *Daily Mirror* was the Hun I brought down. There was a better picture in the *Daily Mail* which I saw afterwards, but I think they might have left the pilot out of the picture.[16] *Lieutenant Leslie Horridge, 7 Squadron, RFC*

The work was seemingly endless and the corps aircraft were constantly in the air. As the massed bombardment prior to the September offensive opened they could see the results of their efforts.

We have been very busy lately. I was up for over six hours yesterday. This is the most I have ever done in one day. When it was getting dark in the evening, I saw one of the biggest bombardments of the war. I could see the guns flashing on a front of about twelve miles. It was one continual flicker. How anyone could live down below I can't imagine.[17] *Lieutenant Leslie Horridge, 7 Squadron, RFC*

The Corps aircraft knew what lay ahead of them and as ever they were determined not to let the infantry down in any way.

A very big push is starting tomorrow and we have to be ready to do almost anything. I hope it will be fine and that we shall see a lot.[18] *Lieutenant Francis Cave, 4 Squadron, RFC*

The Battle of Flers-Courcelette was intended to capture the German Third Line from Morval to Le Sars. The blood, sweat and tears of the previous two months had achieved a start line close enough to the old German Third Line to offer some chance of success, but of course the Germans had not been idle. There were no longer open 'green fields' behind the Third Line; it was just the first in a series of three more fully-fledged trench systems. These trench systems were not as formidable in themselves as those that had faced the Fourth Army on 1 July. They had been under heavy fire since July and were often reduced to amorphous chains of shell holes with few deep dugouts where the garrison could attempt to sit out the barrage. Nevertheless they were still formidable defence works and, although ground had been gained during the course of the long drawn out summer battle, the essential problems that would be encountered in rupturing the three lines remained the same. However, Haig and Rawlinson were about to unveil a secret weapon – the tank – that offered them some hope of loosening the strangulating grip of trench warfare. The male tanks were armed with 6 pdr guns; the females with machine guns and it was hoped that their armour and caterpillar tracks would allow them to cross No Man's Land unscathed to wreak havoc on the Germans. The early tanks were slow, prone to breakdown at the drop of a hat and of course none of their crews had battle experience in their new ironclads. Rawlinson decided to use them for their shock value with the intention of attacking and subduing difficult German strongpoints that might otherwise hold up the British advance. He saw them not as a weapon of breakthrough, but one that would speed up the overall pace of the advance and thus keep up the whole momentum that was so important to Haig.

The artillery barrage was correctly identified as the real key to success. For three days, the first two German trench systems were pounded all along the 9,000 yard front that was to be assaulted and, although the intensity of fire used on 14 July was not achieved, it was comfortably in excess of that attained for 1 July. When the infantry attack was under way the creeping barrages were to be greatly

*British troops march past the new weapon – a male tank armed with 6 pdr guns – during the Somme offensive.*

strengthened by increasing the rates of fire of each participating gun and at the same time reducing the speed at which the barrage moved forward. Such barrages would be fired all along the line with the sole exception of the 100 yard 'lanes' which were left for the approach of the tanks. This paradoxically left the German strongpoints that the tanks would try to subdue less inconvenienced by artillery than the rest of the line. It was questionable, given the mechanical unreliability of the tanks, whether this was a fair exchange for the benighted infantry.

Great lumbering beasts that they were, the tanks could be heard from miles around, so a cunning plan was used to conceal their approach to the front line.

Why are all the FE2 Bs learning to night-fly so suddenly? Nobody knows. But within a week or so all the FE2 B squadrons were night flying, and then they started to drop an occasional 20-lb bomb on some wretched village just over the lines. Why are the FEs flying tonight? They don't even know themselves, except that they were told to go and fly up and down the lines from Arras to Albert; and when one machine came back another went out to drop a bomb that could do no-one any harm. It's an interesting fact that the 120 hp Beardmore engines fitted into the early FE2 Bs made almost exactly the same noise as the Daimler engines fitted into the first tanks. And it was in this way that the tanks were brought right up to the trenches, when the Boche knew nothing about them. The reason that the FEs always took a small bomb with them to drop on the Hun was merely to avoid suspicion.[19] *Lieutenant Robin Rowell, 12 Squadron, RFC*

Finally, Trenchard briefed his officers as to what was expected from the RFC in the coming assault.

On the afternoon of September 14 all the officers of our aerodrome were summoned to an empty shed. There we found our own particular General, who said more to the point in five minutes than the rumourists had said in five weeks. There was to be a grand attack next morning. The immediate objectives were not distant, but their gain would be of enormous value. Every atom of energy must be concentrated on the task. It was hoped that an element of surprise would be on our side, helped by a new engine of war christened the Tank. The nature of this strange animal, male and female, was then explained. Next came an exposition of the part allotted to the Flying Corps. No German machines could be allowed near enough to the lines for any observation. We must shoot all Hun machines at sight and give them no rest. Our bombers should make life a burden on the enemy lines of communication. Infantry and transport were to be worried,

whenever possible, by machine-gun fire from above. Machines would be detailed for contact work with our infantry. Reconnaissance jobs were to be completed at all costs, if there seemed the slightest chance of bringing back useful information. No more bubbles of hot air were blown around the mess table.[20]
*Lieutenant Alan Bott, 70 Squadron, RFC*

The officers' mess of 70 Squadron was a quiet place that night.

Only the evening was between us and the day of days. The time before dinner was filled by the testing of machines and the writing of those cheerful, non-committal letters that precede big happenings at the front. Our flight had visitors to dinner, but the shadow of tomorrow was too insistent for the racket customary on a guest night. It was as if the electricity had been withdrawn from the atmosphere and condensed for use when required. The dinner talk was curiously restrained. The usual 'shop' chatter prevailed, leavened by snatches of bantering cynicism from those infants of the world who thought that to be a beau sabreur of the air one must juggle verbally with life, death and 'Archie' shells. Even these war babies (three of them died very gallantly before we re-assembled for breakfast next day) had bottled most of their exuberance. Understanding silences were sandwiched between yarns.[21] *Lieutenant Alan Bott, 70 Squadron, RFC*

At 06.20 on 15 September, the infantry went over the top. Once again, Lieutenant Cecil Lewis was aloft on contact patrol at the vital moment.

There was a half hour hurricane bombardment and then the tanks were put over. From the air at about 5 or 6,000 feet behind the lines watching this whole scene, there was this solid grey wool carpet of shell bursts, but it was just as if somebody had taken his finger in the snow and pulled it through the snow and left a sort of ribbon. There were four or five of these ribbons between Fricourt and Boisselle, and running back toward High Wood. Through these lanes at Zero Hour we saw the tanks beginning to lumber. They'd been cleared for the tanks to come in file. They came up three or four in file, one behind the other. Of course they were utterly unexpected, the first lot went sailing over the trenches and we thought, "Well this is fine!" Because the whole thing was the year was getting a bit late, "If we don't get through now, we never shall!" This was the great opportunity and hope was high. We thought, "If they can get through the third line defences, we can put the cavalry through and the whole war will become mobile again!" And so we watched pretty carefully to see how things went. By this time all this area had been shelled for the best part of three months and it was contiguous shell holes for miles and miles. The ground looked from above like a pock marked skin. All the trees had been shot, there was no greenery, there was nothing. Except amongst the grey wool of shell burst these lumbering chaps. One or two of them with red petrol tanks on their back; one even with a little mascot, a little fox terrier running behind the tank. Then one would stop and we had no idea why. Obviously it had been hit, or somebody had thrown a grenade at it, or it had a breakdown. At the end of two hours they had moved about a mile and we thought everything was going well and we came back because our petrol was finished.[22]

*Lieutenant Cecil Lewis, 3 Squadron, RFC*

Lieutenant Routh flew a contact patrol across the battlefield a little later, at about 08.30.

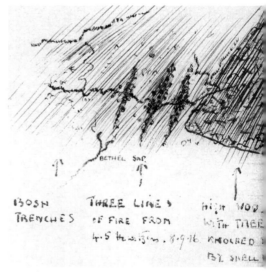

At High Wood things were not going so well. Just behind the wood a battalion had put out 'XX' denoting 'held up by machine gun fire'. This was immediately taken back and dropped at Railway Copse, the Corps artillery station. Returning we found same place had put out 'OO' which means barrage wanted but before we could send it, it was taken in. It therefore remained unsent. The first signal would probably get what was required. The tanks in High Wood were not successful. One had gone over both trenches, rather beyond the Bosche line and there had stuck. It was very heavily shelled for about ten minutes, probably by a trench mortar, so much so that after smouldering for some time it burst into flames. The other two turned over on their side in our own trenches.[23]

*Lieutenant E J D Routh, 34 Squadron, RFC*

Further along the front he began to see the potential value of the tanks.

Probably a great deal of the day's success has been due to these tanks, they went over five minutes before the infantry and as the Bosche had never seen them before, must have come as the devil of a surprise to them. Another tank engaged a battery just our side of Gueudecourt, it succeeded in knocking out three of the German guns but was knocked out by the fourth. This duel was taking place at about 100 yards. Another tank 'male' and 'relation' got astride of a trench, one at each end and simply wiped out the whole darn crowd. They are great things and have done wonders.[24] *Lieutenant E J D Routh, 34 Squadron, RFC*

The young pilots of 70 Squadron awoke to face their responsibilities in the Somme skies.

An orderly called me at 4.15am for the big offensive patrol. The sky was a dark grey curtain decorated by faintly twinkling stars. I dressed to the thunderous accompaniment of the guns, warmed myself with a cup of hot cocoa, donned flying kit, and hurried to the aerodrome. There we gathered around Captain Cruikshank, the patrol leader, who gave us final instructions about the method of attack. We tested our guns and climbed into the machines. By now the East had turned to a light grey with pink smudges from the forefinger of sunrise. Punctually at five o'clock the order, "Start up!" passed down the long line of machines. The Flight Commander's engine began a loud metallic roar, then softened as it was throttled down. The pilot waved his hand, the chocks were pulled from under the wheels and the machine moved forward. The throttle was again opened full out as the bus raced into the wind until flying speed had been attained, when it skimmed gently from the ground.[25] *Lieutenant Alan Bott, 70 Squadron, RFC*

The flight flew across No Man's Land towards Bois D'Havrincourt at a height of 12,000 feet.

An aerodrome just East of the wood was the home of the Fokker star, Boelcke. Cruikshank led us to it, for it was his great ambition to account for Germany's best pilot. While we approached, I looked down and saw eight machines with black Maltese crosses on their planes, about 3,000 feet below. They had clipped wings of a peculiar whiteness, and they were ranged one above the other, like the rungs of a Venetian blind. A cluster of small scouts swooped down from Heaven-knows what height and hovered above us; but Cruikshank evidently did not see them, for he dived steeply on the Huns underneath, accompanied by the two machines nearest him. The other group of enemies then dived.[26] *Lieutenant Alan Bott, 70 Squadron, RFC*

Cruikshank had the chance to achieve his ambitions as amongst the German scouts was Boelcke himself...

A squadron of seven English Sopwith Biplanes flew over our aerodrome on their way home. I took off at once and chased them. I came up with them near Hervilly, eastward of Peronne, but could do nothing for the moment because I was flying below them. The fellows took advantage of this to attack me. Impudence! I soon turned the tables on them and got one in my sights. I came nicely up to him and gave him about 50 rounds from close range – about 20-40 metres. Then, having had enough, he went down – after

Lieutenant von Richthofen had also given him a few superfluous rounds – into a wood near Hesbecourt and crashed.[27] *Captain Oswald Boelcke, Jasta 2, German Air Service*

Lieutenant Bott was being hard pressed. His pilot once again was Lieutenant Vaucour.

I looked up and saw a narrow biplane, apparently a Roland, rushing towards our bus. My pilot turned vertically and then side-slipped to disconcert the Boche's aim. The black crossed craft swept over at a distance of less than 100 yards. I raised my gun mounting, sighted and pressed the trigger. Three shots rattled off – and my Lewis gun ceased to fire. Intensely annoyed at being cheated out of such a splendid target, I applied immediate action, pulling back the cocking handle and pressed the trigger again. Nothing happened. After one more immediate action test, I examined the gun and found that an incoming cartridge and an empty case were jammed together in the breech. To remedy the stoppage, I had to remove spade grip and body cover. As I did this, I heard an ominous ta-ta-ta-ta-ta from the returning German scout. My pilot cart-wheeled round and made for the Hun, his gun spitting continuously through the propeller. The two machines raced at each other until less than 50 yards separated them. Then the Boche swayed, turned aside, and put his nose down. We dropped after him, with our front machine gun still speaking. The Roland's glide merged into a dive and we imitated him. Suddenly a streak of flame came from his petrol tank and the next second he was rushing earthwards, with two streamers of smoke trailing behind. [28] *Lieutenant Alan Bott, 70 Squadron, RFC*

Vaucour and Bott managed to survive this vicious dogfight after further adventures, but overall it was a bad day for 70 Squadron. Captain Cruikshank was dead, perhaps shot down by his intended quarry Boelcke, who was credited with shooting down two of the four Sopwiths lost in the fighting. It would be another quiet night in the 70 Squadron mess – but new pilots would ensure that there were no empty seats at breakfast on 16 September.

Lieutenant Albert Ball had been home on leave and returned to France on 11 September. By this stage he had been awarded the DSO and Bar to join his MC. He commanded 'A' Flight of 60 Squadron and although he conscientiously performed the duties of flight commander he still continued to fly as many additional solo offensive patrols as possible. On 15 September, he went up on several missions and had a brisk but deadly meeting with five Roland two-seaters.

Five Rolands seen over Bapaume in formation. Nieuport dived and fired rockets in order to break up the formation. Formation was lost at once. Nieuport chased the nearest machine and got under it, firing one drum at 20 yards. Hostile Aircraft went down quite out of control and crashed North East of Bertincourt.[29] *Lieutenant Albert Ball, 60 Squadron, RFC*

Ball had been on a patrol intending to attack German observation balloons, but he had found an effective alternative use for the incendiary Le Prieur rockets he was carrying fixed to his wing struts and fired by means of an electric switch. He would frequently use these rockets to disrupt German formations over the next few weeks.

Throughout the day the usual extensive bombing raids were carried out and the Martinsydes of 27 Squadron went out in pairs.

A Canadian, by name Sherren, and I set off together, crossed the lines at a good height and came down low to look for trains. We spied one steaming along on a single line near Gouzeaucourt and I flew along behind it at about 500 feet, 'pulled the plug' and let go my two 112lb bombs. The first fell at the side of the train, but the second seemed to make a direct hit on the engine, which stopped, emitting clouds of smoke and steam, Sherren dropped his two bombs on the rear coaches and round we flew to examine the damage. I was flying one of the newly delivered planes with a 160 horse-power engine and circling over the village of Gouzeaucourt I realised that I was being machine gunned from the ground and that bullets were hitting the plane. So I quickly opened the throttle and as I passed over the village let fly with my Lewis gun which was carried pointing down to earth. I saw a German soldier walking with a girl in the street, but I don't suppose my bullets disturbed them. Determined not to run any further risks, I climbed steadily until I reached an altitude of 15,000 feet, which was pretty well the Martynside's ceiling. On landing at Fienvillers I thought I bumped more than usual and on taxiing to a halt found that both tyres had been punctured by bullets and one of the longerons behind my seat had been severed. So I was lucky to get away unscathed as there were several bullet holes in the wings.[30] *Lieutenant Hugh Chance, 27 Squadron, RFC*

As ever the railways were the target and 12 Squadron, was directed at Bapaume Station.

There was argument as to who should carry 20lb bombs and who should have those of 112lb. We carried either nine of the former, or two of the later. We preferred the big ones, because they made such a glorious splash. Three machines had big ones, and Philpott and myself were two of them. I had not been very successful with the bomb sight, so I went low to drop mine. Philpott always went low. Even then I missed the line with the first bomb, but got a siding and some wagons. I dropped the second fair and squarely, and was just pulling up and round when I saw a machine dive on the station and drop a big bomb from about 50 feet. "Philpott", thought I, and envied him the magnificent demolition of the station buildings. Our targets had been carefully allotted to save waste. I circled round Bapaume at about a 1,000 feet and admired our handiwork. Then I saw a Hun and made for him, getting in a long burst from my Lewis gun before he knew I was near. He turned away and put his nose down, and I dived after him, swinging sideways occasionally to get in a few more shots. Then my drum finished. I could not reload in a dive, but did not like to leave him. While I was still thinking, I suddenly saw him stop and his tail go up in the air. I mechanically eased back the stick and flew over him, and only then realised that he was on the ground, well up on his nose, I had very nearly been with him in my excitement. I flew round and saw the pilot and observer get out. My gun was empty, and I'm not sure that I should have used it even if it had been loaded. They had not fired a shot at me, and I felt more amused than anything else. So I went home and found them beginning to wonder what had happened. Everyone else was back.[31] *Lieutenant Raymond Money, 12 Squadron, RFC*

On the ground the attack could hardly be called a pushover, for there were severe problems with surviving German machine guns, especially in those shell free 'lanes' visible from the air. The infantry were left badly exposed in these 'lanes' whenever the tanks broke down or were held up, as was frequently the case. The German artillery fire also crashed out to flay the British jumping-off positions and to catch the infantry in the wastes of No Man's Land. However successful the RFC had been in directing counter-battery fire, it was self-evident that not enough British guns were being devoted to this most essential of tasks. It was not so much that either the RFC or Royal Artillery had failed; rather that the whole gargantuan scale of the counter-battery question had not yet been fully grasped. The consequence was appalling casualties – nearly 30,000 in total.

Nevertheless, the German front line positions were seized all along the 9,000 yard front and 4,500 yards of their new 'Second Line' was also lost around Flers where the tanks had performed well. This it should be noted was the exception to the rule as many of the tanks suffered mechanical breakdowns, but here twelve of the tanks managed to get forward and they famously led the advance down what remained of the main street of Flers.

The 'push' commenced today. Now at 9.30pm we have captured Courcelette, Martinpuich, High Wood, Flers, Lesboeufs and probably Combles. We are also advancing on Guedecourt. The 'caterpillars' have been an immense success, being always in front of the infantry. I went up with Duke at 10.40 but it was

*Mark I tank D17 at Flers. One of the four that assisted in the capture of the village, it was hit by two shells and abandoned on the eastern outskirts.*

rather dud and we could do nothing. I dropped a bomb on 'F. 69' and caused a small explosion there. I am on early patrol tomorrow with Duke and with luck there is no saying where our troops may be.[32] *Lieutenant Francis Cave, 4 Squadron, RFC*

Cave's diary entry was the usual mixture of optimism and outright rumour. Once again the German line had been bent, bashed, reshaped and bitten into – but it retained its overall integrity. The morale of the defending troops was dented, but it endured; German manpower reserves were stretched, but still the reserve divisions moved forward to counter-attack, obstruct and eventually once more halt the British advance. During the battle the RFC broke new records for the amount of hours flown and the intensity of the aerial fighting: the contact patrols, artillery observation work, deep searching reconnaissance patrols, bombing raids – all covered by the aggressive posture of the scouts seeking out their prey. Yet the aerial operations in early September marked the median point before the pendulum of aerial warfare swung decisively back towards the Germans. Just a few days later, the changing pattern of the aerial conflict was painfully apparent.

*173*

From 1 July 1916 to, at any rate, 15 September 1916, a bomb raid or a reconnaissance on the Third Army battle front even 25 miles West of the lines, by such easily vulnerable aircrafts as BE2 Cs, had not been by any means suicidal affairs, thanks in great measure to the magnificent work of escorting machines. In our own case No 60 Squadron (Morane single-seater fighters) and No 11 Squadron (FE2 B two-seater pusher fighters) did most of this work. But the attacks they beat off, though gradually increasing in intensity during the first fortnight in September, were not remarkably well co-ordinated, nor were they pushed home with extremity of vigour. On 17 September 1916, we were to learn what a powerful and dangerous enemy the Germans still could be.[33] *Lieutenant Raymond Money, 12 Squadron, RFC*

The impetus for change was the delivery on 16 September of the Albatross D I earmarked for Boelcke's Jasta 2. Although new German scouts, such as the Fokker D II and the Halberstadt D II, had been arriving on the front throughout the summer of 1916, they all had only one fixed forward firing machine gun. The Albatross DI was the first scout to be armed with twin Spandau machine guns firing through the propeller without a corresponding loss in aerial performance, due to its careful streamlining and the awesome power of its 160hp Mercedes engine which took it up to speeds of nearly 110mph. This new aircraft was clearly superior to any Allied scout then flying on the Western Front and its sleek appearance and deadly bite soon earned it the nickname of 'shark'. Boelcke was delighted with his new machines.

*Albatross D I.* IWM Q 61061

Yesterday at least six arrived, so that I shall be able to take off with my Staffel for the first time today. Hitherto, I have generally flown Fokker biplanes, but today I shall take up one of the new Albatrosses. My pilots are all passionately keen and very competent, but I must first train them to steady team-work – they are at present rather like young puppies in their zeal to achieve something.[34] *Captain Oswald Boelcke, Jasta 2, German Air Service*

That day, untrained or not, the 'puppies' were to leave their mark on the battlefield!

On 17 September, the BE2 Cs of 12 Squadron were ordered to bomb the Marcoing railway junction lying just to the south of Cambrai. They were escorted by the FE2 Bs of 11 Squadron led by Captain Grey. Lieutenant Money was not in the best of tempers after an earlier attempt that day to carry out the mission had been cancelled due to light mist. His petrol pump malfunctioned forcing him to use the hand pump. Inevitably, he lost pressure and consequently both speed and height as he approached Marcoing, trailing far behind the main BE2 C formation.

I dropped my bombs and watched them go down, disregardful of Archie which was bursting very close all round me. I knew that I should be very lucky to get back across the lines. While I was still watching for the burst of my last bomb, I heard a terrific burst, and the machine was borne suddenly upwards. In the same moment, my engine ceased and I became the centre of black smoke and flying fragments. A few seconds later I realised that I was only keeping the machine on an even keel by pushing the stick as far forward as it would go, and that most of my engine was no longer there. Apart from a gaping hole in the right bottom plane and an inside strut dangling, the machine seemed alright. So that was the finish of the morning's exploits![35] *Lieutenant Raymond Money, 12 Squadron, RFC*

With his engine destroyed by the burst of anti-aircraft fire and losing height rapidly, Money knew he had no chance of regaining the British front line. Unfortunately, he soon became aware that his comrades were also seriously threatened as a number of the new German scouts dived down on them. Months later, the leader of the ill-fated 11 Squadron patrol, Captain D S Grey, wrote to the mother of Lieutenant Lionel Morris to explain what had happened to her son in the unforgiving skies of France.

The escort of six or seven machines which I was leading engaged them (and your son second leader). I was ahead with two other machines and one of them which I believe was your son turned back to assist those in the rear. I was then attacked myself and knew no more of the fight until I reached the ground.[36] *Captain D S Grey, 11 Squadron, RFC*

Gray seems to have been been shot down by Boelcke himself, although there are obvious discrepancies between the British and German accounts as to the number of German scouts involved in the dogfight.

> This morning I ran into an enemy squadron with two of my pilots (Lieutenants Reimann and Richthofen). We cleaned them up thoroughly; each of us got one. I engaged the leader's machine, which I recognised by its streamers, and forced it down. My opponent landed at Equancourt and promptly set fire to his machine. The inmates were taken prisoner; one of them was slightly wounded. The pilot had to land because I shot his engine to pieces.[37] *Captain Oswald Boelcke, Jasta 2, German Air Service*

As his BE2 C slowly fell to earth, Money looked on horror struck as the Jasta 2 pilots tore into his escort.

> Suddenly I heard the rattle of machine gun fire. I looked up and saw one of the escorting FEs from No. 11 Squadron going down in a steep spiral with two Huns on his tail. I cursed in impotent anger, and even let off a few rounds from my Lewis gun in their direction. Suddenly I saw another FE going down, and a third going to its assistance, although he himself was being attacked by two more Huns. The air was thick with Huns. Out of harm's way, bunched together on the horizon, was the little group of four BEs. Six FEs were holding up 30 or 40 Huns, and I cursed and raged furiously at my impotence to help. It was a sickening and heartrending sight.[38] *Lieutenant Raymond Money, 12 Squadron, RFC*

Alongside Boelcke, was Lieutenant von Richthofen, who was desperate, almost obsessive, in his desire and determination to shoot down his first victim – but he was also inexperienced. Nevertheless, he managed to get behind the FE2 B crewed by the veterans Lieutenant Lionel Morris and Lieutenant Tom Rees.

> Boelcke had come very near the first English machine, but he did not yet shoot. I followed. Close to me were my comrades. The Englishman nearest to me was travelling in a large machine painted in dark colours. I did not reflect very long, but took my aim and shot. He also fired and so did I, and both of us missed our aim. A struggle began and the great point for me was to get to the rear of the fellow... Apparently he was no beginner, for he knew exactly that his last hour had arrived at the moment I got at the back of him. At that time, I had not yet the conviction, "He must fall", which I have now on such occasions, but, on the contrary, I was curious to see whether he would fall. My Englishman twisted and turned, flying in zig-zags. At last a favourable moment arrived. My opponent had apparently lost sight of me. Instead of twisting and turning, he flew straight along. In a fraction of a

*Manfred von Richthofen.*

second, I was at his back with my excellent machine. I gave a short burst of shots with my machine gun. I had gone so close that I was afraid I might dash into the Englishman. Suddenly I nearly yelled with joy, for the propeller of the enemy machine had stopped turning. Hurrah! I had shot his engine to pieces; the enemy was compelled to land, for it was impossible for him to reach his own lines. The English machine was swinging curiously to and fro. Probably something had happened to the pilot. The observer was no longer visible.[39] *Lieutenant Manfred von Richthofen, Jasta 2, German Air Service*

The Albatross totally outclassed the FE2 Bs and gave them a margin of error that more than compensated for any lack of combat skills. It allowed the fledgling German pilots to prosper and take their kills almost at will.

The 'circus' had done its work only too well. It must have come up from behind and below the BE2 Cs, and gallant No. 11 had dived to the rescue. This would be just what the Germans wanted. It looked to me as though they opened out to let the FEs get among them, and then closed in in bunches of three or four on the tails of the FEs. Naturally these, as pushers, had no field of fire behind, and the Germans were too well mounted and in too great numbers to give the FEs opportunity to turn and bring guns to bear. All this, as far as I was concerned, had only occupied about three-quarters of a minute, and I would not have believed it possible that in so short a time I could have been filled with so great a desolation and rage.[40] *Lieutenant Raymond Money, 12 Squadron, RFC*

Money, after all, had problems of his own as his plane fell out of the sky.

I was descending gently, like a lift, almost stalled; and with the noise of my engine and propeller silenced, I could hear the infernal rat-tat-tat of the enemy machine guns and the occasional running trill of one of our own. I looked down to see where I was going to hit the ground, and saw a train derailed and smoking, and the remaining BE, almost on the ground, turning and twisting to get away from a Hun on his tail. It looked hopeless, and even as I watched, the BE hit the ground and turned right up on its nose. I would have given my life for ten minutes and a DH2. I threw my ammunition drums overboard and the breechblock of my Lewis gun. I had a week's supplies of subversive propaganda in the machine which I had, day after day forgotten to drop. "Well, they'll get it all at once," I thought grimly. Another half minute had elapsed, and I was no more than a thousand feet up. I speculated over what kind of a crash I should have, for I had not sufficient control to land properly, and realised that if it had not been such a perfect day, I should probably be spinning. The trees of the Bois d'Havrincourt came nearer and I saw a field telegraph line. "May as well dish that," thought I, and in a last flicker of rage I let the stick go right back. The poor old machine reared up and then crashed heavily, and things went black. The next thing I knew I was sitting in the back of a touring car, and a voice was saying in English, "Well, the War is over for you."[41] *Lieutenant Raymond Money, 12 Squadron, RFC*

Richthofen's first victims crashed into the ground at Villers Plouich. After setting fire to his machine Captain Grey saw the last act.

About a minute after landing I saw another one of our machines come down and disappear behind some trees and houses not far about 500 yards from us. We subsequently passed this machine when we were driven off in a car under escort. It was crashed beside the road which was here on an embankment and a crowd of people round. The car drew up and I gathered from the German officer that the observer was killed and the pilot injured and had already been removed in an ambulance. The car only stopped for a few seconds and we could get no more information (neither of us spoke German). Helder, my observer, says we passed the ambulance a little farther on but I do not remember this. Your son must have been removed in the ambulance almost immediately it could be brought to the spot. We arrived that night at midnight at Cambrai and were told that there was a pilot named Morris in hospital brought down that morning, his observer being killed. The man who told us spoke English and walked up from the station with us to the prison and was I believe connected with the hospital. We saw no-one again until I think the next afternoon when we were told Morris had died that morning. He had been wounded in the air and injured by the crash. His observer had been repeatedly hit by machine gun bullets and must have been killed outright. We were told Morris was conscious most of the time and when admitted into hospital and was able to give his name etc. He was very quiet and I think suffered little pain. I would have liked to have seen him but he was already dead before we knew very much about it and we were somewhat dazed and put out by our experiences ourselves. An officer who was at Cambrai with us visited a brother officer wounded in hospital (Patterson) and gave a good account of the conditions and treatment there. I should like you to feel assured that your son met with a most gallant end, going as I believe to the assistance of his comrades and that his sufferings were not great and that he got all the attention possible. I do not think it possible to obtain any of his effects but it might be done through the International Red Cross, Geneva. I knew your son at the first two flying schools he was at

*Lionel Morris who died in a German hospital after crashing at Villers Plouich.*

at home and of course in the Squadron. He had done a great deal of work and was one of the most reliable and brave pilots I have met. I say this without exaggeration and not merely through a desire to gratify. As you know his manner was quiet and unassuming but it covered a very stout heart and steady nerve and I am certain he gave a good account of himself. No officer in the Flying Corps could wish to meet with a better end.[42] *Captain D S Grey, 11 Squadron, RFC*

Richthofen was on his way to become the greatest scourge of the RFC. Lieutenants Morris and Rees were just the first victims of his illustrious career. Boelcke was delighted at the results of the day's work.

The Staffel is making itself! We have got five English machines since yesterday evening! In view of these many 'numbers', mother will be saying again that it is not right to number our victims in this unfeeling way. But we don't really do it – we do not number the victims who have fallen, but the machines we have brought down. That you can see from the fact that it only counts as one victory when two inmates are killed, but that it still remains a 'number' when both the inmates escape unhurt. We have nothing against the individual; we only fight to prevent him flying against us. So when we have eliminated an enemy force, we are pleased and book it as one up to us.[43] *Captain Oswald Boelcke, Jasta 2, German Air Service*

On the same day, Lieutenant Hugh Chance was ordered to carry out a bombing raid on Valenciennes which lay far behind the German lines.

We set off at 07.00 and were soon flying in formation towards our target. It was a fine sunny autumn day and 'Archie' was more troublesome than usual. When we were about 20 miles inside German-held territory, we were heavily shelled and the air was full of black crumps. Almost immediately my engine stopped and I began to lose height. I thought that perhaps the air pump, which delivered fuel from the main tank to a small tank which supplied the carburettor by gravity, had packed up. So I feverishly worked at the auxiliary hand pump and after a short interval the engine picked up again. Then I was in a dilemma – should I try to rejoin the formation, which was now disappearing into the distance, or turn home. However fate decided, and the engine stopped again and refused to start in spite of my efforts to put pressure into the tank. So there was nothing to do but to glide down as flatly as possible and try to get back over the lines. But soon I realised I was not going to make it – I had already dropped my bombs on a wood – and would have to make a forced landing. We had just been issued with tracer bullets for our Lewis guns and were warned that the Boche were claiming that they were explosive and contrary to the rules of the Hague Convention. So before landing I fired off my machine guns and threw out the spare drums of ammunition. Picking a likely looking stubble field, I landed without difficulty and clutching the incendiary torch with which we were equipped in case of a forced landing, jumped out – set the torch alight and poked it into the canvas of the main planes. But this proved ineffective, so I climbed back into the cockpit – broke the glass of the petrol gauge, dipped my handkerchief into the stream of petrol which poured out, lit it from the torch and flung it back into the cockpit. There was a great gush of flame and I ran headlong to be clear of the burning plane and flung myself down, as some German troops, exercising some distance away, started loosing off.[44] *Lieutenant Hugh Chance, 27 Squadron, RFC*

Chance was captured and taken to the Citadel at Cambrai where he met several RFC officers including Raymond Money.

Boelcke had been pleased with his young pilots but he recognized that they had much to learn before they could confidently take on the DH2s and Nieuports.

I have to give my pilots some training. That is not so simple because they are all inspired with such fiery zeal that it is often difficult to put the brake on them. They have certainly all learnt that the main thing is to get the enemy in your power and beat him down at once instead of arguing with him. But until I get it into their heads that everything depends on sticking together through thick and thin when the Staffel goes into battle and that it does not matter who actually scores the victory as long as the Staffel wins it – well, I can talk myself silly, and sometimes I have to turn my heavy batteries on to them. I always give them some instruction before we take off and deal out severe criticism after every flight and especially after every fight. But they take it all very willingly.[45] *Captain Oswald Boelcke, Jasta 2, German Air Service*

Boelcke's practical lessons were deadly affairs. On 19 September, he and his Jasta disrupted a reconnaissance mission of FE2 Bs escorted by the Moranes of 60 Squadron. The results were predictable.

Six of us rattled into a squadron consisting of eight or ten FEs and several Moranes – the fat lattice tails down below and the Moranes above as a cover. I engaged one of the latter and pranced about the air with him – he escaped me for a moment, but I got to grips with him West of Bapaume; one of my guns jammed, but the other shot all the better. I shot up that monoplane from close range until he broke up in flames and fell into the wood near Grévillers in fragments.[46] *Captain Oswald Boelcke, Jasta 2, German Air Service*

*Morane Parasols of 3 Squadron, RFC at La Houssoye, September 1916.* IWM Q11844

The Morane was flown by Captain H C Tower who was killed in the burning crash.

Gradually, the British found that everything was becoming much harder. Thus on 22 September, 4 Squadron, RFC was ordered to attack the German observation kite balloons.

In the morning, Scott told us that there was going to be balloon strafing in future with phosphorus bombs. Carroll and I did it this afternoon. There were six of us in all and five de Havillands. They make a splendid burst and probably do in anything near them. After dropping mine, I missed the others and suddenly found a Hun diving on my tail. He was very fast and practically had me on toast as I only had a forward mounting. He held his fire until about 20 yards away and then circled about, firing from all directions. I got into a spinning nose-dive and temporarily lost control of the machine. Eventually I got it out and got behind him and let him have about 15 rounds right into him, causing him to nose dive, but probably under control. I then made straight for home. I had absolutely given up all hope of living through it, or at any rate of landing this side of the lines.[47] *Lieutenant Francis Cave, 4 Squadron, RFC*

After the Battle of Flers-Courcelette on 15 September, the Fourth Army had wanted to launch the next assault as soon as possible. Unfortunately, the inevitable delays caused by moving forward the guns, coupled with an unfortunate break in the weather, led to the attack being postponed until 25 September. The plans

*The trail of smoke from the burning remnants of a German observation balloon.*

adopted showed a further tactical advance. Objectives were limited to the German front line, which had originally been their Third Line when the offensive began in July. This automatically increased the density of shells falling on the German garrison. The augmented creeping barrages were further developed. In the area of counter-battery work some 124 German batteries were located by the RFC and other sources. Of these the hard pressed gunners managed to engage 47 and it was claimed that 21 batteries were silenced. This of course meant that 103 were still in action. When the Battle of Morval was launched on 25 September, the results were impressive. The British troops stuck close behind the mangling curtain of detonating shells that guided them forward across No Man's Land and hit the German survivors before they had chance to think or do anything. A further development was that the concentrated fire of some 60 field guns shattered the German counter-attack launched next day. Gradually the idea of using a wall of artillery shells to defend captured positions was taking hold. This would prove a vital part of the 'bite and hold' methods developed in 1917 – use artillery to guarantee the capture of desirable, but restricted objectives, within the range of the British field artillery, consolidate these gains and then sit back to let the German take severe casualties in trying to regain their lost positions. Overall, lessons were slowly being learned, although it is important to recognise the 'two steps forward, one step backwards' nature of tactical thinking. Every battle had different features and it was hence difficult for the senior commanders to separate the effects of special circumstances from the results of the application of sound tactical principles. Red herrings abounded and the fog of war was very real over the Somme.

On 26 September, the focus of the battle began to shift once more to the northern Somme sector. Originally given a holding role, the Reserve

*Morval, captured by 5th Division on 25 September 1916.*

*Aerial photograph, of Morval on 30 September.*

Army under General Sir Hubert Gough had gradually become more active as the campaign ground through the summer and into the autumn. In July, there had been severe fighting to capture the village of Ovillers and to gain the Pozières Ridge. Once consolidated on Pozières Ridge they had directed their activities towards isolating the German garrison holding Thiepval. Finally, on 26 September, the time was considered ripe for a final assault to be made to pinch out the Thiepval thorn in the British side. Here too, new tactics were tried, with mortars used to fire gas shells and for the first time massed Vickers machine guns fired indirectly over the German front line onto the rear areas to complement the artillery barrage. Still there were problems and heavy casualties occurred when the infantry were unable to keep up with the creeping barrage during the bitter fighting in Thiepval itself. Nevertheless the village fell, together with several neighbouring strongpoints, leaving the Gough's Army safely ensconced on the Thiepval Ridge overlooking the German trenches in the Ancre Valley to the north.

* * * *

Despite all the odds, as the fighting boiled, Lieutenant Albert Ball remained alive and still causing mayhem amongst the Germans. His Nieuport 17 was not as fast or powerfully armed as the Albatross DI, but it had a tighter turning circle and was more agile in close combat. The Nieuport was therefore clearly inferior, but in the hands of a skilled pilot like Ball, it was more than capable of holding its own. His combat reports, couched in the normal, dry impersonal language, conceal rather than illuminate the dramatic events that they were recording. On 21 September he had run into a formation of six Roland scouts.

Hostile Aircraft (H.A.) seen North of Bapaume in formation. Nieuport dived and fired rockets. Formation was lost. Nieuport got underneath nearest machine and fired a drum. H.A. dived and landed near railway. Nieuport then attacked another machine and fired two drums from underneath. H.A. went down and was seen to crash at side of railway. After this the rest of the H.A. followed Nieuport towards the lines. Nieuport turned and fired remainder of ammunition, after which it returned to aerodrome for more. Second machine was seen to crash by Lieutenant Walters.[48]
*Lieutenant Albert Ball, 60 Squadron, RFC*

Two days later, on 23 September, he was in the thick of it again this time carrying the new Buckingham tracer-incendiary ammunition.

Four Rolands were seen coming from Cambrai towards Mory. Nieuport got behind them and fired a drum at 30 yards range. This made them separate. Nieuport then made for the nearest machine and got underneath it, firing one drum. This drum had no effect on the H.A. for Nieuport could not get near enough. Nieuport then made for another and succeeded in getting within 15 yards underneath, at which range 90 rounds of 1 in 3 Buckingham were fired. H.A. was on fire before 15 rounds were fired, but it was observed to go out before crashing on the ground near Mory. The remainder of the H.A. surrounded the Nieuport after this, for it had no ammunition. Nieuport only got 13 hits on its planes.[49] *Lieutenant Albert Ball, 60 Squadron, RFC*

On 25 September, at around mid-day he had a splendid tussle with a humble two-seater with what was obviously a top class German crew. His usual tactics were thwarted by the skill of the German pilot and he could not close to the usual deadly range. These were the first reports he signed following his promotion to Captain.

We kept on firing until we had used up all our ammunition. There was nothing more to be done after that, so we both burst out laughing. We couldn't help it – it was so ridiculous. We flew side-by-side laughing at each other for a few seconds, and then we waved adieu to each other and went off. He was a real sport that Hun.[50] *Captain Albert Ball, 60 Squadron, RFC*

In the early evening of the same day, Ball had another desperate tussle. At this stage he was using a Lewis gun fitted with the newly issued double drums of ammunition.

Nieuport could not see any H.A. over Bapaume at a reasonable height, so it went along the Cambrai Road. After being there for a few minutes, two formations came along. Nieuport attacked the first. The H.A. ran with noses down, but, when another formation came near it turned towards the Nieuport. Nieuport fired one drum

all's Nieport 17
F MUSEUM P20432

ieuport 17.
F MUSEUM P19392

to scatter formation after which it turned to change drums. One of the drums dropped into the rudder control and for a few seconds Nieuport was out of control. Nieuport succeeded in getting drum on gun and attacked an Albatross which was then flying at its side. Nieuport fired 90 rounds of 1 in 3 Buckingham at about 15 yards range underneath H.A.. H.A. went down, quite out of control and crashed. The remainder of H.A. followed Nieuport, but in the end left. In order to keep them off at safe range Nieuport kept turning towards them, each time this was done H.A. made off with noses down.[51] *Captain Albert Ball, 60 Squadron, RFC*

Just as Ball preyed on German formations and isolated his victims with deadly precision within the chaos that his whirlwind attacks created, so the German maestro Boelcke was meting out punishment on the RFC. On 27 September, Boelcke led an attack on six Martinsydes of 27 Squadron over Bapaume; but as the leader of a formation, he multiplied the practical as opposed to moral effects of his actions.

I was on patrol with four of my gentlemen; when we reached the front, I saw a squadron which I first took for a German formation. But when we met to the South East of Bapaume, I recognised them for enemy aircraft. As we were lower than they, I turned away to Northward. The Englishmen then passed by us, crossed our lines, circled round a bit behind our captive balloons and then wanted to go home. Meanwhile, however, we had climbed to their height and cut them off. I gave the signal to attack and the fun started. It was a mighty scrap. I got to grips with one and blasted him properly, but came up too close and had to pass out below him. Then I went into a turn, in the course of which I saw the Englishman go down and fall like a sack somewhere near Ervillers. I engaged another immediately – there were plenty of them. He tried to get away from me, but it did not avail him – I hung on close behind all the time. Yet I was surprised at this opponent's tenacity – I thought I really must have settled him some time before, but he kept on flying round and round in the same sort of circles. At last I could stand it no longer – I said to myself that the man must be dead and the controls are jammed so as to keep the machine in a normal position. So I flew quite close up to him – then I saw the man sprawling over in the cockpit, dead. I left the machine to its fate, having noted its number – 7495.[52] *Captain Oswald Boelcke, Jasta 2, German Air Service*

*Oswald Boelcke as Staffel leader*

In fact, another of his pilots, Sergeant L Reimann, had the temerity to put in a claim for the same aircraft! In the circumstances the victory was left uncredited to avoid any embarrassment. Second Lieutenant S Dendrino who was flying the Martinsyde had obviously lapsed into unconsciousness from the effects of his wounds. He died shortly after crashing behind the German lines. Boelcke however was still not satisfied.

> I took on another. He got a good dose from me, but after a series of fighting turns managed to escape behind his own lines. When I had to pass out under him, I saw how my bullets had cut his fuselage about. He will remember that day for a long time! And so shall I, for I worked like a nigger and sweated like a reserve officer.[53] *Captain Oswald Boelcke, Jasta 2, German Air Service*

The battered Martinsyde was flown by Second Lieutenant R W Chappell. He was lucky to be personally unharmed for his aircraft was riddled with bullets splattering through the petrol tank, his seat, radiator, engine, planes, centre section strut and flying controls.

By this time, Richthofen was also beginning to score regularly in his own right. He had shot down his second victim, Sergeant Herbert Bellerby of 27 Squadron on 23 September. A week later he scored again.

> He plunged down in flames. One's heart beats faster if the opponent, whose face one has just seen, plunges burning from 4,000 metres. Arriving below, I found very little remaining of either the men or the machine. I took a small piece of the insignia from this one as a souvenir. I had taken the machine gun from my second also to keep as a souvenir; it had a bullet of mine in the bolt, which rendered it useless.[54] *Lieutenant Manfred von Richthofen, Jasta 2, German Air Service*

*Boelcke reporting on his thirty-fourth victory.*

The pendulum had swung back to the Germans. Second Lieutenant Edmund Lewis, having recovered from his wound, was sent back to his beloved DH2s, this time with 24 Squadron. He immediately recognized that the situation had changed, but he was a philosophical young man.

It rather feeds you up to see all this newspaper talk about our supremacy in the air. We certainly had it last June, July and August, but we haven't got it now. The Huns still keep to their side of the line while we venture over their lines, but if they wished they could sit over our aerodromes (with their fast machines) and we could do nothing against them. Perhaps this is a bit of an exaggeration, as we would certainly fight them and not run away as they do, but I don't think the Hun is good enough to face equal numbers over our side even if they have got better machines. What I mean is that a DH2 is no longer attacking but is fighting for its life against these fast Huns, and that at present we have only about half a dozen machines to cope with them. Thank the Lord they haven't got many of these fast ones and that given equal numbers our machines would still put up a good – very good in fact – fight against them on account of superior 'guts'. But I suppose war in the air will always be like that. First one side has the best machines and then the other, and the side which shows most guts all through will be the winners. During this War, first we had the lead with BEs and Vickers; then the Germans got it with the Fokkers. After that we got it with the DHs and now the Huns are a bit superior with their fast scouts. But whereas formerly one side or the other had the mastery for many months, now it is only a few weeks, as the rate of production is much faster and new machines come out daily. At any rate I hope new machines are coming out from our side – we can't rest as we are.[55] *Second Lieutenant Edmund Lewis, 24 Squadron, RFC*

Despite the failure of the BE12 scout, the British did have access to new scout designs that could have at least given the German Albatross a run for its money. But, not unnaturally, the French had a near monopoly on the production of Nieuports and those few that eluded them were hoovered up by the Royal Naval Air Service. Only 60 Squadron were re-equipped with the Nieuports. The new Sopwith Pup and Triplane Scouts seemed promising; but caught up in the tangled politics of the British aircraft production industry they were also destined for the RNAS.

Of course, Trenchard was quickly aware of the new situation. However, he was determined that the RFC would continue to do its duty. As he saw it, they had been through the bad times before and they would do it again. The RFC still had a considerable numerical superiority and the Germans still rarely crossed the British front line, so they were automatically on the back foot as far as reconnaissance and artillery observation was concerned. Trenchard was not the type of man to bend with the wind, he stood firm and he pushed back against it.

I have come to the conclusion that the Germans have brought another squadron or squadrons of fighting machines to this neighbourhood and also more artillery machines. One or two German aeroplanes have crossed the line during the last few days . . . With all this, however, the anti-aircraft guns have only reported 14 hostile machines as having crossed the line in the 4th Army area in the last week ending yesterday, whereas something like 2,000 to 3,000 of our machines crossed the lines during the week.[56] *Major General Hugh Trenchard, Headquarters, RFC*

Trenchard had always supported his master, Sir Douglas Haig. Now Haig recognized that Trenchard's concerns were legitimate and backed his urgent request for an increase in new scout aircraft to counter the deadly Albatross.

I have the honour to request that the immediate attention of the Army Council may be given to the urgent necessity for a very early increase in the numbers and efficiency of the fighting aeroplanes at my disposal. Throughout the last three months the Royal Flying Corps in France has maintained such a measure of superiority over the enemy in the air that it has been enabled to render services of incalculable value. The result is that the enemy has made extraordinary efforts to increase the number, and develop the speed and power, of his fighting machines. He has unfortunately succeeded in doing so and it is necessary to realise clearly, and at once, that we shall undoubtedly lose our superiority in the air if I am not provided at an early date with improved means of retaining it . . . The result of the advent of the enemy's improved machines has been a marked increase in the casualties suffered by the Royal Flying Corps, and though I do not anticipate losing our present predominance in the air for the next three or four months, the situation after that threatens to be very serious unless adequate steps to deal with it are taken at once.[57] *Sir Douglas Haig, Commander in Chief, BEF*

Both in the air and on the ground the Battle of the Somme was reaching a crucial phase.

1 The Germans had been so impressed by the Vickers Fighter earlier in the war that they continued to refer to British pusher aircraft such as the DH2 and FE2 B as Vickers types
1. IWM SR: H. Taylor, SR 307, Reel 1
2. J. Werner, 'Knight of Germany: Oswald Boelcke German Ace', (London: John Hamilton Ltd, 1933) pp183-184
3. B. G. Gray, 'Number One of Jasta 2: An account of Oswald Boelcke's Twentieth Victory', (Cross & Cockade, Vol 22), pp127-128
4. J. Werner, 'Knight of Germany: Oswald Boelcke German Ace', (London: John Hamilton Ltd, 1933) p205

5. J. Werner, *'Knight of Germany: Oswald Boelcke German Ace'*, (London: John Hamilton Ltd, 1933) pp206-207

6. J. Werner, *'Knight of Germany: Oswald Boelcke German Ace'*, (London: John Hamilton Ltd, 1933) p205

7. J. Werner, *'Knight of Germany: Oswald Boelcke German Ace'*, (London: John Hamilton Ltd, 1933) p207

8. IWM DOCS: H. Chance, typescript memoir, 'Subaltern's Saga', pp13-14

9. RAF MUSEUM: E.G. A. Bowen collection, 8/9/1916

10. J. Werner, *'Knight of Germany: Oswald Boelcke German Ace'*, (London: John Hamilton Ltd, 1933) p209-210

11. J. T. B. McCudden, *'Five Years in the Royal Flying Corps'*, (London: Aeroplane & General, 1918), pp107-108,

12. IWM DOCS: Hinchin, *'Lecture on Aerial Tactics From the Point of View of an Artillery Observer'*, notes attached to papers of Robin Rowell, 85/28/1

13. IWM DOCS: L. Horridge, Manuscript letter, 13/9/1916

14. IWM DOCS: L. Horridge, Manuscript letter, 13/9/1916

15. IWM DOCS: L. Horridge, Manuscript letter, 26/9/1916

16. IWM DOCS: L. Horridge, Manuscript letter, 30/9/1916

17. IWM DOCS: L. Horridge, Manuscript letter, 18/9/1916

18. IWM DOCS: F. O. Cave, Manuscript diary, 14/9/1916

19. IWM DOCS: H. Rowell, typed Manuscript

20. A. Bott, *'Cavalry of the Clouds'*, (New York: Doubleday Page & Company, 1918), pp28-29

21. A. Bott, *'Cavalry of the Clouds'*, (New York: Doubleday Page & Company, 1918), pp28-29

22. IWM SR: C. Lewis, AC 4162

23. IWM DOCS: E. J. D. Routh, Manuscript diary, 15/9/1916

24. IWM DOCS: E. J. D. Routh, Manuscript diary, 15/9/1916

25. A. Bott, *'Cavalry of the Clouds'*, (New York: Doubleday Page & Company, 1918), pp33

26. A. Bott, *'Cavalry of the Clouds'*, (New York: Doubleday Page & Company, 1918), pp35-36

27. J. Werner, *'Knight of Germany: Oswald Boelcke German Ace'*, (London: John Hamilton Ltd, 1933) p211

28. A. Bott, *'Cavalry of the Clouds'*, (New York: Doubleday Page & Company, 1918), pp36-37

29. RAF Museum: A. Ball Combat Report, 15/9/1916

30. IWM DOCS: H. Chance, typescript memoir, *'Subaltern's Saga'*, pp14-15

31. R. R. Money, *'Flying and Soldiering'*, (London: Ivor Nicholson & Watson Limited, 1936) pp97-98

32. IWM DOCS: F. O. Cave, Manuscript diary, 15/9/1916

33. R. R. Money, *'Flying and Soldiering'*, (London: Ivor Nicholson & Watson Limited, 1936) p100

34. J. Werner, *'Knight of Germany: Oswald Boelcke German Ace'*, (London: John Hamilton Ltd, 1933) p209

35. R. R. Money, *'Flying and Soldiering'*, (London: Ivor Nicholson & Watson Limited, 1936) pp101-102

36. RAF MUSEUM: D. S. Grey, manuscript letter, 25/11/1916

37. J. Werner, *'Knight of Germany: Oswald Boelcke German Ace'*, (London: John Hamilton Ltd, 1933) pp211-212

38. R. R. Money, *'Flying and Soldiering'*, (London: Ivor Nicholson & Watson Limited, 1936) p102-103

39. M. von Richthofen, *'The Red Airfighter'*, (London: Greenhill Books, 1990), p93-94

40. R. R. Money, *'Flying and Soldiering'*, (London: Ivor Nicholson & Watson Limited, 1936) p102-103

41. R. R. Money, *'Flying and Soldiering'*, (London: Ivor Nicholson & Watson Limited, 1936) pp103-104

42. RAF MUSEUM: D. S. Grey, manuscript letter, 25/11/1916

43. J. Werner, *Knight of Germany: Oswald Boelcke German Ace'*, (London: John Hamilton Ltd, 1933) p212

44. IWM DOCS: H. Chance, typescript memoir, 'Subaltern's Saga', pp15-16

45. J. Werner, *'Knight of Germany: Oswald Boelcke German Ace'*, (London: John Hamilton Ltd, 1933) p213

46. J. Werner, *'Knight of Germany: Oswald Boelcke German Ace'*, (London: John Hamilton Ltd, 1933) p213

47. IWM DOCS: F. O. Cave, Manuscript diary, 22/9/1916

48. RAF Museum: A. Ball Combat Report, 21/9/1916

49. RAF Museum: A. Ball Combat Report, 23/9/1916

50. A. Ball, quoted in Chaz Bowyer, *'Albert Ball, VC'*, Bridge Books, Wrexham, 2nd edit, 1994, p91

51. RAF Museum: A. Ball Combat Report, 25/9/1916

52. J. Werner, *'Knight of Germany: Oswald Boelcke German Ace'*, (London: John Hamilton Ltd, 1933) pp213-214

53. J. Werner, *'Knight of Germany: Oswald Boelcke German Ace'*, (London: John Hamilton Ltd, 1933) p214

54. M. von Richthofen, *'The Red Baron'*, (Folkestone: Bailey Brothers & Swinfen Ltd, 1974), p52

55. G. H. Lewis, *'Wings over the Somme'*, (Wrexham: Bridge Books, 1994), p191

56. H. Trenchard quoted in H. A. Jones, *'Official History of the War: The War in the Air, Being the Story of the part played in the Great War by the Royal Air Force*, (Oxford: Clarendon Press, 1922-1937), Vol II', pp283-284.

57. H. Trenchard quoted in H. A. Jones, *'Official History of the War: The War in the Air, Being the Story of the part played in the Great War by the Royal Air Force*, (Oxford: Clarendon Press, 1922-1937), Vol II', p296-297

*190*

Chapter Seven

# October: Clinging on...

Whatever the tactical gains and theoretical advances made in the September attacks, one thing remained clear. The British were as far from a strategic breakthrough as ever. The Fourth Army had carried the original German Third Line system after three months of intensive fighting; but they now faced yet another trench system built by the Germans along the ridge stretching from Le Transloy to Thilloy, whilst two more trench systems were under construction stretching back towards Bapaume and beyond. The Reserve Army on top of Thiepval Ridge still faced multiple German trench lines, bolstered by the all too familiar fortified woods and villages. Yet, Haig was convinced that the German Army was ready to collapse. Intelligence reports had indicated problems of morale amongst the hard-pressed German infantry and Haig was determined to carry on the offensive. The decision having been taken, Rawlinson's Fourth Army continued to batter itself senseless against the German lines.

On 1 October, III Corps and the left hand Division of XV Corps were launched against the German lines at Eaucourt l'Abbaye. Above them flew the contact patrol observers of 3 and 34 Squadrons. They had a perfect view that simply and clearly illustrated the benefits for the infantry of sticking close to the creeping barrage - and the penalties of failing to do so.

At 3.15pm the steady bombardment changed into a most magnificent barrage. The timing of this was extremely good. Guns opened simultaneously and the effect was that of many machine guns opening fire on the same order. As seen from the air the barrage appeared to be a most perfect wall of fire in which it was inconceivable that anything could live. The first troops to extend from the forming up places appeared to be the 50th Division who were seen to spread out from the sap heads and forming up trenches and advance close up under the barrage, apparently some 50 yards away from it. They appeared to capture their objective very rapidly and with practically no losses while crossing the open. The 23rd Division I did not see so much of owing to their being at the moment of Zero, at the tail end of the machine. The 47th Division took more looking for than the 50th, and it was my impression at the time that they were having some difficulty in getting into formation for attack from their forming up places, with the result that they appeared to be very late and to be some distance behind the barrage when it lifted off the German front line at Eaucourt l'Abbaye, and immediately to the West of it. It was plain that here there was a good chance of failure and this actually came about, for the men had hardly advanced a couple of hundred yards apparently, when they were seen to fall and take cover among shell holes, being presumably held up by machine-gun and rifle fire. It was not possible to verify this owing to the extraordinary noise of the bursting shells of our barrage. The tanks were obviously too far behind, owing to lack of covered approaches, to be able to take part in the original attack, but they were soon seen advancing on either side of the Eaucourt l'Abbaye-Flers line, continuously in action and doing splendid work. They did not seem to be a target of much enemy shell fire. The enemy barrage appeared to open late, quite five minutes after the commencement of our own barrage and when it came it bore no resemblance to the wall of fire which we were putting up. I should have described it as a heavy shelling of an area some 300-400 yards in depth from our original jumping off places. Some large shells were falling in Destrémont Farm but these again were too late to catch the first line of attack, although they must have caused some losses to the supports. Thirty minutes after Zero the first English patrols were seen entering Le Sars. They appeared to be meeting with little or no opposition, and at this time no German shells were falling in the village. Our own shells were falling in the Northern half. To sum up: the most startling feature of the operations as viewed from the air was:

1) The extraordinary volume of fire of our barrage and the straight line kept by it.
2) The apparent ease with which the attack succeeded where troops were enabled to go forward close under it.
3) The promiscuous character and comparative lack of volume of enemy's counter-barrage.[1] *Major John Chamier, 34 Squadron, RFC*

It was at this moment, just as the German resistance finally seemed to be weakening, that the weather broke. The autumn weather deteriorated from mellow fruitfulness to cold rain and soon the battlefield had turned into a morass of mud.

*John Chamier.*
RAFM/RAeC 340

I have never seen such desolation. Mud, thin, deep and black, shell holes full of water, corpses all around in every stage of decomposition, some partially devoid of flesh, some swollen and black, some fresh, lying as if in slumber. One bolt upright, a landmark and guide, another bowed as if trying to touch his toes. Our trenches are little more than joined up shell

*By the autumn of 1916 the battlefields had become a morass of mud. A working party of British troops illustrate the conditions the men had to work in.* Q.1616

holes, mostly with 12 inches of water above 12 inches of mud . . . Several times this filthy slime has been well above my field boots and my legs and feet are, and have been for hours, completely wet and numbed with cold. In my own misery I feel intensely for the men who, with puttees only, are worse off than the officers. They are marvellous in their uncomplaining fortitude but I think I understand the secret. Contrary to what one might believe to be the case, I have found that the desire to live is strongest when the conditions of existence are most dangerous and depressing.[2]
*Lieutenant Alfred Bundy, 2nd Battalion, Middlesex Regiment*

In the air, the RFC lost one of their best pilots on the return of Captain Albert Ball to England. Towards the end of September, Ball had become aware that the risks he was taking in combat had moved from the intrepid, through rash, to the frankly suicidal. He had carried on fighting, but some of the sights he saw seem to have affected him deeply.

She was a two-seater and I fired five rounds into her. She burst into flames and fell upside down. Although she dropped like a stone, I saw her observer climb out of his seat and jump clear of the flames. He must have preferred that kind of death to the chance of being roasted.[3] *Captain Albert Ball, 60 Squadron, RFC*

He was tortured, at least to some extent, by the knowledge of the murderous nature of his trade.

I feel so sorry for the chaps I have killed. Just imagine what their poor people must feel like . . . However it must be done, or they would kill me.[4] *Captain Albert Ball, 60 Squadron, RFC*

His nerves were stretched ever tighter; he was exhausted and in short was suffering, not surprisingly, from combat fatigue. He therefore asked his Squadron Leader, Major Smith-Barry, if he could go home. This time, his request was treated with due respect and swiftly approved by higher command. His final flight on 1 October was as active as ever and resulted in three more claims. On his return he had some 31 victories by the standards then prevailing in the RFC. There is no doubt that whatever the actual total Albert Ball brought down, he was very much the genuine article – the first high scoring British 'ace'. At that stage in the war, the RFC did not accept the classification of 'ace' for pilots who had scored more than five victories. It was considered that the scout pilots were just doing their duty, as were all the Corps' pilots with equal, if not greater, chance of being killed and far less means of defending themselves. This was a rational response, but it could not last as the Great British public began to salivate over the emerging press reports of the young Nottingham lad and his dramatic feats of arms. Yet, Albert Ball never was, and never would be, the future of the RFC. His 'lone wolf' methods were already slightly outdated, as the concept of disciplined formations of scouts working together under the direction of experienced tacticians was already beginning to dominate aerial tactics. But logic has no place in hero worship. Ball reached a pinnacle of popular acclaim that, although slightly unfair to others in its exclusivity, he certainly deserved as a genuine hero. It was his personal example, not his tactics, which inspired a whole generation of RFC pilots throughout the war as the true benchmark of courage.

The next land attack was perforce postponed due to the prevailing bad weather. Observation was difficult, both on the ground and in the air; the mud interfered with the bringing up of shells; it was almost impossible to move the guns; and as they sank in the mud their accuracy declined radically. Brief breaks in the weather encouraged Haig and Rawlinson to order repeated assaults on 7, 12, 18, 23, 28 and 29 October. All failed abjectly and barely any gains were made. The infantry had to force their way through the mud in addition to all the other manifold dangers and difficulties of going 'over the top'.

The barrage started and crept forward. The men were rather slow in starting and so losing the advantage of the barrage. They only advanced 100 yards, after which they sat down in shell holes, while the barrage still crept back, leaving the Bosche in perfect comfort. We went to drop a message about this and then returned going down the line again, being greeted by machine-gun fire this time. Saw reinforcements going over, who also stopped in the shell holes . . . Gordon Kidd and Phillips were flying a Morane Parasol, I happened to be watching them at the moment a shell appeared to strike the wing amidships which immediately folded

SEE NEXT PAGE THIS CROSS MARKS THE SPOT (APPRO
HERE GORDON KIDD & PHILLIPS WERE KILLED
OBY FROM PHOTO TAKEN 3·11·16 et ABOUT 1000 FT
M 17 SEE TEXT.

BAPAUME
THILLOY
X
LIGNY THILLO
LE BARQUE
WHEAT TR
No MANS
LAND
MI7a
SUTTE de WARLENCOURT

up, the machine going into a spinning nose dive and continued in this manner until the ground was reached. It was a horrid sight. They must have been killed instantaneously. The barrage during this attack is the worst I have ever flown in. Flying in the thick of it at a thousand feet was terrifying, both beyond ourselves when we got back.[5] *Lieutenant E J D Routh, 34 Squadron, RFC*

With the infantry hamstrung by the mud and with the artillery not operating at full efficiency the British were effectively back to 'Square One'. But this was not the only reason for failure. The Germans had brought in fresh divisions, reinforced their artillery and adjusted their tactics on the ground to protect their machine-gunners from the creeping barrage by positioning them further back. The successful methods of September could not work when the weather had effectively neutralised the British artillery.

Of course the poor weather made it extremely difficult for the RFC to carry out its duties. Indeed, often it was just too wet and windy to fly at all.

We have had quite a lot of nice wet days lately, although it has usually cleared up a bit in the afternoon. It has been very windy too. I found I could make the machine go backwards if I wanted to. On one shoot I was doing it took me more than half an hour to get from the target to the ground station near the battery. It would have taken three minutes as a rule.[6] *Lieutenant Leslie Horridge, 7 Squadron, RFC*

During this period of rough weather, Horridge had a heaven sent opportunity to take his revenge on one of the staff officers who indirectly ruled their lives.

A staff colonel wanted to be taken up yesterday to have a look at the trenches. He was given maps and told what to look out for so as to find where he was. He was up for about an hour and a half. He was taken over the trench he wanted to see about three times and also was over a large town for about twenty minutes. He was so ill that when he came down he hadn't the faintest idea where he had been! I think it is very amusing. Anyhow it will increase his respect for the Flying Corps.[7] *Lieutenant Leslie Horridge, 7 Squadron, RFC*

When there were gaps in the weather the RFC continued its work undaunted day and night.

Crossed line at 11.55pm at Gueudecourt. A number of red lamps in Le Transloy at about N.30b.7.8 Followed road from Bapaume to Cambrai. Reached Cambrai at 12.20am. Had a good look at Cambrai and found a train with steam up in station on East side of the town. At 12.25am dropped three 20lb Hales HE on train. A beauty. Hit train just behind engine. All lights immediately went out and AA guns and searchlights became very active. We hovered about for a few minutes and then dropped remaining three bombs on railway line which is on the West of the station running parallel. The AA fire was hellish. A strong searchlight played on us from Sailly on the Northern side of the Cambrai-Arras road, so we dived on him and I gave him a drum of the best. The searchlight then went out and another one got on us. We then returned and AA fire kept on us for a long time. We then got away from the searchlights although a number tried to pick us up. Over Hermies at 12.45am a strong searchlight was looking for us so I opened fire on him. The drum was of tracers accidentally and gave our position away. AA fire and searchlights followed us until 1am when we re-crossed the line at Morval at 3,000 feet. Beautiful night and observation good.[8] *Captain Joseph Callaghan, 18 Squadron, RFC*

The Germans also began to indulge in night bombing and it was soon realized that precautions had to be taken to prevent the RFC landing fields becoming easy targets.

During night flying operations we were particularly vulnerable as our position was disclosed by having to use petrol flares for getting off and landing and we had to take special precautions. The flare party of five men, each with his tin of petrol, old rag and a sousing blanket, stood by to light up when ordered by Sergeant Major Patterson who knew that the aircraft were ready to take off and to extinguish immediately the aircraft had gone. On return each aircraft had to fire the Verey pistol signal for the night, then Patterson would shout the order to light up. When the machine had perched, the flares would again be immediately extinguished. It was not long before the Germans grasped our plan, looked out for our recognition signal for the night and copied it. As soon as we lit up, down came a shower of bombs. Only one night, however, did bombs actually straddle our positions, and then fortunately, without causing any casualties or damage to aircraft. To counter this we created a dummy aerodrome with canvas sheeting to simulate sheds during daytime and lit flares there at night. On one occasion this drew a low attack of machine gun fire sweeping up and down the dummy, empty aerodrome.[9] *Major George Carmichael, 18 Squadron, RFC*

Major Hawker was still breaking the rules by undertaking regular combat patrols, as and when, he felt like it. On 10 October, 24 Squadron had plenty of action.

As the Offensive Patrol reached Beaulencourt Andrews dived, so followed and saw HA doing contact patrol over Eaucourt. Dived inside him to cut him off and gave him a drum from 75-100 yards as he crossed, chased by Andrews. Changed drums and gave him a second at 2,000 feet over Bapaume but at too great a range. Returning climbed above the patrol and saw HA diving on an FE. The FE dived straight and I could not get within range, but chased him towards Bapaume and gave him a drum at about 150 yards. Patrol followed Andrews back to Albert and I was left alone on the lines for some time. Picked up Kelly and dived on a Hun over Rocquigny firing half a drum at 100 yards but he walked away from me. Saw two DHs flying from Suzanne to Albert so flew in and picked them up and went back beyond the Bapaume-Peronne road. A Nieuport type HA came overhead without seeing us, so turning I raised the mounting and fired a few ineffectual shots as the mounting was very wobbly – this finished my ammunition. Saw Nieuport type HA dive on a DH's tail, and dived after it, but the DH went down too quickly for me to catch up, the HA however dived East. Andrews rejoined the patrol so followed him. Some roughhouse with several Nieuport type HA, dived on three or four, frightened them off DH's tails but could not do much without ammunition. The HA all retired East and climbed and probably came back as soon as DHs left the lines.[10] *Major Lanoe Hawker, 24 Squadron, RFC*

It was apparent that Lanoe Hawker, in common with Albert Ball, did not let a mere triviality like running out of ammunition stop him from continuing to actively engage in a dogfight.

Young and inexperienced pilots were still arriving at the front on a daily basis. There was no easy way to introduce them to the realities of aerial conflict over the Western Front. Even familiarization flights on the British side of the line posed a considerable risk, for a small navigational mistake could send a disorientated pilot miles over the

German lines in a matter of minutes.

I was sent out to get my bearings and got lost in the clouds over the German trenches. The worst of all was the engine wouldn't climb – we were then at 2,000 feet. Then something happened and we nose dived to within a few feet of the ground and had to come down. How it was we never got properly done in I can't tell as we appear to have been over the German trenches the whole time and the shelling was terrific. I should think we had about 300 at us besides the rifle fire. They were bursting absolutely all round, above and below us. We never had a chance to look at the machine properly but the petrol tank was pierced in two places – there must have been more damage as we felt ourselves chucked into the air several times and I can tell you I was pretty busy dodging 'Archie'. Had the engine been good I think we could have got off all right. The clouds were at 1,000 feet and we could not even reach them again. You can imagine our disappointment when we found ourselves down

*Caspar Kennard.* RAFM B9

on the wrong side of the lines. You can imagine how we feel – it was my first flight to the lines and to have to come down without even having had a decent scrap for it.[11] *Second Lieutenant Caspar Kennard, 16 Squadron, RFC*

The corps machines undertaking artillery reconnaissance and photographic observation were finding that the German scouts were increasingly making their presence felt over the key areas. They too, knew that the archaic BE2 Cs plying their trade up and down the battlefield, were doing more to harm the German cause than any scout pilot ever could. On 20 October, Second Lieutenant Cotton was acting as observer when the German scouts pounced.

The five HA turned and dived upon us, two of the machines opening fire at about 500 yards. I did not reply until they were within 150 yards and opened fire on the leading machine who immediately turned North on a steep bank. Then I emptied about 25 rounds into him and immediately emptied the remainder of the drum into the second machine which had turned South. The first machine made a steep nose-dive for about 1,000 feet and then glided down apparently under control to the ground.[12] *Second Lieutenant William Cotton, 7 Squadron, RFC*

On 21 October, Lieutenant Bell-Irving flying a Nieuport 17 of 60 Squadron, was escorting a number of FE2 Bs and BE2 Cs when German scouts approached. He immediately turned to face them.

After firing about 8 rounds my gun stopped and I was temporarily unable to rectify it. I turned West, and climbed, trying to put the gun right and reach another Nieuport which was higher and further West. The Hostile Aircraft (HA) turned and out-climbed me so I put my nose down to get over the lines. A bullet then hit my tank and I stopped up one of the holes with my hand, having to leave the gun. The HA shot away a flying wire and damaged my planes on the right side so that my machine became uncontrollable. After falling for some distance, I regained partial control with my engine off and full rudder and aileron. I glided across the lines without directional control at about 100 feet, landing between the front and support lines. I jumped clear as the machine ran into a trench and turned over.[13] *Lieutenant Alan Bell-Irving, 60 Squadron, RFC*

It was clear that even the best available RFC scout, the Nieuport 17, was demonstrably slower and could also be out-climbed by the Albatross DI and DII scouts. This was a serious situation. The German aircraft were also hampered by the weather, but their newfound sense of purpose was symbolized by the formal creation of the German Air Force on 8 October. The German aviators were once again taking heart, cheered by the arrival of the new scouts and the inspirational successes of Boelcke and his Jasta 2. As the Verdun operations at last diminished in scale, the German aircraft there were redeployed to the Somme and soon they had some 333 aircraft at their disposal. The RFC had lost both their qualitative and numerical advantage, for they deployed in total just 328 aircraft – a rough equality of numbers. The British reinforcements that arrived offered nothing new and some of the replacement aircraft were obviously useless. Thus, the ill-fated BE12 scout was completely withdrawn from the fray after only the briefest exposure to the grim reality of the aerial combat zone. Although some flights of 19 Squadron were already re-equipped, the flight led by Captain Tidswell had to make just a few more bombing raids. On 16 October, they took off again and Tidswell's luck finally ran out after having undertaken more flights over the German lines than anyone left serving in his Squadron.

All the machines of the formation that your son was leading became engaged over the Bois d'Havrincourt at 4pm, October 16th. There was a strong northerly wind blowing, and the fight drifted South. The formation was broken up and none of the other pilots saw what happened to Captain Tidswell. Lieutenant C G Baker, who is now at home, reported that he saw Captain Tidswell dive on a Hun, and that he attacked and drove off another Hun machine which was following Captain Tidswell, but did not see what happened after. Our returning machines crossed the lines near Peronne, and the general opinion at the time was that your son must have landed South or South West of Bois d'Havrincourt, and at least eight miles behind the German lines.[14] *Lieutenant C E*

As was usual, his Squadron Leader wrote the formal letter of notification to Tidswell's family.

> I regret to inform you that your son, Captain C. R. Tidswell has not returned from a flight over the enemy's lines on the 16th. I have waited two days because it is difficult to make certain for a short time whether a pilot has not had a forced landing a long way off. Your son was the leader of a bomb raid about seven miles over the lines. He was seen to have dropped his bombs and had turned to come back when some hostile machines were encountered. These were driven off after a short combat and the last that was seen of the leader was when he was gliding down apparently to attack a Hun, but quite as possibly from engine failure. No-one saw him attacked or hit by anti-aircraft, and it seems likely that he must be a prisoner. We all feel his loss and I particularly heavily, because he was the Senior Flight Commander and my right hand man; he was a great asset to the Squadron and to the Mess and in another month he would probably have been promoted to Squadron Commander. Your son left instruction about the disposal of his letters and kit; these are being carried out and his personal belongings will be forwarded to you in due course. Please accept my sympathy in your loss which I believe to be only temporary.[15] *Major Reginald Rodwell, 19 Squadron, RFC*

*William Read.* IWM HU 64547

It was not to be however, for Tidswell had been killed.

Against this background of heavy losses, Trenchard made every effort to rush in more reinforcements to the Somme. One unit selected was 45 Squadron, under the command of Major William Read and equipped with Sopwith 1½ Strutters. Unfortunately, many of his crews were not properly trained or, to say the very least, inexperienced. The consequences became painfully apparent on 22 October. The day started badly when they suffered their first casualty on the morning patrol.

Griffith with Surgey got mixed up in a brawl with five Huns. Surgey behaved very well. He was shot in the stomach early in the fight but brought down one Hun. Their machine was shot about badly and although badly hit too he kept the Huns off with his gun and then turned his attention to stopping the flow of petrol from a bullet hole in the tank. They landed safely.[16] *Major William Read, 45 Squadron, RFC*

Orders had to be obeyed, so Read sent off another offensive patrol at 10.15.

Mountford returned early but Porter with Samuels, Wade with Thuell and Sergeant Snowden with Fullerton have not returned and I'm afraid they have been brought down on the other side. Porter was a very good Flight Commander, very efficient. A hot headed Irishman with very pronounced views, but very sound and his Flight was the best run of the three. Wade was very keen and I do not think he knew what fear meant. They would have been a hot pair to tackle. Sergeant Snowden was not a good pilot and had not a great amount of confidence. His Observer Fullerton was the best observer I had. A sad day's work.[17] *Major William Read, 45 Squadron, RFC*

They were all dead. Porter, Wade and the hapless Snowden had run into

*45 Squadron.* IWM HU 62452

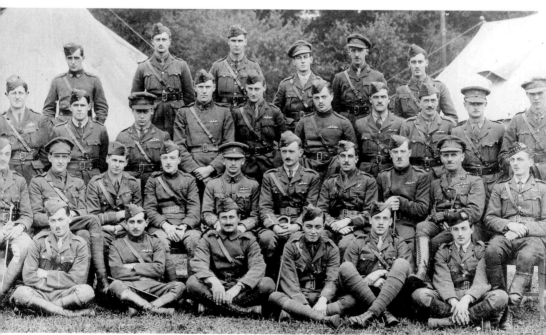

Boelcke's Jasta. Boelcke himself dealt with Captain Porter.

> Flying with several gentlemen of my Staffel, I cut off two enemy biplanes on their way from the East, meeting them South of Bapaume. Both were brought down. The machine I attacked broke to pieces under my machine gun fire and went down in flames.[18]
>
> *Captain Oswald Boelcke, Jasta 2, German Air Force*

On the same day, while escorting a photographic reconnaissance aircraft over Bapaume, Lieutenant F L Barnard and his observer Lieutenant F S Rankin became involved in a series of desperate running fights. The dangers faced by an observer standing up in the exposed front cockpit of the FE2 B were never more clearly demonstrated.

> When these had been driven off we turned for home but found three more HA on our tail. The observer put one drum into one which was passing straight over our heads at very close range and this machine immediately became out of control, the tail and back of the fuselage being on fire. It went down in a spin. The remaining two HA were now firing from behind and the observer stood up to get a shot at them, one more HA was seen to go down in a nose-dive with smoke from its engine. The observer was still firing when he was hit in the head and fell sideways over the side of the nacelle. I managed to catch his coat as he was falling and by getting on the front seat pulled him back. I then got back in the pilot's seat. The engine and most of the controls had been shot but I managed to get the machine over our lines and landed 200 yards behind our front line.[19]
>
> *Lieutenant F L Barnard, 18 Squadron, RFC*

Not surprisingly, this terrifying incident had a marked effect on Barnard, but fortunately his commanding officer took an understanding approach.

*George Carmichael.* RAFM

> Lieutenant F L Barnard was in combat when his observer, Lieutenant F S Rankin who was standing up to fire back over the top plane was hit and would have fallen out had not Barnard seized his coat and dragged him into the cockpit. He actually held him there until with almost superhuman strength and skill he brought his machine to our landing area. The observer, Rankin, unfortunately did not survive. Lieutenant Barnard was so affected by his experience that I had to arrange for his posting home, and his nerves were so badly affected that I do not think he was able to return to the Western Front.[20] *Major George Carmichael, 18 Squadron, RFC*

Yet, for all their problems and casualties on 22 October, there was another side to the day's actions. The RFC had stuck to their task and continued to perform the various roles for which the infantry were dependent upon them.

> I dropped two bombs on Star Wood and fired the machine gun into their trenches. The whole time was one mass of spurts of flame so insistent was our bombardment. The air was literally swarming with our machines – there must have been a 100 to every mile of trench. In one place there was 17 Observation Balloons.[21] *Flight Sergeant Shepherd, 5 Squadron, RFC*

The weather closed in again, which was rather a mixed blessing. Every day without their eyes in the sky was a disaster for the British attacks against the Transloy Ridge. On the other hand, it did provide a bit of a break for the hard-pressed pilots and they would not have been human if they did not welcome the rain.

> Here we are again. It is another wet day and of course we stop in doors all day. Being out here makes you very selfish. It is always a relief when it is raining, although it is not much fun for the infantry and it also stops active operations.[22] *Lieutenant Leslie Horridge, 7 Squadron, RFC*

Major Read took the chance to try and assess what was left of his squadron. Sadly, he found that the overall standard of flying in his squadron was extremely poor.

> A day of rain and no flying – except in the afternoon when some of my pilots flew round the aerodrome. That shocking pilot Flight Sergeant Webb crashed another machine and Gomes broke a propeller getting off the ground. Some of my pilots are cruel bad. Flight Sergeant Webb, Gomes, Rodwell and Sergeant Malcolm are awful. Have put in an application today to get rid of them. They also lack ginger.[23] *Major William Read, 45 Squadron, RFC*

In fact, some of the more inadequate pilots in his squadron went sick, some gave up flying and the others struggled as best they could. Soon Read's squadron was reduced to just five or six effective aircraft and crews. In circumstances like these, Trenchard could not afford to indulge in inter-service rivalries. In desperation, he requested assistance from the Royal Naval Air Service. To the eternal credit of the RNAS their response was immediate.

> The Admiralty have decided, on the urgent representation of the Army Council, to detach at once a Squadron of 18 Fighting Aeroplanes from the Dunkirk command for temporary duty with the British Expeditionary Force.[24]

Taking a flight from each of the Dunkirk wings, the RNAS formed 8 Squadron flying a mixture of Sopwith Pups, Nieuports and Sopwith 1½ Strutters. On 26 October, the composite squadron moved down to Vert Gallant airfield where they were attached to the 5th Brigade, RFC.

Despite this appearance of harmony, inter-service rivalry and jealousies had not been entirely dissipated, as Trenchard and Baring found when they paid an inspection visit next day.

> We went to the Naval Squadron which is now attached to us, and which is on the same aerodrome as No. 32. They said they would like the oil used by No. 32 for machine guns. It was better than their own naval oil. We then went on to No. 32. They asked if they might have the naval oil, which they said was better than their own military oil. When the matter was investigated later there was found to be not the slightest difference between the naval and the military oil.[25] *Captain Maurice Baring, Headquarters, RFC*

One of the Naval Flight Commanders, Captain Roy Mackenzie, showed an intuitive grasp of the essence of successful combat techniques.

> He told us that when we were having a fight with another aeroplane we must bear in mind that there were two very frightened men in the picture, but the other man was the more frightened of the two. What excellent advice! For surely, if one could truly believe this, a battle was half won before the start.[26] *Captain Robert Compston, 8 Squadron, RNAS*

The 'Naval Eight' Squadron would settle in for a week before entering the fray in early November, when they provided a welcome addition to the depleted RFC scout squadrons.

But, even in the midst of the late October clouds, there was one silver lining for the hard-pressed British. On 28 October, Boelcke and his Jasta took off during a gap in the stormy weather. Soon they clashed with their opposite numbers of 24 Squadron.

> I had just begun a game of chess with Boelcke – then, about 4.30pm, we were called to the front because there was an infantry attack going on. We soon attacked some English machines we found flying over Flers; they were fast single-seaters that defended themselves well. In the ensuing wild battle of turns, that only let us get a few shots in for brief intervals, we tried to force the English down, by one after another of us barring their way, a manoeuvre we had often practised successfully.[27] *Lieutenant Erwin Böhme, Jasta 2, German Air Force*

Richthofen was also closely involved in the fight.

> We were six against their two. If they had been twenty we would not have been surprised to receive the signal of attack from Boelcke. The usual battle began. Boelcke went after one and I the other. Close to Boelcke flew a good friend of his. It was an interesting fight. Both fired and at any moment the Englishmen had to fall.[28] *Lieutenant Manfred von Richthofen, Jasta 2, German Air Force*

*A G Knight.* RAFM/RAeC 2063

Later Major Hawker, who was not there, compiled a report detailing the fight as seen by his pilots.

Lt Knight was at 8,000 feet and Lt McKay, who had been delayed by engine trouble, was about 1,500 feet lower down. Six HA fast scouts appeared at about 10,000 feet over Pozières. They hesitated about five minutes before they attacked. One then did a side-slipping dive under the top DH, but Lt Knight did not attack as he was suspicious of this manoeuvre. The HA then all dived at Lt Knight, who promptly spiralled to avoid their fire. During the fight, six other scouts joined in, making a total of twelve against two DHs, and some went down and attacked Lt McKay. The HA dived in turn on to the DH's tail, but the DH promptly turned sharply under the HA, which usually switched on and climbed again. The DHs were very careful to avoid diving straight at any HA that presented tempting targets, but fired short bursts as HA came on their sights.[29] *Major Lanoe Hawker, 24 Squadron, RFC*

As the scouts twisted and turned, trying to get into the ideal shooting position behind their opponents, manoeuvres were conceived and carried out by instinct, relying on split second reactions and a preternatural sense of awareness of where the other combatants were in this aerial three dimensional chess.

Boelcke and I had just got one Englishman between us when another opponent, chased by friend Richthofen, cut across us. Quick as lightning, Boelcke and I both dodged him, but for a moment our wings prevented us from seeing anything of one another – and that was the cause of it. How am I to describe my sensations from the moment when Boelcke suddenly loomed up a few metres away on my right! He put his machine down and I pulled mine up.[30] *Lieutenant Erwin Böhme, Jasta 2, German Air Force*

Then it happened, a trifling glancing blow, but the consequences were significant.

Suddenly I noticed an unnatural movement of the two German

*The last photograph of Boelcke.*

*Boelcke takes off on his last flight.*

flying machines. Immediately I thought, "Collision!" I had not yet seen a collision in the air. I had imagined it would look quite different. In reality, what happened was not a collision. The two machines merely touched one another. However, if two machines go at the tremendous pace of flying machines, the slightest contact has the effect of a violent concussion.[31] *Lieutenant Manfred von Richthofen, Jasta 2, German Air Force*

From their own hard pressed and distinctly unsympathetic perspective, the British pilots looked on before more pressing matters required their undivided attention.

It was after about five minutes strenuous fighting, that two HA collided. One dived at Lt Knight, who turned left handed. The HA zoomed right handed and its left wing collided with the right wing of another HA, which had started to dive on Lt Knight. Bits were seen to fall off; only one HA was seen to go down and it glided away East, apparently under control, but was very shortly lost to sight, as the DHs were too heavily engaged to watch it.[32] *Major Lanoe Hawker, 24 Squadron, RFC*

After the impact, both pilots fell earthwards.

It was only the faintest touch, but the terrific speed at which we were going made it into a violent impact. Destiny is generally cruelly stupid in her choices; I only had a bit of my undercarriage ripped, but the extreme tip of his left wing was torn away. After falling a couple hundred metres I regained control of my machine and was then able to observe Boelcke's, which I saw heading for our lines in a gentle glide, but dipping a bit on one side. But when he came into a layer of clouds in the lower regions, his machine dipped more and more, owing to the violent gusts there.[33] *Lieutenant Erwin Böhme, Jasta 2, German Air Force*

Gazing down at the falling master, his protégées prayed that the Albatross would hang together just a few more moments until Boelcke could execute an emergency landing. All could still be well.

Boelcke drew away from his victim and descended in large curves. I had not the feeling that he was falling, but when I saw him descending below me I noticed that part of his planes had broken off. I could not see what was happening afterwards, but in the clouds he lost an entire plane. Now his machine was no longer controllable. It fell accompanied all the time by Boelcke's faithful friend.[34] *Lieutenant Manfred von Richthofen, Jasta 2, German Air Force*

There was nothing Böhme could do.

I had to look on while he failed to flatten out to land and crashed near a battery position. Men came running to the rescue

from the battery's dugout. My attempt to land close to my friend
was impossible on account of the trenches and shell holes there.[35]
*Lieutenant Erwin Böhme, Jasta 2, German Air Force*

Böhme was beside himself in anguish and noticed nothing of his
surroundings. He could himself have been killed, as he made a careless
landing on his weakened undercarriage.

I flew quickly to our aerodrome. They did not tell me till the
following day that my machine turned over on landing – I certainly
knew nothing about it when it happened. I was absolutely
distracted, but still cherished hopes. But when we arrived at the
scene of the accident in a car, they brought the body along to us.
He must have been killed outright at the moment of the crash.
Boelcke never wore a crash helmet and never strapped himself in
tight in an Albatross – otherwise he might have survived the
crash, which was not too bad a one.[36] *Lieutenant Erwin Böhme, Jasta
2, German Air Force*

Jasta 2 was stunned by the news. Boelcke had been their mentor; a
stern task-master, but a true hero figure to his men. Böhme, of course,
felt a particular anguish, although it was clear the accident was
unavoidable in the chaotic circumstances of the dogfight.

I have now regained a superficial control of myself. But in the
silent hours my eyes see once again that ghastly moment when I
had to watch my friend and master fall from beside me. Then the

*Boelcke's Funeral.*

*The funeral service in Cambrai Cathedral.*

torturing question comes up once more: why was he, the irreplaceable, doomed to be the victim of this blind destiny?[37] *Lieutenant Erwin Böhme, Jasta 2, German Air Force*

The funeral was a miserable affair. The RFC recognised the death of their scourge with a chivalrous gesture. Lieutenant Thomas Green of 3 Squadron risked his life to drop a wreath over the German lines.

A further floral tribute was sent by the British

TO THE MEMORY OF CAPTAIN BOELKE, OUR BRAVE AND CHIVALROUS OPPONENT.

FROM, THE ENGLISH ROYAL FLYING CORPS.

RFC pilots languishing in the Osnabruck POW Camp – including Captain Robert Wilson who had been Boelcke's twentieth victim.

* * * *

With one less fearsome enemy to worry about, the work of the RFC went on as before. Endless photographic reconnaissance missions, relentless never-ending artillery observation duties. Whenever the weather broke for long enough to allow the Corps' machines to get aloft, then off they would go.

> Got up at five to do my first shoot with Sergeant Lawford. I had to range a battery of 9.2" Howitzers. The call letter being 'K'. The clouds were very big and a strong wind was blowing (50mph). We started at 7.00am and got to 1,000 ft and I had just finished ringing up the aerodrome when the engine cut out and we had to make a forced landing and just got into the aerodrome. We were at one time just before we landed, travelling at 100mph about 50ft up and goodness knows how we came down safely. This was one of the nearest goes I have ever had to having a complete smash up.[38] *Flight Sergeant Shepherd, 5 Squadron, RFC*

The endurance of some of the pilots who had been in almost continuous action for six months had been severely tested. But, for the most part, they bore their trials and tribulations with courage and fortitude.

> The old Hun has been rather more active lately, but I expect he will be squashed again before long. He breaks out periodically, especially if the Kaiser has been stirring him up, but he is usually put in his proper place before long.[39] *Lieutenant Leslie Horridge, 7 Squadron, RFC*

So they worked on, getting ready for one last effort. The baton of the offensive was finally passed from the exhausted Fourth Army to the Reserve Army, (now renamed Fifth Army) which was getting ready to launch an attack on Beaumont Hamel.

> There is going to be a very big push in a few days. Bigger than July 1st. It will be North of the Ancre and South. We hope to get Miraumont, Grandcourt, Pys and some say Achiet-le-Petit. There is a possibility of the cavalry getting through.[40] *Lieutenant Francis Cave, 4 Squadron, RFC*

Truly hope sprang eternal to the youthful breast!

1. H. A. Jones & W. Raleigh, *'The War in the Air'*, 6 Vols., (Oxford: Clarendon Press, 1922-1937), Vol. II, pp298-299
2. IWM DOCS: A. Bundy, Diary, 19/10/1916 & 24/10/1916

3. A. Ball, quoted in Chaz Bowyer, *'Albert Ball, VC'*, (Bridge Books, Wrexham, 2nd edit, 1994), p93

4. A. Ball, quoted in R. H. Kiernan, *'Captain Albert Ball, VC, DSO'*, (London: The Aviation Book Club, 1939), p121

5. IWM DOCS: E. J. D. Routh, Manuscript diary, 15/9/1916

6. IWM DOCS: L. Horridge, Manuscript letter, 8/10/1916

7. IWM DOCS: L. Horridge, Manuscript letter, 8/10/1916

8. RAF MUSEUM: J. C. Callaghan, Manuscript Log Book, 9/10/1916

9. RAF MUSEUM: G. I. Carmichael, Typescript memoir, p154-155

10. T. M. Hawker, *'Hawker V.C.'*, (London: The Mitre Press,1965), pp215-216

11. IWM DOCS: C. Kennard, Manuscript letter, 12/10/1916

12. W. M. V. Cotton quoted in S. F. Wise, *'Canadian Airmen and the First World War: The Official History of the Royal Canadian Air Force Volume I'*, (Toronto: University of Toronto Press), pp385-386

13. A. D. Bell-Irving quoted in S. F. Wise, *'Canadian Airmen and the First World War: The Official History of the Royal Canadian Air Force Volume I'*, (Toronto: University of Toronto Press), p389

14. C. E Morgan quoted in C. R. Tidswell, 'Letters from Cecil Robert Tidswell', (Privately published), p38

15. R. M. Rodwell quoted in C. R. Tidswell, 'Letters from Cecil Robert Tidswell', (Privately published), p37

16. IWM DOCS: W. R. Read, Manuscript diary, 22/10/1916

17. IWM DOCS: W. R. Read, Manuscript diary, 22/10/1916

18. J. Werner, *'Knight of Germany: Oswald Boelcke German Ace'*, (London: John Hamilton Ltd, 1933) p225

19. F. L. Barnard quoted in S. F. Wise, *'Canadian Airmen and the First World War: The Official History of the Royal Canadian Air Force Volume I'*, (Toronto: University of Toronto Press), p388

20. RAF MUSEUM: G. I. Carmichael, Typescript memoir, p153

21. RAF MUSEUM: Flight Sergeant Shepherd, Manuscript Diary, 22/10/1916

22. IWM DOCS: L. Horridge, Manuscript letter, 29/10/1916

23. IWM DOCS: W. R. Read, Manuscript diary, 24/10/1916

24. Various, *'Naval Eight: A history of No. 8 Squadron, RNAS'*, (London: The Signal Press, 1931). p.5

25. M. Baring, *'Flying Corps Headquarters, 1914-1918'*, (Whitstable: Blackwood, 1968), p189

26. Various, *'Naval Eight: 'A history of No. 8 Squadron, RNAS'*, (London: The Signal Press, 1931). pp76-77

27. J. Werner, *'Knight of Germany: Oswald Boelcke German Ace'*, (London: John Hamilton Ltd, 1933), pp228-229

28. M. von Richthofen, *'The Red Baron: Translated by Peter Kilduff'*, (Folkestone: Bailey Brothers & Swinfen Ltd, 1974), p53

29. IWM DOCS: L. Hawker, Combat report, 28/10/1916

30. J. Werner, *'Knight of Germany: Oswald Boelcke German Ace'*, (London: John Hamilton Ltd, 1933), p229

31. M. von Richthofen, *'The Red Airfighter'*, (London: Greenhill Books, 1990), pp96-97

32. IWM DOCS: L.Hawker, Combat report, 28/10/1916

33. J. Werner, *'Knight of Germany: Oswald Boelcke German Ace'*, (London: John Hamilton Ltd, 1933), p229

34. M. von Richthofen, *'The Red Airfighter'*, (London: Greenhill Books, 1990), p97

35. J. Werner, *'Knight of Germany: Oswald Boelcke German Ace'*, (London: John Hamilton Ltd, 1933), p229

36. J. Werner, *'Knight of Germany: Oswald Boelcke German Ace'*, (London: John Hamilton Ltd, 1933) pp229-230

37. J. Werner, *'Knight of Germany: Oswald Boelcke German Ace'*, (London: John Hamilton Ltd, 1933) pp230-231

38. RAF MUSEUM: Flight Sergeant Shepherd, Manuscript Diary, 30/10/1916

39. IWM DOCS: L. Horridge, Manuscript letter, 29/10/1916

40. IWM DOCS F. O. Cave, Manuscript diary, 30/10/1916

# Chapter Eight

# November: Full Circle

By November, the state of the war in the air over the Somme was clearly defined. The arrival of German reinforcements; the reorganisation and refocusing of the German Air Force; the fighting legacy of Boelcke bequeathed to the young pilots of Jasta 2; but most of all the swing of the technological pendulum – they had all combined to leave the RFC in a position of marked inferiority. It was obvious that the DH2s had had their day. The use of pusher aircraft to overcome the lack of an effective machine gun synchronisation mechanism had been a successful stratagem, but now more powerful and faster tractor aircraft were dominating the skies.

I know I felt very uncomfortable with two HA well above me, and in spite of the fact that I climbed to about 13,500 they were still above, which is very demoralising. We shall have to bring out some very fine machines next year if we are to keep up with them. Their scouts are very much better than ours now on average . . . the good old days of July and August, when two or three DH2s used to push half a dozen Huns onto the chimney tops of Bapaume, are no more. In the Roland they possessed the finest two-seater machine in the world, and now they have introduced a

*Albatross DII.* IWM Q 54406

few of their single-seater ideas, and very good they are too, one specimen especially deserves mention. They are manned by jolly good pilots, probably the best, and the juggling they can do when they are scrapping is quite remarkable. They can fly round and round a DH2 and made one look quite silly.[1] *Second Lieutenant Gwilym Lewis, 32 Squadron, RFC*

Lieutenant Francis Cave had been showing signs of stress in mid-summer, and this increased, as he witnessed many less fortunate pilots perish. On 1 November, he was on an artillery observation patrol with his regular observer Lieutenant Duke when he saw another machine go down.

We were just calling up 80th Siege when we saw a Hun chasing a BE2 C right down to the ground. It crashed near Courcelette before we could get up, but we fired at the Hun as he went off; but he got so low that we had to zoom over some trees near Miraumont. The BE2 C belonged to No. 7 Squadron, the pilot had shell shock and the observer was wounded.[2] *Lieutenant Francis Cave, 4 Squadron, RFC*

The pilot was Second Lieutenant Percival and the Observer Air Mechanic Brindle.

One obvious tactic to try and bypass the German superiority was to

*Group of Pilots; Vert Galand, 1916. Behind them is a DH2.*

increase the night bombing of the lairs of the Albatrosses – to get them on the ground where they were helpless.

Crossed the line at Le Sars at 8.50pm at 4,500 feet. Velu at 9.00pm. No activity at Velu but could see conspicuous lights on the ground in a northerly direction. So went to see what they were. They were at Villers Lez Cagnicourt. There were three lights on the ground – two white ones and one red one. The two white ones were about 50 yards apart and the red one formed the apex of an isosceles triangle and were about 200 yards distant from the white lights. The red light pointed into the wind. Green and white Verey lights were being fired into the air at long intervals. We had a good look at the place and could see hangars on the Western side of the flares. The position of this aerodrome is (51B) V.4b 4.c (centre of the landing ground). At 9.15pm from 5,000 feet dropped 3 Hales 20 lb HE bombs. The first two burst about 200 yards South of the hangars and the other two were about 100 yards South of the hangars. All lights were immediately put out and as we hovered over the aerodrome to drop our remaining bombs a machine was wheeled out of a hangar and took off into the wind. We followed him and by keeping our nose down kept him in sight. We were getting quite close to him (we were at 4,000 feet and he was about 1,500 feet) when he turned sharply and we turned to get on top of him. He was drawing away from us so I opened fire on him and gave him a drum. He then went out of sight and we followed in his direction. As we came over the aerodrome again we dropped our remaining three bombs – two burst on the aerodrome and the third one hit a hangar. No fire was caused. We hovered round but could not see the hostile machine.[3] *Captain Joseph Callaghan, 18 Squadron, RFC*

*ord Lucas.* RAFM/RAeC 1747

Yet the flow of casualties could not be staunched. In early November, the RFC suffered a significant loss. Captain Lord Auberon Lucas, the Flight Commander of B Flight, 22 Squadron, had an enormous personal hinterland in comparison with most of the young pilots in the RFC. Already aged 40, he had rowed for Oxford and acted as war correspondent for *The Times* during the Boer War, where he had the misfortune to lose his leg. This inconvenient mishap did not however stop him, for he continued to ride in steeplechases and indeed joined the Hampshire Yeomanry. In 1908, his political career took off when he joined the Liberal Government, where he served in various capacities as an Under Secretary, before joining the Cabinet as President of the Board of Agriculture in 1914. Even such a political animal as Winston Churchill, was impressed by the power of his vivacious personality.

To know him was to delight in him. His open, gay, responsive nature, his witty, ironical, but never unchivalrous tongue, his pleasing presence, his compulsive smile, made him much courted by his friends . . . Young for the Cabinet, heir to splendid possessions, happy in all that surrounded him, he seemed to have captivated Fortune with the rest.[4] *Winston Churchill, First Lord of the Admiralty*

Lucas had played a constructive role early in the war in the deliberations of the munitions committee, but could not resist the lure of active service. On the formation of the coalition government in May 1915, he retired from politics to enlist and train as a pilot with the Royal Flying Corps. He may have been young for the Cabinet but he was an old man in the officers' mess. Offered command of a squadron he refused until he had had active combat experience as a Flight Commander on the Western Front. At last he was posted out to join 22 Squadron.

He had an artificial leg and had to use a pair of steps to get into the nacelle of his FE2 B. I remember his tall figure mounting the steps one at a time.[5] *Flight Sergeant H Stoddart, 22 Squadron, RFC*

Lord Lucas was a personal friend of Maurice Baring.

On October 30th, 1916, I went to Bertangles and saw Bron Lucas. We walked across the Aerodrome to Hawker's Mess. It had poured with rain all day, but in the evening the clouds lifted over the horizon, leaving a low gold wrack, against which the sheds stood out black. Above there was a great tumult of clouds drifting and streaming and reflecting the light below, with here and there a rift. I said to Bron that it was like one of my pictures. He laughed and said, "Yes". I wondered what it meant.[6] *Captain Maurice Baring. Headquarters, RFC*

Perhaps Baring suspected that Auberon Lucas was not always so chivalrous with that ironic tongue of his! Lucas was delighted to throw himself into the thick of the fray – to test himself in the new battleground in the sky.

He was an undergraduate once more and an active soldier, as active, as athletic in the air as he had ever been on the ground. His youth had been given back to him with interest, and for his disabilities he had received a glorious compensation. Apart from the work and his keenness and whole-hearted interest in the war, in his Squadron, in his mechanics, and in his machine, he enjoyed himself with all the great gift of enjoyment and fund of gaiety with which he had enjoyed everything else in his life: his houses, his fishing, his pony-hunts, his steeplechases, his horses, his pictures, his dinner parties, the performances of the Follies, or, so long ago, the days, whether of strenuous rowing or idle punting on the river at Oxford.. They could not keep him out of the air . . .[7] *Captain Maurice Baring, Headquarters, RFC*

At 13.37 on 3 November, Lucas and his observer Lieutenant A Anderson took off with two other FE2 Bs from their airfield for a photographic reconnaissance of the German rear areas. Lucas and Anderson were soon separated from their comrades and forced to carry out their risky trade below the broken cloud cover and tormented by stiff breeze. It was then that fortune chose to cast aside her favourite.

We could see no sign of the formation, so we made for the lines and picked up three of our escort about two miles this side of the lines. Of the other escort we never saw anything and after waiting about ten minutes we decided to go over with the other three machines and as we knew we were faster than they, we were going to circle round after every half minute or so to allow them to catch up. We went in over Pierre St Vaast Wood and we started taking our photographs with two of our machines sitting on our tail and the third a little under us. It was then I noticed how strong the

*Lord Lucas in a Martinsyde.* IWM Q 58613

wind was which was blowing approximately from the South West and which kept blowing us further over. After taking our third photograph, I saw that we had drawn rather far away from our escorting machines and so I signalled to Lucas to turn round and we turned into the wind. It was then as we were half way round that one enemy aircraft came out of the clouds for our tail. We had to turn to meet him but as we were firing at him, two more machines dropped out of the clouds on to our tail firing steadily. The first burst blew half our service tank away, so Lucas swung her round and put her nose down for our lines. I fired away over the top plane but they did very good shooting and our machine was simply riddled with bullets. Suddenly the machine started side-slipping violently and at the same time the engine gave a jar and stopped dead. Looking down I saw that Lucas was bending down in his seat and, thinking that he was working with his switches, I put out my hand to shake him, but then I discovered he was hit through the back of the head and was unconscious. At this time we must have been at about 6,000 feet and so I set to work to try to get his left foot off the rudder bar, as she was still side-slipping. This I eventually managed to do but at this time we were only about 3,000 feet and the three German machines were still on our tail firing away. I saw that with a head wind and no engine we could not hope to reach the line as we were then over Haplincourt, so to avoid the machine guns (we were also being fired at from the ground) I put her down very steeply. Unfortunately Lucas half slipped off his seat and when I tried to land I found I could not flatten out enough, the undercarriage was swept off and she crashed on the wing. I was thrown clear and Lucas was brought in a few minutes later, but never recovered consciousness and died about 4pm.[8] *Lieutenant A Anderson, 22 Squadron, RFC*

From the victory claims made that day, it appears that pilots of Jasta 2 had shot down Anderson and Lucas as well as the other two FE2 Bs on the mission. The Germans buried Lucas that night with due ceremony in a little cemetery just half a mile outside Haplincourt. Ironically, Trenchard had that very day, written out the telegram that would have given Lord Lucas his own squadron had he returned safely. His governmental experience would have been invaluable to the Royal Flying Corps in many capacities over the next two years had he survived.

On 13 November, the Battle of the Ancre was launched as the last gasp of the Somme Offensive. General Sir Hubert Gough's relatively fresh Fifth Army lunged forward into the valley of the River Ancre to the north of the Somme. Assisted by a reasonably effective artillery

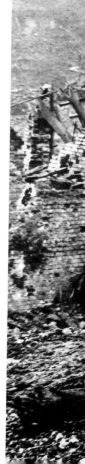

bombardment, the infantry made considerable initial progress. Beaumont Hamel fell at last, Beaucourt was captured and the positions on the Thiepval Ridge further developed. However, the attack on the Serre and Redan Ridges further North had failed. The attacks continued for a few days, but the weather worsened and it soon became obvious that nothing more of real value would be achieved. And so, on 18 November, Haig suspended the attacks – at long last the agony that was the Battle of the Somme was over.

Of course, conflict on this gigantic scale cannot just be cut off abruptly. The metaphorical corpse of the Somme battles carried on twitching for several more weeks. Hard fighting continued on the ground and in the air, only gradually dying down as winter took its icy grip. So it was that Lord Lucas was not to be the last grievous loss to the RFC above the Somme battlefield. At 13.00 on 23 November, Major Lanoe Hawker VC, who had led his squadron from the front throughout the long battle, took off for yet another patrol. Hawker, as the first British ace, as both a VC and as a man had been a fine example to his squadron.

*Ruins of Beaumont Hamel in November 1916.*  TAYLOR LIBRARY

From the earliest days he was an inspiring leader and its devoted 'parent' and friend. Before we left Hounslow, he had moulded the raw material on the right lines and it was in the beginnings that the seeds of its future greatness were sown. Those early runs in the morning which he himself led, those parades which we at the time thought rather unnecessary, those modest, almost confidential lectures, and equally those 'rags' when all of us, himself included, dashed off to town for an evening's amusement – all went to form that 'character' which was peculiar to 24 Squadron from it's earliest days. When we met with our first reverses, three of our best had gone west, his was the grit and determination that controlled us all. His personal example as a fighter was first and foremost the cause of his Squadron's success. As a friend and man he was delightful – wonderfully childish in many ways, but at the same time, always its correct, calm Commanding Officer with ample reserve when required. Although the Commanding Officer, nothing amused him more than an orange thrown at someone's head, or a soda water syphon fight, and in what we jokingly called 'the Battle of Bertangles', between ourselves and 22 Squadron, he used I know more syphons than anyone.[9] *Captain A M Wilkinson, 24 Squadron, RFC*

On that fateful day, Captain John Andrews led the 'A' Flight patrol of four DH2s across the German lines on an offensive patrol to cover a photographic reconnaissance necessitated by the final death throes of the offensive. With him were Lieutenant Robert Saundby, Lieutenant Crutch and Major Hawker himself, who once again was making up the numbers to ease the situation for his hard-pressed pilots. As they took off, Crutch was forced to turn back as his engine failed him, but the remaining three carried on regardless. It had been arranged that two other squadron pilots – Lieutenants Long and Pashley – would reinforce the patrol at 14.00. After gaining altitude to around 11,000 feet the patrol crossed the lines heading towards Bapaume. Here, at about 13.50, they sighted two German aircraft flying below them at about 6,000 feet.

> I attacked two Hostile Aircraft (HA) just North East of Bapaume and drove them East when I observed two strong patrols of HA Scouts above me. I was about to abandon the pursuit when a DH2 Scout Major Hawker, dived past me and continued to pursue.[10] *Captain John Andrews, 24 Squadron, RFC*

We will never know why Hawker continued to pursue the decoys, he may not have seen the lurking German hunting pack above him, or perhaps he was just carrying out his own dictum to attack everything.

*John Andrews.* RAFM/RAeC 1

*DH2.* RAF Museum P019425

> We were at once attacked by the HA, one of which dived on to Major Hawker's tail. I drove him off firing about 25 rounds at close range. My engine was immediately shot through from behind and I was obliged to try and regain our lines. When on the lines another DH2 came diving past me from our side and drove the HA off my tail. I last saw Major Hawker at about 3,000 feet near Bapaume, fighting with an HA apparently quite under control but going down.[11] *Captain John Andrews, 24 Squadron, RFC*

Andrews had been rescued by Lieutenant Saundby.

> We were dived on by a patrol of seven or eight Walfischs. One followed by another, dived on me. I spiralled two or three times and the HA zoomed off. Then I saw patrol leader being attacked by Walfisch and went to his assistance, diving on to the HA's tail, I emptied three-quarters double drum into him at about 20 yards range. He suddenly wobbled and dived so steeply with engine on that I could not follow him, although I dived up to 130mph. I flattened out and looked round but could see no other DH2s and the HA appeared to have moved away East, where they remained for the rest of the patrol. I turned to see if patrol leader was all right and saw him go down and land at the French landing ground behind Guillemont. I continued the patrol defensively, alone until two other DH2s joined me at 2.30pm.[12] *Lieutenant Robert Saundby, 24 Squadron, RFC*

Both Andrews and Saundby had lost contact with Major Hawker who had come face to face with Lieutenant Manfred Von Richthofen – Boelcke's heir apparent. It was to be a desperate duel to the death. It was not a fair fight, but that was irrelevant. All that the DH2 could offer in aerial combat against the Albatross DII was the ability to turn fast in tight circles without losing too much height. This was an essentially defensive attribute and the DH2's single Lewis gun provided inadequate firepower in contrast with the belt fed, twin German Spandau.

So we circled round and round like madmen after one another at an altitude of about 10,000 feet. First we circled twenty times to the left, and then thirty times to the right. Each tried to get behind and above the other. Soon I discovered that I was not meeting a beginner. He had not the slightest intention to break off the fight. He was travelling in a box which turned beautifully. However, my packing case was better at climbing than his. But I succeeded at last in getting above and beyond my English waltzing partner. When we had got down to about 6,000 feet without having achieved anything in particular, my opponent ought to have discovered that it was time for him to take his leave. The wind was favourable to me, for it drove us more and more towards the German position. At last we were above Bapaume, about half a mile behind the German front. The gallant fellow was full of pluck, and when we had got down to about 3,000 ft he merrily waved to me as if he would say, "Well, how do you do?" The circles which we made round one another were so narrow that their diameter was probably no more than 250 or 300ft. I had time to take a good look at my opponent. I looked down into his carriage and could see every movement of his head. If he had not had his cap on I would have noticed what kind of a face he was making. My Englishman was a good sportsman, but by and by the thing became a little too hot for him. He had to decide whether he would land on German ground or whether he would fly back to the English lines. Of course, he tried the latter after having endeavoured in vain to escape me by loopings and such tricks. At that time his first bullets were flying around me, for so far neither of us had been able to do any shooting. When he had come down to about 300ft he tried to escape by flying in a zigzag course, which makes it difficult for an observer on the ground to shoot. That was my most favourable moment. I followed him at an altitude of from 250ft to 150ft, firing all the time. The Englishman could not help falling. But the jamming of my gun nearly robbed me of my success. My opponent fell shot through the head 150ft behind our line.[13] *Lieutenant Manfred von Richthofen, Jasta 2, German Air Force*

*Lanoe Hawker shot down and killed by Richthofen.*

Hawker was dead, just a few yards and seconds from safety. The circle was complete. The death of Immelmman in June 1916, just prior to the start of the great battle, had signified the rise to ascendancy of the RFC and the supremacy of the DH2s over the Fokker EIII. Now Immelmann had been avenged, as the death of Hawker marked the swing back of the pendulum and the eclipse of the DH2 by the Albatross. To add piquancy, the instrument of revenge, Richthofen, was the pupil of Immelmann's hunting partner Boelcke. Richthofen would go on to lead the slaughter of the outclassed RFC machines throughout the next six months before the next generation of Allied aircraft made their belated appearance in May 1917.

The Battle of the Somme will never escape the infamy generated by the horrendous losses of 1 July. Yet, despite all the doom and gloom gestated by the appalling casualty lists, the British Army was beginning to make rapid strides up the military learning curve of competence. The use of artillery to chaperone the infantry to their objectives with a crushing combination of preliminary, creeping and standing barrages had shown the way forward. The difficulty in piercing the fog of war meant that the British High Command did not always draw the right conclusions from their successes and failures, but they did not have the benefit of hindsight and our criticism should be muted by a fair minded recognition of the difficulties that they faced. There would be many more disasters and false dawns, many more errors of commission and omission in the planning process before they became fluent in the new language of war.

Haig always considered that the break in the weather in October had denied his armies the victory they had deserved. He believed with some justification, that the German Army was rocking on its heels, as it attempted to cope with the long attritional nightmares on the Somme and Verdun fronts.

The fighting had made the most extraordinary demands both on commanders and troops. The relief arrangements inaugurated at Cambrai, and the new system of reserves projected for the West Front, no longer sufficed. Divisions and other formations had to be thrown in on the Somme front in quicker succession and had to stay in the line longer. The time for recuperation and training on quiet sectors became shorter and shorter. The troops were getting exhausted. Everything was cut as fine as possible! The strain on our nerves in Pless was terrible; over and over again we had to find and adopt new expedients. It needed the iron nerves of Generals von Gallwitz, Fritz von Below, von Kuhl, Colonels von Lossberg and Bronsart von Schellendorf, to keep them from losing their heads, to systematically put in the reserves as they came up, and, despite all our failures, eventually to succeed in saving the situation. Above all, it needed troops like the Germans! [14] *General Erich Ludendorff, German Headquarters*

Ludendorff recognised that the British and French offensive on the Somme was not the end of the matter but just the first instalment.

GHQ had to bear in mind that the enemy's great superiority in men and material would be even more painfully felt in 1917 than in 1916. They had to face the danger that 'Somme fighting' would soon break out at various points on our fronts, and that even our troops would not be able to withstand such attacks indefinitely, especially if the enemy gave us no time for rest and for the accumulation of material. Our position was uncommonly difficult and a way out hard to find. We could not contemplate an offensive ourselves, having to keep our reserves available for defence. There was no hope of a collapse of any of the Entente Powers. If the war lasted our defeat seemed inevitable. Economically we were in a highly unfavourable position for a war of exhaustion. At home our strength was badly shaken. Questions of the supply of foodstuffs caused great anxiety, and so, too, did questions of morale. We were not undermining the spirits of the enemy populations with starvation blockades and propaganda. The future looked dark.[15] *General Erich Ludendorff, German Headquarters*

Thus, ringed by their enemies, desperate for a way out, Germany was tempted to use unrestricted submarine warfare to try and implement their own blockade.

As for the RFC, the Battle of the Somme marked the point where it finally came of age as a fighting service. Its reconnaissance and observation role had been clearly defined earlier in the war. But the Somme was its first real air campaign fought in the teeth of a skilful, well equipped and determined opposition. General Gough summed up the general appreciation of the role played by the RFC.

During all the three months of fighting, the Air Service had been increasingly active and efficient. Fighting was not confined to operations on the ground and in the muddy trenches. Much went on in the air. Gradually and surely our Air Service established a moral and material superiority over the enemy, though at the cost of many gallant young lives. But the work done was invaluable – especially in the direction of 'blanketing' the enemy's observation of his artillery fire, while they assisted, guided and directed ours most helpfully. No one of the complicated miscellany of services which comprise a modern army so commanded the respect and admiration of the infantry as did our air service.[16] *General Sir Hubert Gough, Headquarters, Fifth Army*

Haig, Rawlinson, Gough and their respective staffs greatly valued the regular, detailed photographic reconnaissance of the trench systems facing their forces; they recognized the crucial role in artillery work; they appreciated the harassing raids on the German billeting sectors;

they looked for bombing raids on strategically significant railway junctions to disrupt the German movement of reserve divisions; and of course they insisted that the RFC scouts should deny similar facilities to the Germans. The RFC could, and did, look back on the whole Somme campaign with considerable pride.

I have often heard officers of other arms state that at times the supremacy of the air passed to the enemy. I challenge this statement. The side possesses the supremacy of the air which is able to keep army cooperation machines in the front and to prevent the enemy from doing so. The question of which side has most casualties in doing so is immaterial to this question.[17]

*Lieutenant Robert Archer, 42 Squadron, RFC*

Most of the 583 RFC casualties suffered on the Western Front between June and December 1916 were over the Somme battlefields. These figures pale into insignificance compared to the crippling losses suffered by the infantry, but as a proportion of those involved it bore a grim comparison. In the tragic ledger of the Somme, the losses they suffered were set against the enormous value of their work. For the RFC at least it was 'Somme Success'.

1. G. Lewis, 'Wings Over the Somme', (Wrexham: Bridge Books, 1994), p75 & 78
2. IWM DOCS F. O. Cave, Manuscript diary, 1/11/1916
3. RAF MUSEUM: J. C. Callaghan, Manuscript Log Book, 9/11/1916
4. W. Churchill, 'World Crisis', 1911-1918 (London: Odhams Press, 1938) p189
5. W. F. J. Harvey, 'Pi in the Sky: A history of No. 22 Squadron, Royal Flying Corps and RAF in the War of 1914-1918', (1969), p147
6. M. Baring, Flying Corps Headquarters, 1914-1918, (London: William Blackwood and Sons Ltd, 1968), pp188-189
7. M. Baring, Flying Corps Headquarters, 1914-1918, (London: William Blackwood and Sons Ltd, 1968), pp194-195
8. W. F. J. Harvey, Pi in the Sky: A history of No. 22 Squadron, Royal Flying Corps and RAF in the War of 1914-1918, (1969), pp170-171
9. IWM DOCS, A M Wilkinson typescript memoir
10. T. M. Hawker, 'Hawker V.C.', (London: The Mitre Press,1965), p250
11. T. M. Hawker, 'Hawker V.C.', (London: The Mitre Press,1965), p250
12. T. M. Hawker, 'Hawker V.C.', (London: The Mitre Press,1965), pp250-251
13. M. von Richthofen, 'Red Air Fighter', (London: Greenhill Books, 1990), pp100-101
14. E. Ludendorf, 'My War Memories, 1914-1918', (London: Hutchinson), p278
15. E. Ludendorf, 'My War Memories, 1914-1918', (London: Hutchinson), p307
16. H. Gough, 'The Fifth Army', (London: Hodder & Stoughton, 1931), p149
17. IWM DOCS: R. A. Archer, manuscript memoir, 'Third tour of duty in France, 8/1916-3/1917'